Fabulous reviews for *Get Hot or Go Home*:

"Fascinating . . . Engrossing . . . Illuminating."
—*Kirkus*

"Humanizes Yearwood."   —*Country Music* magazine

"Gubernick's superior reporting from the country music front makes for a fascinating story."   —*Chicago Tribune*

"Gubernick gets right down to the gritty details of family and Nashville."   —*Grand Rapids*, MI *Press*

"Detail-rich."   —*Nashville Tennessean*

"A savvy combination of thorough reporting and research . . . Gubernick has a remarkable ear for dialogue and an eye for telling detail."   —*Rocky Mountain News*

"Important work . . . Required reading for music business professionals."   —*Nashville Banner*

"Tremendously insightful . . . A must-read for anyone longing for the spotlight."
—*Tampa*, FL *Tribune & Times*

Get Hot or Go Home

TRISHA YEARWOOD:
The Making of a Nashville Star

LISA REBECCA GUBERNICK

ST. MARTIN'S PAPERBACKS

Published by arrangement with William Morrow

GET HOT OR GO HOME

Library of Congress Catalog Card Number: 93-4174

ISBN: 0-312-95397-6

Printed in the United States of America

William Morrow hardcover edition published 1993
St. Martin's Paperbacks edition/February 1995

St. Martin's Paperbacks are published by St. Martin's Press, 175 Fifth Avenue, New York, N.Y. 10010.

10 9 8 7 6 5 4 3 2 1

For Grace Gubernick and the memory of Reuben Gubernick

ACKNOWLEDGMENTS

Get Hot or Go Home began in the office of my editor, Paul Bresnick. He had always wanted to see a book about the making of a rock act, he told me. The next day, I told him, I was heading to Nashville to do a cover story for *Forbes* on the country music boom. Wouldn't it be better to choose a Nashville star? While I was doing the *Forbes* story I asked everyone I interviewed which singers were on the verge of stardom. Trisha Yearwood was mentioned by virtually everyone. When I was in Los Angeles, I spoke with Al Teller, head of MCA Records, the label Yearwood recorded on, and he agreed to let his company cooperate. Several weeks later I met with Yearwood and her manager, Ken Kragen, and they agreed to the project, no strings attached. Garth Fundis was initially reluctant to permit me in the recording studio, but after considerable persuasion he agreed to let me sit in, with the right to ask me to leave. Fortunately, he never did. I am grateful to all of them, especially to Trisha Yearwood for making a wonderful album and letting me come along for the ride.

I borrowed the book's title from the rockabilly singer Joe Clay who shouted it out in the midst of "You Look That Good to Me," recorded in 1956. I'd like to thank Bill Ivey and Ronnie Pugh at the Country Music Foundation for helping me track down its origins—as well as pointing me to the right files for finding information on all matters Music Row. Anything they didn't know, Ed Benson, Janet Williams, or Teresa George at the Country Music Association or Robert Oermann at *The Tennessean* did.

This book would never have been possible without the help of virtually everyone I've written about. At MCA Nashville: Bruce Hinton, Tony Brown, Shelia Shipley, Scott Borchetta, Walt Wilson, Janet Rickman, Sarah Brosmere, Susan Levy, Lorie Hoppers. At Kragen & Company: Laurel Altman, Amy Shachory. At the Sound Emporium: Susan Dey, Scott Paschall, Gary Laney. At Group W: Cheryl Daly, Terry Kelly. Nancy Russell provided help beyond the bounds of any publicist's call. Malcolm Mimms, Sheri McCoy, Tony Conway, and Joe Harris were invaluable as well. Thanks to everyone in the road band, as well as Lisa McLaughlin, Alan Haege, Jarrah Herter, and especially Leonard Arnold, trail boss extraordinaire.

Paul Bresnick at Morrow didn't just help come up with the idea, he was a wonderful editor and enthusiast. I'd also like to thank Ben Ratliff and Mark Garafolo. Eric Ashworth and Barney Karpfinger provided wise counsel.

My editors at *Forbes*, Stewart Pinkerton, Laury Minard, and Jim Michaels, were good enough to listen when I asked to do a story about country music, and generous enough to give me time to write this book. On that first article, Pete Newcomb was a superb cowriter and cohort. I am once again grateful for Martha Trachtenberg's indefatigable research. Thanks to friends and family who were generous enough to put up with my absence and my distraction.

This book would have been unimaginable without my husband, Paul Fishleder. His wit and support (and editing) are the best I could ever wish for.

CONTENTS

This town is full of pretty girls that can sing their hearts out, it's full of country boys with a great song written down in pencil on a sheet of notebook paper folded up real little in their back pocket. Most of those pretty girls will go back to singing in their own hometowns eventually, and then they'll get married. . . . Most of those boys will go back home, too, and get a job doing something else, and sing on the weekends for a while with some old boys they went to high school with, and then they'll quit, too. They'll think about Nashville some over the years, about the time they spent here, they'll make it out in their minds to be better than it was.

Because it was not fun, mostly. It was hard, hard.

—Lee Smith,
The Devil's Dream

PROLOGUE

AT 7:45 P.M. ON THE LAST NIGHT IN FEBRUARY 1992, TRISHA Yearwood, a rush of blond hair and blue sequins, made a nervous run for center stage. She brushed past the placard for Goo Goo Clusters, past the red barn backdrop, under the neon-lit sign for Dollar General Stores, across a six-foot round patch of scuffed flooring set smack center stage. This was Yearwood's debut at the Grand Ole Opry, her first pilgrimage to the mother church of country music.

In a beaded bolero over a low-cut black velvet gown—a piece of strategic satin added to make it just a bit less revealing—she looked like Ann-Margret in training. She had the outfit, but she hadn't quite mastered the attitude. She started singing her first number one record as she moved into the spotlights.

> *Katie's sittin' on the old front porch*
> *Watchin' the chickens peck the ground*
> *There ain't a whole lot going on tonight*
> *In this one-horse town*

> [She fanned her fingers at the right balcony]

> *Over yonder comin' up the road*
> *In a beat-up Chevy truck*
> *Her boyfriend Tommy is layin' on the horn*
> *Splashing through the mud and the muck*

> [Finger fan to left balcony]

Her daddy says he ain't worth a lick
When it come to brains, he got the short end of
*   the stick . . .*
But Katie's young and she just don't care
She'd follow Tommy anywhere
She's in love with the boy . . .

[Back to center stage, another wave]

Katie and Tommy at the drive-in movie
Parked in the very last row
They're too busy hangin' on to one another
To even care about the show . . .

[Back to stage right, fingers still going]

Her daddy's waitin' up 'til half past twelve
When they come sneakin' up the walk
He says young lady get on up to your room
While me and Junior have a talk
But Mama breaks in, says don't lose your
*   temper*
It wasn't very long ago
When you yourself was just a hayseed
*   plowboy*
Who didn't have a row to hoe
My daddy said you wasn't worth a lick
. . .
But he was wrong and honey you are too
Katie looks at Tommy like I still look at
*   you . . .*

She waved to the orchestra seats, every inch the small-town
beauty queen. "Thank you. Oh my. I've been all over the country, and I've performed in front of thousands of people, and I've
never been more nervous than I am tonight. I am at the Grand
Ole Opry, and I listened to Patsy Cline at home before I came."
Deep breath. She looked out as the lights panned the house. The
audience rustled with tepid applause.

Yearwood hadn't much time for her second number; three
minutes later and it was over. She managed a shallow bow, a last
wave, and a thank you, then turned to retreat into the backstage
carnival.

* * *

Behind that two-dimensional red barn, Stoney Mountain Clog-gers, aging Opry stars in gravity-defying toupees, toddlers with mothers in close pursuit, and stagehands wended through the warren of dressing rooms. Over in Makeup Room A, Boxcar Willie leaned back in an elevated swivel chair where he was getting made up for stage.

"Why you wearin' plastic gloves?" he asked the cosmetician.

"New health regulations."

"But we don't have none of that AIDS stuff here."

"It's the rules," she said, rubbing crimson rouge into his cheeks.

Outside the makeup-room door, a woman carrying an oversize tape recorder tried to make her way through to Yearwood. But she was quickly body-blocked by a woman in a short turquoise skirt and black T-shirt, brown ringlets curling halfway down her back. For the last three months Nancy Russell had been Yearwood's publicist, and part of her charge was making sure her client got only the right sort of press. "She says she's with ABC radio," Russell said as she moved into the crowd, "but I know she's been leaking stuff to the *Enquirer*." Danger diffused, Yearwood disappeared into the maelstrom.

Hovering on the edge of the crowd, smiling as the singer passed by, was a sturdy middle-aged woman in an oversize sweatshirt, black slacks, and white sneakers. Gwen Yearwood and her hus-band, Jack, had driven seven hours from Monticello, Georgia (pop. 2,289), to hear their youngest child sing.

Gwen Yearwood's first trip to the Opry had been thirty-seven years ago, for her senior class trip in high school. She recorded the scene in her diary so she could describe the place to her parents. She knew they would be listening to the broadcast on WSM back home in Willacoochee, Georgia, almost five hundred miles away. Static spiked the broadcast, but it didn't really mat-ter. The Opry was the biggest thing happening on Saturday night.

Bonnie Lou Carson sang the "Tennessee Wig Walk" that June night in 1955. Hawkshaw Hawkins, who would die in the same plane crash that claimed Patsy Cline, turned up in a white suit and matching hat for "Rebound." In all, twenty-odd singers joined the night-long procession across the stage of the century-old Ryman Auditorium—the origin of that weathered patch of flooring fixed into the new Opry stage.

The history of that brick tabernacle reads like *The Pilgrim's Progress*. In 1891, Captain Tom Ryman, a riverboat captain who claimed the usual vices of drinking and gambling, heard the Reverend Sam Jones's sermon "Motherhood." The sinner was saved, and, as penance, gave enough money to build a gospel hall for others to be similarly redeemed. In 1897, a balcony was added for the Confederate Reunion, and each week after that, audiences thirty-three hundred strong would come to receive the Word.

The Opry started off in the radio studios at WSM, but they couldn't hold the crowds. For the next few years the show moved to increasingly larger venues, from the Hillsboro Theater to the Dixie Tabernacle in East Nashville to the War Memorial Auditorium, where it was booted out because the crowds got too raucous. In 1941 the show moved into the Ryman, which offered sufficient space, though not much in the way of amenities. The auditorium made few concessions to corporeal comfort. The audience was crammed into twenty-odd rows of stiff-backed pews, and a dozen largely ineffective fans were all that cooled the place in the summer.

The newfangled Opry House, conceived by businessmen, is a tribute to technology. Three 450-ton chillers, 5.4 million BTUs apiece, insure that the temperature never goes above 77, even in the dog days of August. According to the first brochure for the new hall, the engineers installed "especially designed contoured pew-type benches covered in burnt orange–colored carpeting [to] allow whole families to sit together in close proximity." A swatch of the nubbly fabric was even glued into the pamphlet, presumably making it easier to appreciate the innovations.

Yearwood called this place "Six Flags Over Nashville," which seems to match the intent of the men who built it. The Opry hall borders the eastern perimeter of Opryland's 757 acres, country music's answer to Disney's antiseptic paradise. The roller coaster is called the *Wabash Cannonball*; the *Tennessee Waltz* is a German carousel, a dizzying spiral of suspended swings.

The new Opry's only history was its reliquary of performers. There was John Conlee, who worked as a mortician before he got into the music business. He always appeared on stage with pink-tinted spectacles; his big hit, circa 1978, was "Rose-Colored Glasses." The Opry was just about the only place you could hear Jeanne Pruett sing her twenty-year-old standard, "Satin Sheets."

By the winter of 1992, Roy Acuff, eighty-nine, was the Opry's senior statesman, just about the last of his generation still making regular appearances on the Opry stage. At ninety-three, Governor Jimmie Davis showed up for special occasions. Minnie Pearl hadn't whooped "How-dee" or told tales of Grinder's Switch for nearly a year. She was at home, recovering from a stroke; her trademark straw hat, price tag hanging off the side, was presumably collecting dust on some wardrobe-room shelf.

Acuff was already legend by World War II, when, as the story goes, a Japanese banzai charged a Marine position on Okinawa crying "To hell with Roosevelt, to hell with Babe Ruth, to hell with Roy Acuff." Fifty years later his hearing and sight were mostly gone, along with his memory. On this night Acuff napped through the early evening, snoozing in the dressing room labeled "Number One" just behind the stage. He came to life just before ten when a comely assistant in a spaghetti-strapped gown gently awakened him, and led him to the stage. He followed her from behind, hands firmly fixed on her bare shoulders. He couldn't manage his yoyo anymore, the one he pulled out to do "Around the World" when Richard Nixon showed up in the waning months of his presidency back in 1974. But once he hit the microphone, he still managed a surprisingly tuneful "Great Speckled Bird."

Acuff had relinquished the task of opening the Opry's weekly telecast to Porter Wagoner, the sixty-year-old onetime grocery clerk who had his first top-ten single back in 1955. Five years later, Wagoner had his own syndicated country show, and eight years after that he signed on a cotton-candy blonde with an improbable bosom as his cohost. Dolly Parton stayed five years, then left for Hollywood. Wagoner sued to keep her, but Parton never looked back.

Wagoner may have lost his partner, but Lord knows he held onto his style; his get-ups had not changed for nearly a quarter century. He still shellacked his peroxided hair into a high-rise pompadour. His denim suit, spangled with rhinestone wagon wheels, was just a bit flashier than the twenty-year-old lime-green outfit encased in glass at the Country Music Hall of Fame.

This night, Wagoner opened the Opry telecast in the audience, singing his way through the pews.

High on the mountain what do you see
Bear tracks, bear tracks lookin' back at me. . . .
Oh he's big around the middle and he's broad across the rump
Runnin' ninety miles an hour takin' thirty feet a jump
He's never been caught and he ain't never been treed
Some folks say he looks a lot like me.

As he hit that last lyric he hiked up his pants to reveal a pale hairless leg and a bright red sock.

"Right now, I'm fixing to yodel," he declared. "This is the only time I do the yodeling. Seems like when I come down and see you folks, something inside wants to come out. Believe me, if it was inside you, you'd want it to come out of you too." As he let loose with a "Yoodle-olde-hey-hee-hoo," an expression of alarm passed over his face. He glanced down at the bright red kerchief knotted around his neck. "Lord, I thought my tongue was hanging out for a second. Scared the life out of me."

You couldn't hear Wagoner's patter backstage, where Yearwood was still maneuvering her way to the stage-door exit. Two lanky men, one wearing a western-style suit (topstitching detailing the pockets as well as the broad back yoke), the other in a blue windbreaker, gold chain circling his neck, diamond stud in his left ear, cut her off by the back of the barn facade. The first was her manager, Ken Kragen, the man responsible for USA for Africa and Hands Across America, with whom Yearwood had signed on just three months before. ("How's your new manager?" someone asked Yearwood before the show. "The last time we were at a restaurant someone walked up to get *his* autograph," she replied. "My goal is to be as famous as he is.")

"We gotta talk," said the second man. His look was Vegas, his voice straight out of Brooklyn. Joe Layton, the man who directed *Barnum* and *Woman of the Year*, had come to put a little Broadway into country.

"When daya wanna talk?" Layton asked as she moved to the door.

"In a half hour, at the bus," she replied as an overweight teenager pushed a program toward her and implored, "Would you sign this, please?"

Yearwood's bus, a forty-foot-long modified Silver Eagle with "Fantasy" etched in lavender across the back window, was parked just behind the Opry entrance. At the appointed time, Layton made his way on, through the dining area, where the singer's older sister, Beth, was changing her infant daughter's diapers on the sofa, through the narrow hallway between the triple-decked bunks, to the suite in back, where Yearwood was already parked in front of the vanity.

Layton folded into the velour sofa, barely nodding hello. Yearwood looked up. "What did I do wrong?"

"Your hands were everywhere," he said, fingers fanning beneath his nose, under his arms. "I never seen choreography like that. Where's all the staging we've been working on? We have skirts so we can swish them and behinds so we can shake them. . . . You tell the crowd you're nervous—what are you waiting for, applause that you're brave enough to be up there? They look at you and think, 'Next.'

"Liberace was out there eating up the furniture along with the old ladies on it. . . . What does that tell you? You have to sell yourself to the audience."

Yearwood silently took it all in.

Layton's next stop was the dressing room back in the Opry Hall, where Yearwood had joined her five-member band. "You know," he mused as he walked over, "this place is still Mickey Rooney and Judy Garland. 'Let's get ourselves a garage and we'll put on a show.' "

Inside the dressing room, you could hear a fiddle playing "Little Cabin Home on the Hill," an old bluegrass tune. Tammy Rogers, Yearwood's fiddle player, and her drummer, Ric McClure, sidled up to the wall and started singing harmony with the unseen fiddler.

Layton ignored the impromptu performance, clapping as he walked in the door. Class was in session. "Did I tell anyone not to look at Trisha? Did I tell you all that it was time to go back into your own little worlds? What was going on out there?"

"We really slipped back," replied Jay Hager, the bass player. "Do you want to know why it happened?"

"I'm not interested. I just don't want it to happen again. Only madame here," Layton said, pointing at Rogers, "gave body English. She was the only one looking at Trisha. She was the only one who knew what she was trying to sell.

"You," he said, pointing at Hager, "Look at her," pointing at

Yearwood. His pronoun was straight out of the boroughs, the final *r* lost to the ages. "You, you, you," he said, firing his finger at each successive band member, "look at huh. Look at huh. Look at huh."

"And you," he said, turning to Yearwood, "put on a show worth watching."

Yearwood had paid Layton fifty thousand dollars for this abuse. Not so long ago it was enough for a girl singer to stand stock-still on stage and belt lyrics into the microphone, her band strumming behind her. If the light flickered off the satin clinging to her cleavage, that was more than enough. Bring in an outsider—a New Yorker, no less—to reshape a show? Unheard of. But the game in Nashville is swiftly changing.

Nashville has always been a sort of Emerald City, the place where the children of back-roads America go to pursue their dreams. For each country star, there is the blue-collar legend—the dishwasher, the truck driver, the Sears Roebuck salesman, who now lives in a neo-Tudor mansion with a genuine guitar-shaped swimming pool, complete with black tile strings.

Even the last mayor got tangled in Music Row fantasies. When the mayor, improvidently named Bill Boner, dumped his third wife for a 34-year-old country singer, the newspapers gleefully reported not only the size of her engagement ring (2.2 carats) but the length of their romantic interludes (7 hours).

The songs that nurtured those dreams were an exotic, regional music that outsiders—those record executives from New York and L.A.—could never really understand. There was the moment in the sixties when Johnny Cash caught fire; a decade or so later it was John Travolta on a mechanical bull—the soundtrack for *Urban Cowboy*, a double record, sold 1.6 million pairs. But the boom couldn't be trusted. After each crest came a commensurate fall. Between 1981 and 1985, country record sales dropped from 15 percent to 10 percent of the total number of records sold, from 94.2 million to 65.3 million. That year, the *New York Times* declared the Nashville sound dead.

That report turned out to be a bit premature. In the late eighties, while rock music splintered off into hip-hop, technopop, thrash metal, rap, and so on, alienating a healthy percentage of its listeners along the way, Nashville hewed to its roots. ("Thank God for rap," said James "Jimmy" Bowen, head of Liberty Records, Capitol Records' Nashville label. "Every morning when they play that stuff, people come running to us.") Those country songs with their plainspoken lyrics and carefully crafted stories started cutting a wide swath across the American radio waves.

"I'm not sure other formats are remembering that lyrics are what it's all about," was how Garth Brooks, the first performer to have three albums in *Billboard*'s top fifteen since Herb Alpert back in 1966, put it. "We treat the lyrics like the woman any man wants to impress the most."

Country music has probably always been more popular than the industry gave it credit for, but until recently there was no accurate way to count how many albums were being sold. *Billboard*, the music industry bible, used to rely on store owners' estimates when it tabulated its weekly sales charts. In 1991 the magazine switched to a computerized tracking method called Soundscan that includes purchases at stores like Wal-Mart and Kmart, places where the country customer is much more likely to buy his or her music. "It's like someone opened the closet door," says Brooks. "Just because the light is on, does it mean it wasn't that way all along?"

By any measure, at the end of 1991 the American public was happily seduced. The aw-shucks Oklahoman might, as one critic put it, look like a thumb in a cowboy hat, but he was outselling Michael Jackson and Bruce Springsteen.

While New York and L.A. record executives were handing out pink slips, Nashville had its biggest year ever. A clutch of brand new high rises crown the six-block patchwork of Victorian houses and squat brick office buildings that hold the record labels, publishing companies, and recording studios that are Music Row.

Trisha Yearwood was born of this prosperous new world. Her first single was the first debut by a female country singer to go number one; her debut album would be the first to sell a million copies in less than a year. She was no naïf who had pulled into the bus station with a suitcase full of songs. Her strategy for stardom was carefully cloaked in a business plan. Yearwood grew up in small-town America, but her parents had both gone to college. She had got her own diploma four years before—in music business.

She wasn't quite comfortable with the usual accoutrements of country music queens. Her stage outfits were fairly understated. She had to be talked into sequins. Her blond hair was shoulder-length and simply styled, coiffed more Madison Avenue than Memphis. "I don't have big hair, and I don't wear fringe," was how Yearwood put it.

To listen to her sing, you'd barely have known she was country. She didn't twang, she didn't yodel. There was none of that vibration back up in her sinuses; her deep soprano had no backwoods catch. Blessed with power, control, and breadth, she was often compared to Linda Ronstadt.

For the most part, Yearwood's fans belonged to the *Saturday Night Live* generation, more familiar with Madonna than Minnie Pearl. They'd no sooner have caught a rerun of *Lawrence Welk* than spent a Saturday night watching the Opry show. To Yearwood's generation of stars, the Opry was an anachronism—as much a museum as a stage.

Yearwood's Opry debut was almost an afterthought. She'd already had her five minutes on that most sacred of secular shows, Johnny Carson, already been nominated for a Grammy Award, already received seven of the trophies the country music establishment seems to pass out with each changing season.

Her fans might not have watched the Opry, but they bought plenty of concert tickets and T-shirts. In 1992, Yearwood's second in the business, Trisha Yearwood, Inc., stood to gross nearly two million dollars, ten times what Hank Williams was making in his heyday.

But as fast and as high as Trisha Yearwood's career had soared, her fame was not yet assured. As country music was becoming more and more popular, its fans were turning ever more fickle. A number one record used to insure a career; now it means four months or so of airplay.

"If this were five years ago, I'd already be established," she said. "Now you can have a number one record and be gone tomorrow." Nineteen ninety-two would be the year that proved whether Trisha Yearwood could make it, whether she could put out an album that proved her to be a star.

Part I

STARTING OUT

From Monticello to Music Row

> I think people have grown away from hillbilly music. The world has changed. There're not too many of us who can identify anymore with Butcher Holler. There are far more of us who come from a middle or suburban kind of background, and we've got our little memories too.
>
> —Lynn Anderson

CHAPTER 1

THERE ARE ENOUGH OF THEM TO FILL SCORES OF METHODIST church choirs—girls from small-town southern families who have sufficient spunk to head to a big city for adventure, then scurry back after a few years, sated. Trisha Yearwood and her older sister, Beth, were daughters of that world, young women who were expected to update their parents' lives but not significantly alter them. Beth Yearwood hewed easily to that path, marrying a college professor from West Tennessee and bearing their first child before she turned thirty.

Trisha, who played a tentative Scarlett to her sister's Melanie, had a harder time with her parents' conventions. She was a hesitant rebel, testing those bounds but never quite crossing them. Back when she was in high school, the issue was Monticello's town square, the block of stubbly grass surrounding the monument to the Confederate dead that had become the meeting place for the town's rowdier teenagers.

Beth gave the square wide berth. Trisha, though, had designs on one of those local hellions, though they never came to much more than a make-out session in a dark corner of a high school party. She wanted to date the boy, but her father said no. And once Jack Yearwood made his displeasure known, it never occurred to her to disobey. "If I got caught on the square, I'd hear about it from my Daddy," she said, and for her first eighteen years, that was enough.

* * *

Jack Yearwood is a big man, ruddy-faced, with a shock of white hair. From behind he still cuts a narrow figure; in profile a low-slung paunch interrupts that slim silhouette. When she was young, Gwen Yearwood looked like a less dangerous Elizabeth Ashley. Her waist has thickened a bit since then, but her face retains an uncommon brightness. Both Yearwood daughters inherited their mother's flawless complexion. Together they look like a somewhat zaftig version of those Breck shampoo mother-daughter advertisements, the quintessence of American beauty.

Trisha Yearwood is the daughter of Georgia's majority. Gwen and Jack Yearwood are of durable stock, fourth-generation Georgians whose parents were laborers, not the sort of faded gentry who lived off memories of a plantation past. Family is important, but that means present ties, not ancestral reveries. "The Yearwoods are from the next county over," was how Jack Yearwood explained it, "so we don't know too much about them."

Jack was born in Eatonton, just east of Monticello. His father started out as a harness racer. When he was too old to ride, he turned to logging, backbreaking, perilous work. In 1961, a post fell off a truck he was loading and crashed into his skull; he was killed instantly.

Gwen's parents worked a farm just outside Willacoochee, about forty miles from the Florida border. The Paulks were a spirited line; her father, Winnes, bought his first motorcycle, a white-fendered Harley-Davidson, when he was sixty-one. His wife, Elizabeth, bought her first pantsuit so she could ride behind him. For a half dozen years, Lizzie and Winnes Paulk tore through the byways of South Georgia, the most unlikely of backwoods bikers.

Gwen and Jack Yearwood were the first in their families to graduate from college, the first who didn't earn their livings working the land. They met at a high school football game in Jack's hometown. Gwen was teaching home economics at the school; Jack was working as a county extension agent, helping place government subsidies and bank loans with farmers in Monticello.

They married and moved to a small house in Monticello. Jack kept with the county for another seven years, then, when his daughters were seven and ten, he took a job as cashier at the Bank of Monticello, a one-branch institution just off the town square. Its eight-pillared facade, as any of the bank's clerks will tell you, "looks just like Thomas Jefferson's." In 1971, Jack Yearwood was promoted to vice president, and for the past twenty years he has primarily tended to small commercial loans.

Jack Yearwood's grammar belies his education. He uses the rough diction of the men he does business with—farmers, laborers, shopkeepers. Gwen Yearwood's vowels stretch with a regional lilt, but she speaks with schoolteacher precision. She insisted her daughters follow her lead, but her rules were not extended to the entire household, and she took deep offense when a magazine article about her daughter described Jack as having a thick drawl.

The Yearwoods lived in town for their first few years in Monticello. Then, just after Jack took the job at the bank, they built a squat brick ranch house on thirty acres about two miles from the square, the small-town southern version of the postwar middle-class dream. For the first few years, Jack kept a small herd of cattle; he gave them up when he realized they would never amount to more than an agricultural fantasy. He still farms about twenty acres (soybeans in one field, wheat in the other); the rest of the land has been left to run wild, his own deer-hunting preserve.

Deer trophies, bucks Jack shot on his land, grace the living-room walls. The requisite brass bulldog, the mascot from Jack's alma mater, the University of Georgia, is above the dining-room table. Two BarcaLoungers face the television; in the opposite corner sits an ancient hutch Gwen inherited from her mother. No one is quite sure just how old it is. Lizzie Paulk bought it used three quarters of a century ago. The Yearwoods don't have much else in the way of family keepsakes. Among their other heirlooms, if you could call it that, is the front door from the house Gwen grew up in, reclaimed when sharecroppers took over the old farmhouse. Jack installed it in the entry to the makeshift office in the basement, where a formica tabletop, its surface covered by a stack of letters, a fax machine, and a small computer, serves as headquarters for the Trisha Yearwood fan club.

Upstairs, the girls' bedrooms remain virtually unchanged since they moved out. Two posters hang over Trisha's bed. One is a portrait distributed by a teen church group ("the only social life there was," she explained) of a pensive teenager with the words "I'm afraid of tomorrow" above her forehead, and "Don't worry, I've been there before. Jesus Christ" at the bottom. The other, in multicolored script, reads "Never Lose Sight of Your Dreams." On the bulletin board Gwen has pinned a mother's proof of that promise fulfilled: a Xerox of a twenty-thousand-dollar check made out to Trisha Yearwood from MCA Records, her daughter's first royalty advance.

There was always music in the Yearwood household, always a radio playing or a turntable going through a stack of Hank Williams and Patsy Cline. By the time she was in grade school, Patricia (she trimmed it to Trisha when she started looking for a record deal) was doing a passable version of "Your Cheatin' Heart." She was the only one of her friends who listened to the older country singers, the only one who talked about wanting to grow up and become, of all things, a country star. Even in Monticello it was a decidedly eccentric dream.

At thirteen, she broke her ankle, and to pass the time, she started tinkering with an old guitar. By the end of the year she and her sister were doing duets, picking up songs off of Trisha's Linda Ronstadt records: "I Never Will Marry," "I Can't Help It If I'm Still in Love with You."

Rock 'n' roll arrived at the Yearwoods in the late sixties, when a neighbor gave Trisha an Elvis Presley album. The first grader was smitten with the pompadoured rock star in the gilded jumpsuits, and like millions of other girls all over America, she insisted that when she grew up she was going to marry Elvis.

By the late seventies, when Yearwood was in high school, just what qualified as country music was already getting slippery. A few decades before, back when the only way Lizzie Paulk could know what Faron Young was wearing at the Opry was through her daughter's diary, Monticello might have produced a country singer schooled solely at the Saturday night barn dance. But the world that created Kitty Wells, Loretta Lynn, and even Dolly Parton was fast disappearing. Lizzie's granddaughter grew up on television, airwaves jammed with entertainment. The Monkees came and went, Ed Sullivan still had his cavalcade of stars, and Sonny and Cher claimed Tuesday nights from seven to eight. (At six, Trisha was doing her own version of "Gypsies, Tramps and

Thieves," complete with a bath towel draped over her head, her approximation of Cher's waist-length tresses.)

WSM no longer had a lock on the radio. You could still pick up Donna Fargo and Conway Twitty on stations from Macon and Athens, but country had lost its grip. Southern rock came in clear on Atlanta's Z103: The sound was Eagles, Linda Ronstadt, and Emmylou Harris.

Jack Yearwood used to call his daughters out to perform whenever there were guests for dinner, but his ambitions were tightly circumscribed. The sisters sang for church groups and town meetings, but he never let them venture much beyond the outer reaches of Jasper County. Jack Yearwood was no Beau Tucker, who gave up his job as a construction worker in Utah to drag his family to Las Vegas and then to Nashville in hopes of meeting someone who might give his youngest daughter, Tanya, a shot at a record deal. The Yearwoods were above that sort of trailer-park whimsy. No daughter of Jack Yearwood's would drop out of school to chase some farfetched dream.

In 1970, the Yearwoods were one of the dozen local families who founded Piedmont Academy, one of those educational institutions started throughout the South in the late sixties after integration was forced on the public schools. It wasn't the students who alarmed her, Gwen Yearwood was quick to explain, it was that the teaching had slipped. The Yearwoods didn't just help fund Piedmont. Gwen Yearwood taught third grade as well. Both her daughters were straight A students. Her older daughter was valedictorian, her younger was salutatorian, voted "Most Talented," "Most Intelligent" and "Most Likely to Succeed." In the 1982 Piedmont annual Trisha had a twenty-three-line list of club memberships and awards (yearbook editor, music award, business award, and first place in the regional typing contest among them), the longest in her class.

Trisha followed her sister to Young Harris, a two-year college not far from Monticello. She majored in business ("I've always been practical"), but her real ambitions ran close to the surface. In speech class, assigned either to give a presentation speech or accept an award, Yearwood accepted the prize for best female vocalist at the Country Music Association's annual awards.

In her second year, she won the lead in *Little Mary Sunshine*, a Broadway musical (circa 1959) in which the heroine (Mary Sunshine) runs a Rockies lodge, is imperiled by a villainous Indian named Yellow Feather, and is subsequently rescued by the captain of the Colorado Rangers.

Both sisters went onto the University of Georgia, but unlike Beth, who eventually got a master's degree in animal nutrition, Trisha left after a quarter; she simply wasn't interested in anything the school had to offer.

It wasn't enough for her to sing at the occasional wedding or even star in the school play. She had heard her mother's stories of the Opry, she had listened to her records. She knew exactly what she wanted, exactly where she needed to be. "I wanted to sing country," was how she explained it. "I grew up in a little town in Georgia. That was the music I knew best. That's all I ever wanted to be." When she told her parents she wanted to try to make it as a country singer, that she intended to move to Nashville, it was the first time she hadn't done precisely what they expected.

"We just didn't want her to go that far away from home," Gwen Yearwood said, recalling their reaction to her announcement. But Jack Yearwood made his daughter's gumption easy. While he was protective of his youngest child, he was, in equal if not greater measure, indulgent of her. Back when Trisha was in eighth grade, three years shy of driving age, Jack Yearwood was taking his daughters to Atlanta when Trisha spotted a blue '66 Mustang with a FOR SALE sign on the side of the road. She insisted her father buy it for her. "The child wasn't even fourteen," recalled Gwen Yearwood. Three days later, though, the car was hers. Jack Yearwood spent two years tinkering with the engine so it would be in working order by the time his daughter was old enough to drive it. "That should give some idea of her determination," said Gwen. "Or maybe it just shows how good she was at getting around her daddy."

When it came to moving to Nashville, Trisha Yearwood got around her daddy once more. Jack Yearwood could have forbidden his daughter to go, insisted that she stay in the state. But neither parent wanted to derail their daughter's dreams; they just wanted to discipline them. "She was bent on going to Nashville," recalled Gwen, "and we were bent on getting her into some kind of a structured setting." A choir director had told Gwen about a music business program at Ward Belmont, a Baptist college within walking distance of Music Row. It sufficed for a compromise. In January 1985, Trisha Yearwood moved into a dormitory at Ward Belmont College. It was the farthest she'd ever been from home.

CHAPTER 2

FROM THE MOMENT WSM BROADCAST ITS FIRST SATURDAY night barn dance, there have been two Nashvilles. There is the city of the musicians and the songwriters and the men and women who make their records, and there is the city where, as the novelist Peter Taylor described it, "phrases like 'well bred and well born' were always ringing in one's ears."

"I've only been to the Opry once or twice with guests from out of town," was how Charles Elder, a local bookseller, put it. "Frankly I found the whole thing rather embarrassing." Bad enough that the music was the product of those uncouth backwoods hill people. Worse, those guitar-picking hillbillies were making altogether too much money. They flashed gaudy clothes, built ostentatious houses, and flagrantly flouted the primary tenet of Nashville's reigning aristocracy: The more money one had, the less one should be showing it.

The history of Ward Belmont is an effective proxy for the strained relations between the Nashville patriciate and Music Row, a history founded on disdain and sustained by fiscal necessity.

From the 1850s, when Joseph and Adelicia Acklen, a Louisiana planter and his wife, christened their new summer home Bellemonte after the villa in *The Merchant of Venice*, the thirty-room estate was a center for Nashville society. Adelicia Acklen threw annual harvest moon balls, barely pausing for the Civil War (the mansion was used briefly at the end of the war by Union soldiers). On December 18, 1866, she held a reception for

Madame Octavia Le Vert of Mobile, Alabama. According to Mrs. Ellet's *The Queens of American Society*, it was one of those pivotal moments in social history, "the forerunner of a new regime of entertainments, combining intellectual and artistic enjoyment with perfect taste."

Adelicia sold Bellemonte nearly two decades later, and it changed hands again in 1889, purchased by Ida Hood and Susan Heron, two teachers from Philadelphia who envisioned establishing a "Vassar of the South." Belmont College opened on September 4, 1890. According to its catalog, the Belmont education combined "the grandeur of an ante-bellum mansion with the cosy conveniences of modern convention."

Misses Hood and Heron's reign lasted until 1913, when the two retired and merged their school with Ward College, another Nashville school for young ladies. Ward Belmont, as it was renamed, held fast to its original mission. The girls may have been living in dormitories, but their circumstances were hardly institutional: Dinner was served on bone china, Irish linen covered the tables.

It was a life that an economic depression and a world war were fast making obsolete. By the end of the 1940s, enrollment had dropped precipitously. The school was no longer covering expenses. In 1951, Ward Belmont defaulted on its mortgage. It closed at the end of that school year.

The bankers who held the mortgage on the property tried to interest Vanderbilt University, then Fisk. They even approached Tennessee State. No one was interested—no one, at least, in the familiar world of society Nashville, as they knew it.

By the second half of the twentieth century, though, new money was being made in Nashville, much of it by the Baptists who had made the city the center of their lucrative Bible-publishing business. The Baptists had money, but the old-money Nashville, Episcopalians and Presbyterians, thought them faintly vulgar. Still, the bankers had to cover their loan, never mind social niceties. The Tennessee Baptist Convention was looking for a campus; the bankers offered up Ward Belmont. On March 13, 1951, the Baptists bought the school, assuming $650,000 in debt. That September, Ward Belmont reopened as a Baptist college.

Robert Mulloy was one of the new school's first graduates, and through the years he has dabbled in the music business, working sessions as a keyboard player backing up, among others, the Jordanaires. He started teaching at Belmont in 1963, and from the start, he was determined to take advantage of the school's proximity to Music Row. He grouped together courses from the business and music departments and brought in music-industry executives to speak to the students. Eventually, he got the college administration to approve music business as a major course of study; it is now one of the school's biggest draws. Belmont Mansion, that cradle of Nashville society, owes its survival to Music Row.

• • •

When Trisha Yearwood enrolled in the music business program, there was just one performance group sponsored by the department. The Belmont Reasons, a Christian rock group, were Mulloy's curious attempt to marry the school's religious tenets with his music program. Yearwood auditioned for the group, but she didn't make the final cut. "I was looking for a soprano," is how Mulloy explained it, "and her register was too low."

"It was the first thing I ever wanted that I didn't get," Yearwood said. Instead, she started doing vocals in off-campus student bands. She was lead singer in Straight-laced, a band that did a lot of top-forty songs—Amy Grant to Whitney Houston—and an overabundance of Patsy Cline. "It got," she said, "awfully cheesy."

There are plenty of girl singers who had the best voices in their hometowns, lots of girls who had the leads in their school musicals. Mostly, getting that first record is about luck, perseverence, and timing—who you know and when you meet them. Which is why one of the first things Yearwood did when she got to town was call up the only person she knew in the business, a friend of her sister's husband who worked at a publishing company called Grand Music—and she didn't exactly know him.

Yearwood had determined that the way to get noticed was to start singing on demonstration tapes, first-draft performances played for performers and producers so they can get a sense of what the songs sound like. She had made a demo tape as part of a school project, and she sent it out to her connection at Grand Music, along with a letter explaining who she was.

The friend listened, then called to see if she would do harmonies for a demo session they were doing with Barbara Fairchild, a singer whose biggest hit was "The Teddy Bear Song," in 1973. On the recording day, Fairchild had laryngitis, and Yearwood stepped in to do the lead. Kent Blazy, who had written one of the songs, was sufficiently impressed to ask for her telephone number. From then on, every month or so, Blazy would call Yearwood in for a session or two. It wasn't much—still, she was the only one in her class actually singing on Music Row.

Halfway through her junior year, Yearwood met a curly-haired musician named Christopher Latham. Latham, a year her junior, played guitar in a Christian heavy-metal group, as well as classical violin. She was intrigued by his musical taste and comforted by the fact that he absolutely worshipped her. Yearwood had had only one steady relationship before Latham, a tumultuous three-year affair that broke up just as she got to Nashville. When it finally ended—with Yearwood desolate over too many indifferent phone calls—she vowed to find someone easier, someone who treated her well. Latham was attentive, and above all, he seemed benign. They married six months before she graduated from college.

"You are encouraged to get married when you're from a small town," she explained, "and that's what I did, even though I knew it wasn't right. I had met this guy and I thought, 'I am never going to meet anyone who cares about me this much,' which is probably true, so I married him." It was a union born of friendship, not passion, but Yearwood told herself that didn't matter: Marriage meant her personal life was taken care of. "If I had been madly, passionately in love with somebody, I might have been really distracted," she said. "That probably doesn't sound very nice, but the support was there, and I was able to put all my passion into my career."

She took an internship in the publicity department at MTM Records, the short-lived Nashville outpost of the Hollywood television company whose flagship was *The Mary Tyler Moore Show*. When she graduated in January 1987, she was offered a full-time job as receptionist.

The people who worked with Patricia Latham, as she called herself then, remember her as an overweight, bespectacled blonde who served as a perfectly competent monitor for the front desk and the phones. "She was fairly self-effacing," remembered Howard Stark, who headed up the operation. "I guess I knew she was a singer, but she never bothered anyone with her tapes. Whatever she was doing, it seemed to be outside the office."

Yearwood tried out for *You Can Be a Star*, a talent contest televised on The Nashville Network (TNN). By the terms of the half-hour show, the grand champion (chosen every thirteen weeks) won a recording contract, guaranteed appearances on the Grand Ole Opry, Emerald Cruise Lines, and at Gilleys, along with an upright piano, a guitar, a set of matching luggage, and a mandolin. Yearwood turned up on the show with big hair, a bright red shirt and matching pumps, and a faded denim skirt with an unfortunate hip-length ruffle. She won, over a former Miss Shreveport, and made it through three more rounds before she lost out to a bearded tenor in lizard boots who walked off with a recording contract with Capitol Records and hasn't been heard from since.

Yearwood had always figured the show for a long shot. If she wanted to sing, she decided, the best way to do it was to call the songwriters she knew back in college. She got back in touch with Kent Blazy, and she began booking up her lunch hours and evenings doing demo sessions. Trouble was, most demos were recorded during the day, and that was when she was at the office. Then, in early 1989, came a solution. Mike Smith, a steel guitar player who had toured with the Gatlin Brothers, was putting together a band of musicians who had families and so wanted to spend more time at home. Would Yearwood be interested in doing vocals? He offered her $150 a week—a bit more than she was making at MTM. She gave notice the next day.

Their first gig was at a bar called the Eleventh Frame, thus named because it was situated at the end of a bowling alley. Every night it was "Help Me Make It Through the Night," a few Patsy Cline tunes, and endless requests for "Free Bird," the Lynyrd Skynyrd anthem. It wasn't quite what she had in mind, but at least the schedule freed up her days to do studio work.

It didn't take long for word to get around that there was a hot new demo singer in town—and with enough range to sing her own harmonies, she was a bargain besides. By the middle of 1989, she was spending full days in the studio and nights on the bar circuit. "I couldn't get up and sing at ten if I'd been singing in a bar with smoke all night," she said. It was time to choose between performing and session work. The decision was easy. Doing studio work, she would be seen by producers and record label executives who signed acts—why work bars where her best audiences were a bunch of inebriated bowlers?

She generally worked five days a week, three sessions a day. Demonstration tapes are a slapdash affair—go to the studio, listen to the tape, spend an hour working with a single guitarist to lay on a track. There are maybe ten minutes for rehearsals— if you can call it that. Mostly, you get it right the first time or not at all. And since the songwriter or publisher is paying the demo singer to sell his songs, if a singer doesn't get it right, she doesn't work.

Kent Blazy had believed in Yearwood from the beginning, introducing her to everyone he knew, anyone he thought might jump-start her career. One spring morning he invited her over to his house to sing a cut with another demo singer, an Oklahoman named Garth Brooks. Blazy had been wanting to get them together for months; he heard a match in their voices. Both sang country, but they shared a rock legacy—and a rock sensibility— as well.

The match worked. Brooks was taken by the strength of her soprano. Did she have a manager? he wanted to know. Not yet, she told him, so he offered to introduce her to Bob Doyle and Pam Lewis, who had just got him a record deal with Capitol Records. ("I've found her," he announced to Doyle and Lewis when he called them later.) He finished with another promise: If he ever got his own tour, he told Yearwood, he would use her as the opening act.

Nice compliment, she figured, but fairly meaningless. She knew Brooks had a record deal at Capitol, but it didn't amount to much. After all, he had yet to release his first single.

That September, Pat Alger, an architect turned songwriter, heard Yearwood sing backup at one of Garth Brooks' showcases. He had been looking for a harmony singer for a one-shot deal he was doing at a party for another songwriter, Harlan Howard. "I called to see if she was interested," he said, "She was." After that party, the core of that group—the Algerians, they called themselves—started playing together regularly, doing monthly gigs at Douglas Corner. The place wasn't much to look at: a white painted brick facade sandwiched between a dry cleaner and a shoe-repair shop, pressed tin ceiling, thirty-odd tables, linoleum-lined bar. There was no kitchen. People came for the music.

By the time the Algerians took to the Douglas Corner stage, Alger had already written hits for Mickey Gilley and Don Williams. When the group was performing, various producers and singers would turn up in search of new material. Like everything else Yearwood was doing, it was simply one more way to get seen—which is precisely what happened. In March 1990, Terryl Tye, a song publisher who worked with Alger, called a producer friend named Garth Fundis. "You have to see this new girl singer," she told him.

Fundis, as it happened, had some extra time on his hands. He had a small roster, generally two or three performers, and six months before it had been reduced by a full third. His biggest star, a Kentuckian named Keith Whitley, had drunk himself to death. Fundis noted the Algerians' next date and decided he would be there.

Trisha Yearwood, as she always did, stood ramrod straight, just to the right of the band. Her scrubbed face was sufficiently attractive, but there were thirty extra pounds padding her five-feet-eight-inch frame. She was neither glamorous nor obviously sexy. What she had to sell was her voice.

Fundis bought. "There was this big tall blonde with an amazing voice like I'd never heard before," he recalled. Afterward, he went up to her and asked if she "wanted to be an act." Her answer, of course, was yes. They spent a half hour together, talking about what music she liked, what she had been performing, and what she wanted to be, and agreed to meet for lunch a week later.

Garth Fundis is what Nashville calls a song man, an insatiable customer of songwriters and publishers, constantly searching for the next perfect tune. He's like a magpie. Songs are his shiny objects, tape cassettes stored away for performers he has yet to record, perhaps even yet to meet. "You never know who will come along," is the Fundis philosophy, and Trisha Yearwood demonstrated its wisdom.

"I find things I like and I hope singers pick up on it," he said. "I'm not the type of person to shove something down someone's throat." One of the things he had liked for about a year was a tune by a writer from Colorado, a song about a headstrong small-town girl called "She's in Love with the Boy." He had held on to the song, not quite sure what to do with it. It was a song only a woman could sing, and he had no women on his roster.

At that second meeting with Yearwood it was the first song he played. Even before the second verse came on, she looked up and smiled. "I love this," she said. "This is my life." And so they agreed to work together, agreed to try to get a record deal.

CHAPTER $\boxed{3}$

PRODUCERS' PROMISES COME CHEAP, THE PRICE OF DRINKS OR maybe even a dinner tab. Each year, the Country Music Association figures, thousands of hopefuls find their way to Nashville, and for nearly every one of them there is someone who will promise, "I'll make you a star." A goodly number even manage to get signed to deals, Nashville deals—a couple of free record sides in exchange for a signature, a piece of the action should some money actually come in, which has about as much chance of happening as Willie Nelson turning up in a brush cut.

Yearwood had heard plenty of that talk by the time she met Garth Fundis. She had already signed one deal, a yearlong exclusive, with the Gatlin Brothers' producer. He cut a few songs and told her he was sure he could come up with something. Nothing, of course, came of it. She was invited to take the lead singer's place in Highway 101. Paulette Carlson, the vocalist, had decided to set out on her own. Yearwood went out to Colorado to meet with the group's manager. On the flight back home she decided she wasn't going to pursue it. "If I went with Highway 101, it would be saying I couldn't make it on my own; it would be giving up," she said. "No way was I ready to do that."

It took considerable fearlessness to let that opportunity pass, to hold out for a shot at stardom, where the odds make the state lottery look like a sure thing. "There are twenty thousand people in Nashville who are three minutes away from being stars," said Otto Kitsinger, who works for *Nashville Now*, country music's answer to *The Tonight Show*. Any one of them who gets past the hoping, the promising, and the praying can find the hard truth in the numbers. In any given year the major labels in Nashville release recordings of no more than a couple of dozen new acts.

Come the cold light of day, there are only two ways anybody gets signed to a record deal. One is to produce a demo tape, send it to an artists and repetoire (A&R) executive at a record company, and pray it stands out from the dozen others in the stack that came in that day. The other is to do a showcase: Rent out a club, invite a few label representatives, and hope to God they show up and are impressed enough to make a deal.

Yearwood had cut hundreds of demos since she'd got to Nashville five years before. Adding one more to that pile wouldn't make the difference. "We needed to put on a show," said Fundis.

The only decision remaining was the guest list.

• • •

Today Ralph Peer is considered one of the forefathers of Music Row, but he never did claim to know much about country music in 1923, when he came down from New York scouting for talent with a couple of recording engineers from General Phonograph Corp. An Atlanta record salesman convinced him to record Fiddlin' Jack Carson, a North Georgia performer who'd been playing at fiddle contests and political rallies for the last half dozen years. Peer didn't think much of the songs Carson played—"The Little Log Cabin in the Lane" and "The Old Hen Cackled and the Rooster's Going to Crow." All he knew was that that salesman ordered five hundred copies, unlabeled and uncatalogued, and when those sold out he ordered five hundred more. Peer put the record on his national catalog and invited Carson to New York to record twelve more sides.

Carson wasn't the only fiddler in the hills, so Peer went down looking for more. He brought along a sound engineer and some primitive recording equipment, setting up shop in deserted general stores or grain sheds, whatever he could find. Peer brought Jimmie Rodgers and the Carter Family into his traveling studio, recording their mountain songs on wax disks, shipping them on dry ice back to New York, where they would be turned into so many thousand 78s. Peer was the first one to make an industry of it, the first out-of-towner who decided which hillbillies to record, the first to set them out for America to buy.

Nobody is recording in backwoods sheds anymore, but in some ways, not much has changed in the last seventy-odd years. Nashville now has its own record companies, but they're still owned by out-of-towners—the Dutch, the British, the Japanese. And though most of the people choosing which music gets made live in Nashville now, most have arrived by way of the big city, these days as likely to be Los Angeles as New York.

In June 1990, it was up to Fundis to choose among the carpet-baggers, to figure out which record labels would be interested in Yearwood, which she should be working with.

Capitol Records was an obvious contender. The reason was Garth Brooks. Since that first meeting at Kent Blazy's, Brooks had recorded his second album for the label and invited Yearwood to sing harmonies on it. The relationship went beyond the studio; Yearwood had taken up Brooks's offer to introduce her to his managers and had begun, informally, to work with them.

Pam Lewis and Bob Doyle are an odd match, sort of like Bea Arthur and Bill Macy on *Maude*. Doyle is a soft-mannered former ASCAP executive, the first to hear Brooks, the first to believe he could be a star. While he was still at ASCAP, Doyle tried to get Brooks a songwriting deal, and when that failed he started up his own publishing house—"It was time to move out on my own," he explained afterward. Brooks was the first songwriter signed to Major Bob Publishing, named for Doyle's rank in the air force reserves. But Doyle wanted to be more than a song plugger, and with Brooks as his first client, he branched out into management. He knew the operation needed someone with marketing expertise. He had seen Lewis in action, and he had been impressed. She could sell the talent he picked. A partnership was born.

Lewis is a sort of a New Age Margaret Dumont—fairly big, fairly forceful, given to washed silk rather than cocktail dresses, crystals instead of pearls. She started as a secretary at MTV, then went to work at RCA in public relations; in 1985 she was transferred to Nashville. She was fired a year after she got there. Joe Galante, who headed up the label's Nashville office, never told her why. "I just got shut out," is all Lewis knew. Forced out on her own, Lewis made the most of her credentials. She started her own PR firm and ended up with a small, impressive roster, including Lyle Lovett, Dan Seals, and Steve Earle.

If it had been up to Pam Lewis, Yearwood would probably have gone with Capitol. She thought that Brooks would make it easier to get signed; his success should have assured that attention be paid. But Yearwood was not convinced Capitol was where she wanted to be. For one, she didn't want it to seem that she was being signed as a favor to Brooks. Just as important, the head of Capitol, James "Jimmy" Bowen was, to put it mildly, not someone she wanted to work with.

Then, as now, Jimmy Bowen, fifty-five, was the most powerful executive in Nashville. He cuts a figure of epic proportions; married five times, he is a bulky six-footer whose uniform generally includes a Greek sailor's cap, aviator glasses, and loose-fitting safari shirts. "I can't fuckin' breathe in a tie," is how he explains his attire. "If I'm in a tie, it's usually because someone died, and I rarely go to those things, either. I do have a tie, two ties now. When you go to New York City you wind up getting a tie. Fear of not being able to eat in a good restaurant will cause me to put on a tie."

Bowen has been called Nashville's answer to T. Boone Pickens, a takeover whirlwind whose assault on studio management has been something less than genteel. In the decade and a half since he arrived in Nashville, Bowen has headed up a half dozen different labels, going from MCA to Elektra/Asylum to Warner Bros. Records back to MCA, over to Universal, and finally to Capitol's Nashville arm, which he has since renamed Liberty. By his own admission, there are executives he has fired two and three times over. "It's the kind of thing that will make you enemies," he says. And it has.

Even in Nashville, where conflicts of interest are so common they've practically become tribal custom, Bowen is considered past the bounds. Unlike their counterparts in New York and Los Angeles, where record company executives rarely handle anything more than their management duties, Nashville's music men have all sorts of side deals. Many produce records on their own, augmenting their salaries with production fees, but few operate on Bowen's scale. There have been years when he has produced as many as fourteen or fifteen albums, along with running a major record company. Bowen denies having a stake in any Nashville studios, but he never hid his interest in Great Cumberland Music, a publishing company that he owned with a manager named Bill Hamm until December 1992. Each time a Great Cumberland song appeared on a record, Bowen stood to make tens of thousands of dollars. Still, he insists he's never pressured an act to use one of Great Cumberland's properties.

"The artists that I produce have the final say in their songs," he says. "If I'm forcing things to happen . . . they'll run me off. They've run people off for years. I'm willing to take that gamble."

Bowen has never shied away from taking chances. Born in Santa Rita, New Mexico, raised in the Texas panhandle, he got his start in music in a college rock band, back when anything seemed possible and often was. In the fall of 1955, Roy Orbison made a stop at West Texas State and sang "Ooby Dooby." "It blew me away," Bowen recalled. It was a time when two college kids could call up a producer and convince him to record their band. The producer was Norman Petty. Bowen's band (he played bass, Buddy Knox did vocals) was The Rhythm Orchids, and the song was "Party Doll." In 1957 it was distributed by Roulette Records, and it climbed to number one on the *Billboard* charts.

It was enough to get Bowen his own record deal. Roulette put out Bowen's eponymous album, and about thirty-five thousand sold. For the time, it wasn't bad, but Bowen never had any illusions about his talent. "I sang a little flat," he said. "When the girls screamed, it was cool; when they didn't, it sounded horrible. Our last four, five jobs there were more of us on stage than there were in the audience. That's always a good clue that something's not working." His future, he decided, was in the hustle, not the song.

He worked his way through a series of jobs at small-time labels before landing in Los Angeles as an A&R man for Reprise, home to Dean Martin and Frank Sinatra. Bowen was assigned to Martin. According to *Dino*, Nick Tosches' biography of the singer, Bowen recorded orchestrations without the singer present. Martin came in later and sang to the recorded music. It may have been unorthodox, but it seemed to work. In 1964, "Everybody Loves Somebody" hit number one. Sinatra, impressed, signed Bowen on to produce for him as well, with similar success: "Strangers in the Night" became his first number one hit in twenty years.

By the midseventies the pop performers who had made Bowen's career were falling out of favor, and Bowen didn't really have a place in the L.A. rock scene. Finally, in 1976, he ended up producing a country singer named Thom Bresch. His first cut, "Homemade Love," hit number six on the country charts. Bowen saw his future in Nashville.

Music Row has been built on a bedrock of boosterism; criticism is not tolerated. From the start, Bowen set himself apart, talking about his troubles with the way things were done. "There's nobody [in Nashville] paying attention to the general record business," he told one reporter. "I don't think they've heard of Springsteen, of John Mellencamp, or Bon Jovi. . . . How can you be a tit on the hog and not know about the whole hog?"

Yearwood had spent enough time circling Music Row to hear all the Bowen stories. The ones that concerned her most were the ones about his reputation as a producer. Despite his experience with Martin (or perhaps because of it), Bowen had come to believe that a performer is primarily responsible for his or her own music. In practical terms that means that Bowen supervised from afar, an absentee landlord. Yearwood wanted a producer who would be involved in how her music was made. More specifically, she was determined to work with Fundis. She was afraid that if she signed with Capitol, Bowen would pressure her to work with him. (In the end, Yearwood's trepidation didn't really matter. Though Lewis spent months soliciting Bowen's interest, he remained lukewarm. He had another young female singer, Suzy Bogguss, who already filled Yearwood's niche.)

Fundis thought Yearwood would be best off at RCA, at the time, the hottest label in Nashville. Not only did RCA have the top-selling roster (K. T. Oslin, Alabama, the Judds, Clint Black) in town, it was also among the smallest, meaning that each of its performers should get the company's attention. Fundis figured RCA for a shoo-in. After producing two RCA albums that had gone gold (certification by the Recording Industry of America that signifies sales of over five hundred thousand; platinum sales over one million), Fundis had an excellent relationship with Joe Galante.

Galante is a compact man, swarthy, with unlikely blue eyes, taut with ambition. Back then, he wore his hair New York New Wave: spiked up, ends bleached blond. He was the most improbable of country music moguls, a child of ethnic America for whom country music was decidedly an acquired taste. Galante's grandparents were born in Sicily, and emigrated to New York at the turn of the century. Galante's father was a postman, his mother a secretary. They sent their son to Catholic schools, and he graduated from Fordham University with a degree in finance.

His first job out of school was as a financial analyst at RCA, reviewing expenses. Two and a half years later he was moved into marketing, where he handled the campaigns for David Bowie and Lou Reed.

It was an unlikely education for Music Row, but in 1974 he was transferred to Nashville and put in charge of operations. Chet Atkins was still in charge when he got there. When Atkins left in 1981, he was replaced by his chief lieutenant, a man named Jerry Bradley.

Bradley has one of the better bloodlines on Music Row. His father, Owen Bradley, produced Patsy Cline. The son got his position as much by virtue of paternity as talent. By the time Galante got to RCA Nashville, costs were running out of control, and there weren't enough hits to cover them.

Galante, being an accountant, did what accountants do. He set up systems to track how much was being spent on a particular act and how effectively. He found ways to get work done on the cheap, getting interns to work free, pressing the staff to work longer hours. When Galante got to Nashville, marketing was a simple matter of finding a star, getting the record on the charts, and hoping it would sell. Galante put a longer-term strategy in place. He was the first Nashville executive to hire a research firm and use focus groups, the first to venture away from Music Row, leasing a bus for a cross-country tour, a door-to-door visit to every major radio station and record seller in America. The point was to establish a relationship with those all-important programmers and retailers, let them know what was coming, make them feel that they were integral to the label's success. In all, he established a reputation as such an effective businessman that in 1981 Bradley was moved aside and Galante took over.

Music Row acknowledged Galante's fiscal success, but his taste was another matter. Sure, he could sell, was the common wisdom, but the man had no ears, no ability to hear a hit before it became one. Fundis didn't worry about Galante's ear. He knew he could make a quality record; what he relied on Galante for was his salesmanship, and that was a proven quantity.

As an afterthought, Fundis invited Tony Brown, executive vice president of A&R at MCA. While RCA was his first choice, he wasn't willing to make it his only bet.

As corporate bloodlines go, MCA's were the best on Music Row. MCA was a sort of collateral descendant of Decca Records, one of the first labels to set up an outpost in Nashville. Decca was incorporated in the U.S. in 1934 by Jack Kapp, the onetime recording director for the Brunswick Company, whose roster included Bing Crosby, Guy Lombardo, and the Dorsey Brothers. It was the beginning of the Depression, and no one had the seventy-five cents to spend on a record. Kapp was convinced that people still wanted to buy records, they just had to be priced to sell. He reduced the price to thirty-five cents and convinced the biggest of Brunswick's performers, Crosby and Lombardo among them, to join him at his new venture. By 1939, eighteen million of the fifty million records sold in the U.S. were produced by Decca.

Jack's brother, Dave, was also in the record business, first as owner of a record store, then as a talent manager. When Jack Kapp formed Decca he asked his brother to join him and start a country division. Jimmie Davis cut his first Decca record in September 1934, just months after the company was formed.

By the early forties, Dave Kapp was increasingly occupied with other areas of the company, and in 1945 he turned over the reins of the country division to Paul Cohen. That same year, Cohen came down from New York to record Red Foley, one of the first recording sessions actually done in Nashville. Under Cohen's watch, Decca became the first record label to do regular sessions in Nashville. Still, the New York–based executive needed a local representative to handle daily business. He delegated that task to a local bandleader named Owen Bradley, and together they signed some of the best-known talents of the day: Ernest Tubb, Kitty Wells, Patsy Cline.

The Kapp brothers' glory was short-lived. Jack died in 1949, and Dave left the company five years later, ultimately forming his own label, Kapp Records. In 1962, the Music Corporation of America (MCA) bought 81 percent of Decca's stock and took control of the operation. By 1973, any remnants of the independent operations had vanished into the corporate maw. All recordings, past and present, were simply labeled MCA.

By mid-1990, MCA's recent corporate history was somewhat less glorious than its past. The label was in the middle of the Nashville pack, with about 20 percent of the market share. There were a handful of established acts, George Strait and Reba McEntire among them. There was a promising young singer named Vince Gill, who had just gone gold with "When I Call

Your Name." But in order to become the force on Music Row, the label needed to bolster its roster of new, younger acts. That job belonged to Tony Brown.

Tony Brown is one of Nashville's cooler customers. He never went to college, but with God and Elvis on his side, how much classroom learning does a man really need? Brown is a preacher's kid from North Carolina who started off playing in gospel bands and ended up working in Elvis Presley's band. He was booked for that last gig in Portland when Presley turned up stone-cold on a Graceland bathroom floor.

Brown hooked up with Presley in 1974; he became the keyboard player for the Voice, Presley's in-house gospel band, on call twenty-four hours a day. The Voice followed Presley from Memphis to Beverly Hills to Palm Springs and back again, generally convening after dark. Presley would ask them up to his bedroom, where they would surround the singer as he put one record after another on the turntable. "When the bass singer would sing a little low line, he would poke you," recalled Brown. " 'Wadn't that great,' he'd say, and play it twenty, thirty times over. Elvis was a sweet guy, he wasn't stupid, but time stopped after awhile. He was encouraged to be Elvis twenty-four hours a day, which made it hard to get out."

Because the rest of Presley's retinue didn't think much of the Voice ("They thought we were a bunch of hangers-on, which maybe we were"), the group was put to work opening for the Sweet Inspirations, who, in turn, opened for Presley. Brown worked his way into playing piano for the Sweet Inspirations. When the singer's pianist, Glen Hardin, left for a new young singer on the country circuit, Emmylou Harris, Brown graduated to Presley's band.

For Brown, Elvis's glamour faded fast. A bloated Presley would do his show. Then, while the audience was still applauding, he was rushed into his limousine, hightailing it for the nearest airport. The band was left to finish and hustle to their bus as the fans hollered, "Was Elvis stoned? What's the man on, anyway?"

After Presley died, Brown graduated to keyboard player for Emmylou Harris (Hardin had left for John Denver). Her band, the Hot Band, became country music's answer to The Band. They were the hottest players in Nashville: Vince Gill, Rodney Crowell among them. "Before that I was pretty much straight gospel," says Brown. "All of a sudden, I was with a bunch of hippies, playing from the heart. I hadn't really been part of all that. Suddenly I was in the middle of country rock. It shaped my whole taste in music." He ended up working with Harris for a couple of years, and when Harris stopped touring after the birth of her second daughter, Jerry Bradley invited him to join RCA. Brown took his first detour from making music to producing it. RCA shipped him to Los Angeles to work in the pop division, not exactly his element. What's more, when he hit L.A. the bands that were second cousins to the music he'd been playing in Nashville—Loggins and Messina and the Doobie Brothers— were fading, and he didn't have much feel for what came next. "It was all B-52's and The Clash," Brown says. "I hated that shit." Two years later he was back in Nashville.

But he wasn't ready to be cooped up in an office. "I hadn't gotten my musician jones out yet," was how he put it, and so, when he got an offer to play backup for Rodney Crowell, half of Nashville's golden couple, he gratefully accepted. Crowell's wife, Rosanne Cash, was not only Johnny's daughter, she had her own gold album. The Cash-Crowell gang was the epicenter of a newer, hipper Nashville. "The rules were pretty simple," recalled Brown. "Were you talented—and could you go to dinner with Bob Dylan as well as George Jones?"

Great atmosphere, but there were problems with the practicalities. Crowell didn't tour much, so Brown ended up playing backup for Cash. But she had two children in just over two years and took time off from touring after each was born. Brown had an ex-wife and two kids to support, so he needed work. He was invited back to RCA, this time by Joe Galante, and he jumped— this time for good. He left RCA when Jimmy Bowen, then in his second incarnation at MCA, offered him a vice president's position. The title was better, but the important thing was that, unlike at RCA, he would be able to produce albums on his own. Bowen even promised that he could start his own label.

Brown created the Master Series, a high-class low-profit jazz label. "It gave me a certain amount of musical credibility," he says. "It also introduced me to a whole new group of people that I'd never been around: the symphony crowd and the jazz crowd. It raised my musical and my social awareness." He proved himself that most rare of Music Row commodities—a label executive with commercial and critical credibility.

* * *

Fundis picked a date for Yearwood's showcase to suit Galante's schedule. June 14 was the hottest day of an unseasonably hot week, and Douglas Corner was filled. Galante and Brown were there, along with a couple of executives from Warner Bros. Records and Capitol who had been invited, unbeknownst to Fundis and Yearwood, by Doyle and Lewis. At the last minute the two had agreed to pick up the twenty-three-hundred-dollar tab for the evening, which included the cost of printing a brief biography for "Tricia Yearwood." Nobody, apparently, had bothered to check the spelling.

She started with "Mr. Radio," a tune Linda Ronstadt had recorded nine years before, then went into "She's in Love with the Boy" and seven more, a soft little "thank you" after each song.

Fundis paced the back of the club, every bit the expectant father. From that first show on, it would be the Garth and Trisha show, performer and producer working as one. "We blew 'em away," he said after the show, then corrected himself: "*She* blew 'em away."

Fundis got phone calls the next day from both Galante and Brown. Galante was impressed with Yearwood's voice, he said, but he had no sense of who she was. Galante was a marketing man, and he didn't know how to sell her. He asked Yearwood to lunch, and brought half his staff with him. "She was all over the place," he recalled. "I asked her what she wanted to do— was she blues, was she aiming at the working woman, just who was she as a singer. . . . She had a great voice but no identity." He already had two good-sized female acts—K. T. Oslin and Lorrie Morgan—and an up-and-comer named Matraca Berg. He wasn't sure where Yearwood would fit in. He called Fundis again the next day. Would Yearwood be willing to do some more demos and hone her style?

"He didn't see the talent beyond the flesh," said Fundis.

Tony Brown called as well, asking if they could set up a meeting. He was interested, he told Fundis, and he wanted to meet with both of them. Brown produced a lot of acts, and he didn't want Fundis to think he was trying to slide in. "I knew it was a package," he said.

When they met, Brown asked about RCA's interest. "They

actually admitted to me that RCA wanted them to make more demos." Brown couldn't believe Galante wasn't interested, but when he thought about it he realized the problem: Galante was reacting more to her image than her voice.

"I just heard twenty this week," Brown told them. "I just heard you sing. Why would I possibly want to hear more demos?" Then he said the one thing Yearwood and Fundis wanted to hear, the one card a record executive keeps closest and longest. "I'll sign you," he told them, "and you can just do an album."

It was almost that simple. Brown wanted her to do one more showcase, for his boss, Bruce Hinton, head of MCA Nashville, as well as the rest of the MCA staff. In August they put on that second show, and as Brown had assumed, everyone loved her. The deal was done.

It was, by all accounts, a whirlwind courtship. "We pulled off the showcase," said Fundis, "and she got this deal and we hadn't even been in the studio yet."

CHAPTER 4

THERE IS NO SHORTAGE OF PRODUCERS WHO REVEL IN EXCESS, chafing to be as flamboyant as the performers they work with. Garth Fundis is not among them. He is a calm, decent man, slow to rile, a steadfast son of the American heartland. He constantly worries that he doesn't spend enough time with his family—his wife, Ann, and three children. His sandy hair has thinned well past his temples and begun to go gray. He has a well-trimmed beard that along with his usual uniform of sports jacket, polo shirt, jeans, and Nikes gives him the look of a recently tenured history professor at a midwestern university. He rarely wears cowboy boots.

Fundis is the second son of a farmer from Baldwin City, Kansas, a tiny town in the eastern part of the state. He played in bands in high school, and when he went on to college in Topeka, spent summers on the road in low-rent rock groups with names like the Heard and Upside Dawn. During performances, an overhead projector cast protoplasmic images of swirling oil and water on a screen behind the stage. "It was," Fundis explained, "the sixties."

By the summer after his sophomore year, though, he thought he had had his fill of low-rent bars and cramped Volkswagen-bus trips to the Great Divide and back. He quit one band mid-summer and figured he was out of the music business for good. Then, three weeks into his junior year, came an invitation to join a band called the Smoke Ring. The group needed a new vocalist, the bandleader, Joe Hupp, told him. How much did Fundis want to be paid, Hupp asked. Fundis came up with the most exorbitant amount he could think of: $150 a week. "No problem," said Hupp, and by October 1969, Fundis was on the road with the Smoke Ring, hitting National Guard armories and sleazy bars from Massachusetts to Colorado.

The Smoke Ring had already recorded its first album when Fundis joined up, but since the original lead singer was gone, it was agreed that Fundis should record a new vocal track. The studio was in Memphis. The producers were Allen Reynolds, then a branch manager for a local bank, now producer for, among others, Garth Brooks; Dickey Lee, whose record about a small-town Romeo and Juliet, "Patches," went to number six in *Billboard* in 1962; and Knox Phillips, son of Sam Phillips, owner of Sun Records, Genesis in the rock-and-roll bible.

The Smoke Ring's record, even with Fundis's new vocals, was not among the studio's more memorable productions. But while it never did much in the way of sales, Fundis kept in touch with Reynolds and Phillips, and after the Smoke Ring dissolved two years later, one of Fundis's first calls was to Reynolds, who had by then moved to Nashville.

"I don't have any work for you," Reynolds told him, "but if you come to town I'm sure you can find something." So, in 1971, Fundis packed his bags and moved into an apartment in southwest Nashville. He ended up with a $2.50 an hour gofer's job at the Jack Clement Recording Studios, which had been built by Cowboy Jack Clement just two years before.

By the time he met Garth Fundis, Clement had done time as a member of the marine corps drill team, and as an Arthur Murray dance instructor, not to mention a stint as the first sound engineer at Sun Records. He had already cut records for Roy Orbison and Jerry Lee Lewis, and written "Ballad of a Teenage Queen" and "Guess Things Happen That Way" for Johnny Cash; already started and folded his own record label, Summer Records ("Summer hits, summer not, hope you like the ones we've got"); and run a radio show in Beaumont, Texas, with Dickey Lee and Allen Reynolds. "There was Cowboy Carl and Cowboy Waliaski," said Clement. "Everybody was Cowboy this or Cowboy that. Mine stuck."

Clement got to Nashville in 1965. By the end of the decade he was operating two of the most successful independent studios in town and producing Charley Pride, the first black country star since Deford Bailey got fired as the Opry's harmonica player back in 1941. His head filled with visions of multimedia moguldom, Clement even bankrolled a film that he insisted would change the course of movie history, a low-rent ax murder flick called *Dear Dead Delilah*, starring Will Geer and Agnes Moorehead.

It was a résumé that hovered somewhere between the improbable and the impossible, an act maintained with style and, back then anyway, sufficient material success to gain Clement an army of followers, students of what he called the Cowboy College of Music. Its precepts were simple; no heavy orchestration, just clean vocals and instrumentals. "Basically, I ignored what everybody told me radio wanted," he said. "I do what I feel and keep my story intact, keep it intact all the way to the poorhouse, if I have to." Which, as it turned out, was pretty much what it would come to.

It took about a year for Fundis to learn the basics of sound engineering. He ended up with the jobs the main engineer didn't want, the contract jobs, the hopefuls who answered the "Cut Hits with the Stars" ads Clement placed in back of various music magazines. These were the farmers, the truck drivers, the assembly-line workers who spent years scrimping to save the two or three thousand dollars it cost to hire a producer, pay the musicians, and rent a studio for their shot at the big time.

"I remember one woman, the wife of a dairy farmer, who had raised her kids, then took what was left of her savings, got in a Winnebago, and came to Nashville," Fundis recalled. "She was in here, next to me, all her hopes and dreams riding on the session. The producer didn't care because he had already got his money, and the musicians were just going through the motions. 'You do this all the time,' she said to me. 'Don't you think it's a hit?' All I could think was, 'I've got to get out of this.' "

Fundis moved over to Jack's Tracks, where he did demo records for the songwriters employed by Jack Music, Clement's publishing company: Wayland Holyfield, Bob McDill, and Don Williams among them. He had a front-row seat as the Cowboy ran through his fortune.

Clement was just finishing his movie when Fundis got to Jack's Tracks, spending five hundred thousand dollars on a film that wouldn't make one tenth that at the box office. There was still money coming in, mostly from Charley Pride ("I sure did make a lot of money off Chuck Pride," Clement said years later), but even gold records weren't enough to cover that half-million-dollar fiasco. By Fundis's second year at the studio, payday had become a weekly lottery. The key to staying ahead of the game was to get your paycheck as early each Friday as possible, then beeline to the bank. If it wasn't cashed by lunchtime, the check was likely to bounce as high as Roy Acuff's yoyo.

Sobriety had never been one of Clement's long suits, and as his finances deteriorated he had an ever-increasing appetite for "liquid refreshments," as he called them. So it was on April 1, 1975. "I'd probably had a little bit of everything that day," Clement recalled, and he had started well before he arrived at Jack's Tracks at noon. Fundis was working in the studio when Clement walked in and insisted he fix a buzz in the monitor. Fundis told him they had tried, that there was nothing they could do, and in any case it wasn't coming through on the recording. Clement wandered off, and the next thing Fundis knew, his ear phones had gone dead. Clement had pulled off the master power switch. "Buzz is gone," he announced.

"What's going on?" asked Fundis.

"You're fired," Clement replied. And, one by one, he walked up to his employees and fired them.

Fundis silently packed up his bag and walked out the door. "I never did have much patience for drunks. . . . It enraged me that this [one] had so much control over my life."

The next day, Clement hired everyone back. Everyone, that is, except Fundis. A few days later, when Fundis finally reappeared at the studio to collect the last of his things, Clement approached him, trying to apologize. "Not acceptable," Fundis told him. "I don't want your apologies. I like you too much to hate you any more." With that, Fundis was through with the Cowboy.

Fundis started engineering free-lance, picking up work from Reynolds, who was then producing Crystal Gayle and Don Williams. Before long, Williams would become the keystone of Fundis's career.

Don Williams, a droopy-eyed, lantern-jawed bassett hound of a man, was the son of a machinist from Floydada, Texas. He had his first top-ten hit in 1964 with the Pozo Seco Singers, and spent the next seven years playing bars and rowdy dance halls before the life became too much for his churchgoing ways. In 1972, after an unsuccessful foray into the furniture business, he moved to Nashville and signed up with Jack Music as a song plugger. He was about as good at pitching tunes as he had been at selling furniture. And so, in 1973, he went back into the studio, recording his first album on JMI, Clement's record label. Two cuts promptly went to the top of the charts, and Williams became the biggest act on Clement's label. Still, his success did not exempt him from the Cowboy's money troubles. After one too many bounced checks—and a lot of frustration with Clement's management style—he went to ABC/Dot Records and announced that he would be producing himself. He kept Fundis on as engineer and, four albums later, promoted him to coproducer.

Williams may have had it with Clement's business practices, but stylistically he remained a disciple. He was the antithesis of the rhinestone cowboys dominating the radio waves in the early seventies. He wanted no part of the treacly orchestrations that backed so many country songs. You could hear the wailing fiddle on "Lord Have Mercy on a Country Boy," the whining steel on "Come a Little Closer," productions that were as much Fundis's creation as Williams's.

That work was what convinced Mary Martin, an executive at RCA Records, to call Fundis in 1987, when their most problematic prodigy, a honky-tonk singer named Keith Whitley, was looking for a new producer.

Whitley had just finished a third album, and it was, by the label's estimation, unreleasable. RCA urged him to find a new producer and start from scratch. Whitley auditioned by song selection: He asked producers to submit material, and he would choose from it. Fundis sent a cassette that included a simple, haunting love song called "Don't Close Your Eyes."

As soon as he heard it, Whitley said later, "it was clear we understood each other. . . . The rest was a matter of getting acquainted."

Fundis had heard about the thirty-two-year-old singer's troubles with alcohol, but RCA executives assured him that those binges were past. Through the production of their first album, Fundis had no reason to disbelieve them. It was the happiest sort of record, a critical and commercial hit, and it became Whitley's first to go gold.

It was when they started preparing for the second album that

Fundis realized that Whitley hadn't quite left the bottle behind him. One of the songs Whitley asked Fundis to get a copy of was "Tennessee Courage," a drinking song by Vern Gosdin. The lyrics were straight-up desperation. To Fundis's mind, it was not the sort of song that a singer with Whitley's reputation had any business recording.

A couple of weeks later, Whitley invited the producer to join him on a leg of his concert tour so they could choose the songs for the new album. One night, after the show, they sat on the bus and worked their way through the pile of tapes. "Didn't you get 'Tennessee Courage?' " Whitley asked after they had finished. Fundis nodded yes.

"What did you think?"

"It's really well written," Fundis hedged.

"It's a great song."

"In light of your situation, don't you think . . . the perspective on the song is from the bottom of the glass."

"Yeah," Whitley answered. "Put it on."

Fundis reluctantly pulled the tape from his bag. After it had played, Whitley leaned back in his chair and smiled. "This is my song, and I'm going to sing it."

Fundis looked over and saw the grin of a drunken man. No matter what he'd been told, alcohol still had a serious hold on Whitley. The conversation trailed off, and Fundis just hoped Whitley would forget about the song.

They went into the studio a couple of weeks later, nothing more said about "Tennessee Courage." Everything went smoothly—until the last day. It was eight o'clock at night, and they had one song left to do, "Heartbreak Highway," a ballad written by Brent Mason, the guitar player working with Whitley that night.

Fundis, the band, and Whitley gathered in the control room to get the lyrics for "Heartbreak Highway."

"I don't want to do that," Whitley announced. "I want to do 'Tennessee Courage.' "

"We're going to do Brent's song," Fundis countered. The sidemen wanted no part of that confrontation. As they filed out, Fundis closed the door after them. "I really don't think this is a song you should do," he said.

Whitley just grinned. "Let's just do it so I can have my own cassette."

"I don't understand what you're doing to me here," Fundis said.

"Can't we just do it so I can have a cassette of it for my car?"

And it went on and on. Finally Fundis relented. "We're going to do Brent's song first, and you'll have to pay the musicians for an extra session's time, but we'll do it."

When they finished "Heartbreak Highway," Fundis called the band into the control room. "There's a song Keith really wants to do. Would you mind staying for one more session?"

The musicians agreed to stay, but they knew Fundis wasn't keen on the song, and their playing showed it. Which brought Fundis out of the control room and into the studio. If he was going to do "Tennessee Courage," he was going to do it right.

"This is a goddamn drinking song," he told them, "and we need to kick the shit out of it." And they did. What he ended up with was a gritty guitar solo and a tough, mournful steel harmony. In the end, it took forty-five minutes, and as Fundis put it, "it was a killer."

The only trouble was Whitley's voice. By the end of the evening it was worn out, and he came off flat and hollow. "I'll come in and sing it in the morning," he promised.

Whitley showed up on time and made a first, unremarkable pass at the song. He tried another take, and when he finished the last chorus, he looked up to Fundis. "You've convinced me," the producer said. "It's your song."

Whitley walked back into the control room. "I have an idea for a recitation," he said, and sat down with a yellow pad and pencil.

"We don't need it. The song stands on its own."

"Let me just try it," said Whitley. "We'll put it together later and see if it works." Whitley taped the reading and was gone ten minutes later.

For the next couple of weeks, Fundis would call with updates, which instruments he had added, which he had pulled off. Whitley would promise to show up at the studio, then call to postpone. "I knew something was wrong," said Fundis, "but I didn't know how wrong."

On the morning of May 9, 1989, Keith Whitley's body was discovered in his Nashville bedroom. His blood-alcohol level measured an incredible .477%. The coroner estimated Whitley had downed the equivalent of twenty shots of 100-proof liquor in less than two hours.

A few lines of Whitley's recitation were included in the liner notes:

You know, sometimes a man can get himself into some pretty strange ways of thinkin'. He can even convince himself that he doesn't have the courage to stand on his own two feet without some help. I used to get my courage out of a bottle. As a matter of fact it used to be exactly like this.

The album went on to sell gold, and one song from the previous album, "I'm No Stranger to the Rain," won Single of the Year at that year's Country Music Association Awards. But Whitley's death had turned Fundis's sense of accomplishment hollow. "No matter what you think you've got, no matter how successful you think you are, it can all vanish in an instant," was how he put it afterward. "After Keith died, I've never taken any success for granted, I know just how fragile it always is."

• • •

December 17, 1990, was Fundis's first day in the studio with Yearwood, his first recording date with a new act since Whitley had died. He was nervous, and by the end of that first day every bit of that anxiety was realized.

He and Yearwood had assembled a five-member band to cut some demos of the songs they were considering for the album, including "She's in Love with the Boy." They spent several hours on the songs, then let the band go home and listened. "She's in Love with the Boy" was meant to capture the rush of first love. It should have bounded with energy. But while the vocals were there, the instrumentation was listless. Yearwood was not happy. Fundis was frantic. Though he had set up the showcase, had helped get her the deal, there was nothing legally binding them. "Here I had gotten it this far," he worried, "and now I'm going to lose her."

Yearwood just kept repeating, "It's just not rocking, it's just not kicking my butt." Then she came in with the last Keith Whitley album and put it on the tape player. "Now that," she said, "kicks butt."

So Fundis started from scratch, rehiring the same band that had played on Whitley's record. It was the first time they had played together since the singer had died.

They went into the studio February 15 and did the first six cuts in two days. After each session, they listened. This time the magic took hold. "We found ourselves saying the same things at the same time," says Fundis. "It's the kind of experience you wish for." The album was virtually finished before she got that first check from MCA.

There weren't any particular problems with Yearwood's contract. It was just that those negotiations, with all their accompanying paperwork, tarried over four months or so. Yearwood was represented in those talks by Malcolm Mimms, a forty-year-old lawyer headquartered on Music Row. Mimms's office, with its massive partner's desk and matching cabinets, appears standard-issue corporate. Mimms himself, with his rumpled corduroys and the point of a blond ponytail brushing just an inch or two from the small of his back, looks like a banjo player in a bluegrass band.

The contract Mimms finally presented Yearwood with at the end of February was fairly routine. She got a $20,000 advance against royalties of 12 percent per album, with a half point more should she sell 500,000, and another half should she go up to 750,000. In all, that's about a full percentage point less than the deal generally given to brand-new pop acts. In addition, according to Yearwood's contract, which is pretty much standard for the industry, her record label also recoups the cost of producing her music as well as a pecentage of the retail price (20 percent for cassettes, 25 percent for CDs) to cover packaging costs.

No movie studio ever had it this good. It's as if the stars and directors didn't have to be paid until the studio had got back every cent of its outlay. "The record companies are in essence venture capitalists," is how Mimms explains it. "If it succeeds, they will get all their money back by having the performer pay for the entire product, plus they will own it for the life of the copyright and only pay out a very small portion of the profits to the artist. It's the damndest business there is."

Yearwood put the final vocals on that first album on May 1. Shortly thereafter, MCA put her on a nationwide bus tour through a dozen midsize midwestern cities, places where the sales managers from Tower Records and Handleman, the nation's largest rack-jobber (so-called because it fills—"jobs"—the racks in discount chains such as Kmart and Wal-Mart) could hear her sing and, the hope was, order her album.

It was Yearwood's first real tour, and it wasn't hard to see she was green. Dramamine did little to help the nausea that set in as soon as the bus set out on the highway. Even though all she did was sing a short acoustic set with a guitar player, she was so nervous before each performance that she broke out in hives. There was no polish, just a small-town girl in blue jeans singing about first love.

"Those branch managers saw her as this simple country girl," said Walt Wilson, the head of marketing at MCA Nashville and her escort on the tour, "and they fell in love."

That marketing tour, as well as it went, was still fairly standard stuff for a brand-new act. After that, there was nothing standard about Trisha Yearwood at all.

One spring morning, Willie Mayhoe, the receptionist at MCA, called Tony Brown. "Garth and Trisha are up here."

Brown had just got off the phone with Garth Fundis and couldn't quite figure out why the producer needed to come by. "Send them back," he said. And Garth *Brooks* and Yearwood appeared at his desk.

"Sir," Brooks said, taking off his hat and placing it in his lap as he sat down, "I'm committed to this project, and I plan to take her on tour with me."

Brown met Brooks's stare. "This guy is serious," he thought.

A brand-new act usually spends the first year or two touring small-time county fairs and midsize honky-tonks, lucky to get a crowd of a thousand or two. But June 1990 found Trisha Yearwood, who had sung a dozen times at Douglas Corner and the Bluebird Cafe—not to mention those memorable months at the Eleventh Frame—standing before a crowd of six thousand at the Universal Amphitheater in Burbank, California, the opening act for the biggest thing to hit country music since Hank Williams. Her first album would still not be released for a month.

She opened fifty shows for Brooks, traveling from Stillwater, Oklahoma, to Springfield, Illinois, to Murfreesboro, Tennessee. And as she toured, her first single, "She's in Love with the Boy" rode higher and higher on the radio charts at *Billboard*, *Radio & Records*, and *The Gavin Report*. By the first week of August, the song had hit number one in all three industry bibles, the first time a debut record by a female performer had ever gone so high.

• • •

Those first two months on the road would have tested the strongest of marriages, and Yearwood's had been shaky from the start. Latham said that he didn't mind her trips, that he was happy with her successes, but she wanted more than support. She wanted someone whose ambitions matched her own.

"I guess I had dreams of playing on the road with somebody," Latham said later, "but I had no thoughts of being in the limelight." For the first couple of years of their marriage, he drove a parts truck for an auto-supply company. At his wife's prodding, he got a job on Music Row, copying tapes at EMI Music Publishing. But it frustrated her that he simply kept on with his low-level position, showing no signs of moving up or moving on. It was hard enough to put up with when she was a demo singer struggling to be heard, but once she had her deal, it became impossible.

"Chris is a smart guy, but not much ambition," said Pat Alger, who is still friendly with both. "Trisha has this thing burning inside her. We're not talking smoldering here, we're talking burning."

Yearwood no longer wanted Latham simply to accommodate her. She wanted out. "There was just no real spark," was how she explained it, "which I think there is supposed to be." She came home after her second stint on the road and told Latham she wasn't sure if she wanted to stay married.

A few months later, Yearwood "stuck a fork in it," in her ex-husband's words. "I tracked down a marriage counselor, but she wasn't interested. She told me, 'I just don't see how I can get back feelings I never had.' That pretty much let me know it was winding down."

"It wasn't show business that broke us up," she said after they had divorced. "We wouldn't still be married if I was back answering phones. . . . But I do feel like there are a lot of things I owe to him."

Back then, though, it was Latham who ended up sleeping on the couch.

• • •

The summer and early fall were a whirlwind: Her album went gold in September, just before her twenty-seventh birthday. Her second single, "Like We Never Had a Broken Heart," marched to the top of the charts, and the rave reviews just kept coming in. She was the next Reba McEntire, raved the *Chicago Tribune*, the Cinderella story of 1991, the Music Row receptionist who had come out of nowhere to stardom.

All the outward signs were fine: good press clips, great sales. Yearwood should have been ecstatic; her career seemed to be well on its way. Instead, she was terrified of the future.

Unlike country performers of years past who had happily let others handle their business affairs, Yearwood considered herself a performer and a businesswoman in equal measure. "If I hadn't become a singer," she said, "I guess I would have ended up being an accountant or something like that." She knew the stories of Dottie West and Willie Nelson, the millions they had made and the millions that had disappeared because someone else had been attending to the numbers.

Yearwood was one of a new Nashville breed that believed in the balance sheet as much as the song. Her degree was in music business, and she had come up behind Garth Brooks, the marketing major who became the most popular singer in country music history. "Country music is a business," she said. "I'm the head of a corporation, and my name is the bottom line."

In the autumn of 1991, Trisha Yearwood, Inc., seven months old, was an organization in need of a plan. Yearwood felt confident of her ability to maintain the status quo, but she had no focus for her future and no one she trusted to help show the way.

Exactly what a manager is supposed to do has always been ill defined. The job is one part Svengali, one part Maxwell Perkins, and a bit of Mama Rose—a little vision, a little order, and a little bit of nudging. Doyle and Lewis, Yearwood felt, provided not nearly enough of any of those things.

She had had qualms about Doyle and Lewis from the beginning. The typo on that invitation for her first showcase might seem like a small thing, but for Yearwood it was part of a larger problem. Lewis was a scattered sort. Everything that needed to get done got done, but it happened in its own good time. It was the worst possible match for Trisha Yearwood, a woman who still balanced her own checkbook, each entry placed with Palmer-perfect handwriting.

It would take days for phone calls to be returned. On one occasion, she said, she missed an interview with the *Atlanta*

Constitution because Lewis's office failed to tell her that she was supposed to call the reporter. Then there were the endless problems on the road. She felt it was Doyle and Lewis's role to find her a proper road manager. They told her she couldn't afford one and should simply appoint someone on the bus to handle those chores.

Yearwood wasn't the only one put off by the Doyle-Lewis style. "Trisha was the first time I ever dealt with Pam and Bob," said MCA's Walt Wilson. "I had seen what they did with Garth and figured they had to be good, but when it came to Trisha they just didn't seem to have an idea for the direction she should be going."

What worked for Garth Brooks was not at all what Yearwood needed. From the beginning, he had a coterie of trusted advisers. A college classmate was his road manager, his brother handled his business affairs. Brooks was a self-guided missile, a juggernaut propelled by public demand. Yearwood didn't have that kind of trajectory. She wanted a manager who could provide her with opportunities she couldn't have come up with on her own. It was Garth Fundis who had helped find her a record deal and Garth Brooks who had offered her a tour. Yearwood needed vision, and she didn't believe that Bob Doyle and Pam Lewis could provide it.

In mid-October 1991, Yearwood decided it was time for a change. Fundis was helping her rehearse with her band. She came in one day looking gray. "I'm losing my mind with these people," she told him. "I can't do this anymore."

Later that day, she met with Malcolm Mimms. She told him that she wanted to fire Doyle and Lewis and that she wanted to do it immediately. It was the week before the Country Music Association Awards, and she couldn't bear the thought of going through the week's festivities with management she had no desire to work with.

Mimms supported the move, but cautioned her that there would be talk. "People are going to say it's a dumb move, that you're ungrateful, that they are the ones that made you."

She then told the executives at MCA of her plans. They had no objections as long as it was legal. That was no problem; there had been no written contract. Yearwood wanted Mimms to do the firing, but he told her that it was something she had to do herself. He would be there for support, he said, but she had to be the one to tell them she wanted out. She called Doyle and Lewis and asked them to meet her at Mimms's office.

"I don't think this is working out," she told them. "I think it's time for me to make other management arrangements."

Lewis, especially, felt that Yearwood was being irrational. She suggested psychological counseling. To Lewis's mind, changing managers was something a performer did when a career was foundering. Yearwood's first album had just gone gold. "She was behaving like a scared young girl," she said. "I couldn't figure out why."

Doyle was less flummoxed. "Sure, I was disappointed," he said, "but why try to push something that's not working?"

As Mimms predicted, people did talk. At every cocktail party during CMA week, you would hear the same tired lines: "Did you hear about Trisha Yearwood? She committed careericide." "Have you heard? Trisha Yearwood shot herself in the foot."

Just as word got out that she had fired Doyle and Lewis, so did the news that she had left her husband. After months of estrangement, Yearwood had finally moved out into a small apartment several floors below Fundis's office in a high-rise apartment building just off Music Row.

The talk didn't stop in Nashville. By the fall of 1991, Garth Brooks was a national phenomenon. His albums were selling millions, and his tour was one of the few successes of the 1991 season. He turned up in *People* magazine, talking about his marriage, how he had strayed during his tours and how he had found his way back to his wife. And there, opening his show, was a soon-to-be divorcée whom he had helped push into the limelight. The tabloids made hay, intimating that the two were romantically involved.

In truth, her professional and personal lives might have been in turmoil, but Brooks had nothing to do with it. "Like I'm gonna have an affair with a married man who's more like my big brother than some kind of sex symbol. Give me a break," she snapped to one of the countless reporters who asked.

The Brooks rumors were an annoyance. The more pressing concern was what she was going to do about management. Fundis filled the gap for a couple of months, and they discussed making that relationship permanent. But before she made any decisions, Fundis told her, she should consider all her options.

A few weeks after the CMA Awards, Fundis, Yearwood, Mimms, and Hinton were discussing those options. Hinton, especially, was worried. "Historically, there has been nowhere to find good management in Nashville," he said later. "Here was this major talent—she needed someone with stature, not someone who was just going to ride *her* coattails."

Months before, Ken Kragen had come in from Los Angeles, where he was based, to give a seminar in Nashville. Yearwood and Fundis attended; both had been impressed. "If we're talking about managers, why not start at the top?" asked the producer.

By the fall of 1991, Ken Kragen had already had been godfather to a dozen careers, had already spent three decades honing his skill at winning publicity, both for himself and the performers he represented. Kragen was the impresario of "good works" who assembled forty-five pop stars in a single room and recorded their anthem against hunger, and lined up seven million Americans, hand in hand, in a well-intentioned gesture of fraternity. Garry Trudeau had immortalized him in *Doonesbury;* Robin Leach had filmed him for *Lifestyles of the Rich and Famous.*

Ken Kragen teaches an annual seven-week course at UCLA called "The Stardom Strategy." Taped editions are available so you can learn at home. Topics include "networking," "investing in yourself," "honesty," "opportunity," and "giving back." It's cheap ammunition for those who write Kragen off as the Dr. Pangloss of Beverly Hills, dismiss his "good works" as just so much self-promotion, consider his overriding optimism so much simplemindedness. But those judgments miss Kragen's savvy. The test of his ability is the road map of his travels. From the Berkeley coffeehouses in the sixties to L.A. pop in the seventies and now to Nashville, Kragen has proven himself a bellwether for popular culture over and over and over again.

Kragen, fifty-six, is a tall man who seems never to have quite grown into his six-foot-two-inch frame. He still has the knobby physique of an adolescent: mostly elbows, more skinny than slim. His auburn hair is just past chin-length, an almost Colonial pageboy—Ichabod Crane with aviator glasses.

His taste tends towards expensive whimsy. He keeps an extensive collection of antique arcade games, stocked to return Tootsie Rolls and matchbox cars for a penny; his collection of ephemera includes a pair of Houdini's handcuffs. His wardrobe includes red leather trousers and a chenille dinner jacket. While he does wear the requisite status watch, Baume & Mercier, his has Mickey Mouse on its face.

Kragen grew up in Los Angeles, where his father, Adrian, was a partner at the law firm Loeb and Loeb. When his son was finishing high school, Adrian Kragen took a professorship at the University of California at Berkeley. His son went along and graduated from the school in 1958.

Those were the years of the hungry i and the Purple Onion, and Ken Kragen was a coffeehouse regular. It was at the Purple Onion that he first heard a group of unknowns called the Kingston Trio. In his first music business venture he brought them to the Berkeley campus for a concert. The show was close to a sellout. The band made $360. Kragen, as promoter, made eighty-two dollars—not a fortune, but not bad until his father told him he had to pay admission taxes. (At that time the government taxed ticket sales). Recalculated, his profit came to two dollars.

Still, the Kingston Trio were sufficiently satisfied to ask Kragen to be their fulltime concert promoter. The problem was, Kragen had just been admitted to Harvard Business School, and while he wanted to work with the musicians, his father wanted him to go to Cambridge. The father won, and during Kragen's first week at Harvard, the Kingston Trio's version of "Tom Dooley" was number one on the *Billboard* charts. "I was convinced I had missed the opportunity of my life."

But it was the sixties, and opportunity was bountiful. Back in Berkeley that summer he went to see another band on the verge, the Limeliters. He had known the leader of the group, Lou Gottlieb, from his concert promotion days at Berkeley. Afterward, Gottlieb called and asked him to be the group's "executive secretary."

"I told them that I had not gone to the Harvard Business School to be someone's executive secretary, and if they wanted a manager they should get in touch." When he returned to school, their letter was waiting. Kragen told the group they would have to wait until he graduated, and they did.

Kragen handled the Limeliters until they broke up in 1963. Just as they were disbanding, Pontiac had offered them ten thousand dollars for a television commercial. Kragen convinced the carmaker that his newest clients, Tommy and Dick Smothers, would be an excellent alternative.

The week the commercial aired, the brothers made three other television appearances. "Suddenly they were on the air a tremendous amount, and their career just exploded. The next forty-nine concerts in a row sold out."

The rise of the Smothers Brothers demonstrated Kragen's first principle of management: One event in a client's life doesn't make much of a difference, but if a manager can get three or more events going in a short period of time he can establish momentum, propel a performer to, in Kragen-speak, a new plateau of stardom.

Kragen hit lots of plateaus through the seventies and eighties. His roster included not only the Smothers Brothers but Lionel Richie, Harry Chapin, and Kenny Rogers, clients whose commercial appeal generally outran their critical success. "Ken Kragen has always handled middle-of-the-road acts," says Timothy White, the editor of *Billboard*. "There's a charm-school touch to what he does. It's the sort of thing that works best in pop and country, where a certain kind of grooming is acceptable."

The Kragen touch meant keeping an act in the public eye through lots of trade ads, lots of appearances on awards shows, probably a commercial sponsorship, or even two. Kragen turned each client into as much of a brand name as any of the products he pitched.

Kragen was one of the first West Coast managers to do business in Nashville. He arrived in '75 when Kenny Rogers left the First Edition (a Kragen client) and started recording on his own. Rogers made his first solo album in Nashville, and Kragen fixed on the market. He cultivated the Nashville oligarchy. He joined the Country Music Association, which elected him to the board of directors and then, in 1982, president.

While Rogers kept him in and out of Nashville throughout the eighties, most of Kragen's attention was focused on his high-profile charitable projects. That didn't sit well with Lionel Richie. Richie wanted to revamp his image, he told Kragen, he wanted to be perceived as hipper, more cutting-edge. Kragen had neither the time, he felt, nor the skills, to aid in that sort of transformation. After six years with Kragen, he left for Freddy DeMann, the same man who managed Madonna.

With Richie's departure, Kragen reduced his client list to one: Kenny Rogers, whose income of ten million to fifteen million dollars a year was enough to keep Kragen prosperous and not too busy. He slipped into a sort of semiretirement, happy to spend time with his wife, Cathy Worthington, a former Playboy bunny whom he had met when one of his clients was performing at the Los Angeles club. ("I never liked the place," he said, "but she handled herself well. It was a great way to make a lot of money without working a lot of hours. I was a lot happier when she started selling real estate.") In 1990, after a number of miscarriages, Cathy Kragen gave birth to a baby girl, Emma, and Ken doted on the child.

Then, in the summer of 1989, Nick Hunter, a Warner Bros. executive in Nashville, sent Kragen a videotape of Travis Tritt, a young country singer from Marietta, Georgia, who had been earning his keep working in an air conditioner plant while he played local bars. He had lots of potential, said Hunter, and he needed a manager. Would Kragen be interested?

Kragen played Tritt's tape to the women in his office and then to his wife. "They thought he was hot," said Kragen. He was seduced by the challenge. "I wanted to see if I could do it again, if I could make him a star."

Tritt recorded his first album, and Kragen helped push it. He even cosigned a hundred-thousand-dollar loan so Tritt could finance the ad campaign. The blitz paid off. Tritt is now Warner Bros.' best-selling country act. His second album sold 2.5 million copies.

Come the fall of 1991, as country music was having its biggest boom ever, Kragen's two clients were both tethered to the Nashville skyline. In October 1991, he made the obligatory appearance for the Country Music Awards. At each stop he heard about a new singer named Trisha Yearwood. Her record had just gone gold, and she had just fired her managers. What could she have been thinking? He even met Yearwood very briefly, but only pleasantries were exchanged. He left faintly offended that no one had asked him if he would be interested in representing her.

Mimms and Hinton had met to discuss Yearwood's management on a Friday. The following Monday, each, unbeknownst to the other, called Kragen in L.A. Kragen, as it turned out, was absolutely interested. He called around Nashville, asked agents and executives at competing labels what they thought of Yearwood. The advice was universal: She had an amazing voice and a weak stage show. Still, she could be the next big thing. "You'd be a fool not to take her," said Jim Ed Norman, who heads up the Warner Bros. Nashville office.

They met on October 21. Kragen asked her what her goals were, and promised a memo to detail how she could accomplish them. "What she wanted was someone who had vision, someone who would tell her what he was going to do and actually do it," said Pat Alger. She went back to Nashville all but decided. But before she made the commitment, she wanted to talk to Fundis.

"You'll be the most talented person he's ever worked with," the producer told her. "He should be able to go farther with this than he's ever gone." What did Fundis think the risks were? He worried about overexposure, he told her, but he trusted her to make the right decisions. "If overexposure was the biggest thing she had to worry about," Fundis said afterward, "there was no reason to say no."

And with his blessing, Yearwood agreed to work with Kragen. There was no written contract; he would receive 15 percent of her revenues.

A week later, Kragen sent her the memo describing *his* goals for her:

Perhaps the most significant moment in our two days together came when Al Teller [head of MCA Records] asked me to put my thoughts about your career image into just one sentence. As you'll recall, my response was "Trisha Yearwood should be seen as a great singer who also is the most stunningly beautiful woman in country music."

Which is certainly one of the last things Trisha Yearwood ever expected herself to be.

CHAPTER 5

TRISHA YEARWOOD WAS NOBODY'S IDEA OF A HOMECOMING queen. She had never even tried out for the cheerleading squad. Instead, she had ended up as a water girl for the football team— the fallback position for a girl with the right attitude and the wrong body. At five feet eight inches, Yearwood was tall enough to be described as statuesque rather than chubby. Still, those extra twenty or so pounds made bouncing around with pom-poms a decidedly bad idea. "Everything jiggled when I jumped," was her answer to why she hadn't gone out for sports.

The 1982 Piedmont Academy *Retrospect* shows a girl whose features have an edge to them—her lips twist slightly downward, almost more smirk than smile—looks more likely to be described as interesting than pretty.

If Yearwood had started out in New York or L.A., that might have kept her from getting a contract altogether. But what plays on Music Row is not what plays in the rest of the music world. Nashville has never liked its women to look too sexy, a reflection of who Music Row believes buys its records. Executives on Music Row believe that 70 percent of all country records are purchased by women, and even though a recent survey commissioned by the CMA put that number at closer to 50 percent, they have stuck by the old saw that women are the tastemakers, the ones who tell their husbands and boyfriends what to buy, the ones who choose which performers they will see in concert. According to that wisdom, they are far more likely to spend their money on male performers, which explains why, last year, just thirty-six female country singers were signed to major labels, 25 percent of the total. Fewer than half those women had records that made it onto the charts—only 12 percent of the total, the fewest since the early sixties, according to Robert K. Oermann, country music columnist for *The Tennessean*. It doesn't seem to matter that of the women currently making albums, 42 percent (better than the percentage for men) have albums that have gone gold or platinum. With very few exceptions, Music Row is convinced that as a rule women don't sell records.

Yearwood had already broken that rule with her first album. Its sales had broken her away from the pack of the other young female singers: Mary-Chapin Carpenter, Matraca Berg, and Suzy Bogguss, none of whom had yet to sell gold. As for new acts, there were hopes for Martina McBride; her album would be coming out in the summer, and she had the same berth on Garth Brooks's tour that Yearwood had had the year before. The biggest competition, everyone figured, would be coming from Wynonna Judd, the younger half of the disbanded mother-daughter duo, the Judds, whose first solo album would be coming out in March. Judd, a short, stocky woman with a Bonnie Raitt voice, hewed to Music Row wisdom that when women do pay to go see another woman perform, they don't want to see a singer who's too sexy, a woman they wouldn't trust alone with their husbands.

"We rarely worry about whether an artist's image is appealing to men," said MCA's Walt Wilson. "From the songwriter to the packaging, almost all our marketing is aimed toward women."

While that strategy may smack of unfortunate stereotypes, it seemed to work. In March 1992, MCA Nashville boasted the largest market share on Music Row, and its two top female performers, Yearwood and Reba McEntire, were the best-selling women in country. As Wilson explained it, the more upbeat the song, the closer a singer came to blues or rock, the greater the appeal to a male audience. The more heartfelt the ballad, the more women will be drawn to the song—as well as to the album that it's on. "When Vince Gill puts out a great up-tempo song with a smoking guitar solo, radio loves it," says Wilson. "But when he comes out with a killer ballad, that's when sales hit."

Tanya Tucker, the rowdiest member of the Music Row sorority, has always had a large male following, but it wasn't until she started to appeal to women that sales really boomed. "When only men were buying her records, she was only selling a couple hundred thousand," says Jimmy Bowen, whose label distributes her albums. "Now that she's a single mother with two kids, women relate to her more—and she's finally starting to sell platinum." When Reba McEntire put out *It's Your Call*, the first single released was up-tempo. Sales did well, but they didn't go through the roof until "The Heart Won't Lie," a slow, sweet duet with Vince Gill.

There are those who believed that "She's in Love with the Boy" would have been a huge hit no matter who sang it, that Trisha Yearwood, her voice notwithstanding, was merely the fortunate messenger. The challenge facing Yearwood and company was to make sure that the singer was perceived as the star.

Female country fans still expect their icons to have their own identities—daughter, wife, mother, working girl made good— an idealized version of what they themselves are, what they hope to become. That identity is a chemistry of music and visual image, three parts song, one part eight-by-ten glossy.

While no one worried about Yearwood being too much of a sexpot, exactly how she would be sold started out as something of a muddle. Walt Wilson got Yearwood's publicity photo just days after that second showcase: It looked like a bad catalog shot from Kmart. She was wearing a cow-print jacket; her hair was styled in a modified Farrah Fawcett shag. You could barely make out her cheekbones. "I saw those and thought, What am I going to do with this?" Wilson recalled. "Trisha looked ten pounds heavier than she was. She had on a horrible set of clothes, and her hair looked awful. I had no idea how we were going to sell her."

The first step toward that sell was hiring Sheri McCoy. McCoy is a small woman whose outfits tend to urban chic: lots of leggings, lots of black, accented with the requisite western accessory or two (a turquoise bracelet, a cowboy-print vest). McCoy calls herself a stylist; she takes charge of the performer's outfits, supervising her look on album covers, videos, and television appearances, as well as outfitting her for performances on the road. Though the profession is a Hollywood staple, such image tinkerers have come to Nashville only in the last few years, and McCoy was among the first.

McCoy had never intended to end up in the music business. She was born in Texas in 1947, married by twenty-three to a ne'er-do-well pool hustler who spent just about every weekend on the rodeo circuit, spending more on entrance fees than he ever brought home. Mostly, he was supported by his young wife, who worked as a hairdresser. At twenty-five, McCoy decided there was life beyond the beauty-parlor door. She went back to school, enrolling in the teaching program at Southeastern State College, in Durant, Oklahoma, a few miles from where she lived.

McCoy's closest friend was her next-door neighbor, a young Southeastern student named Reba McEntire who was dating another rodeo regular ("Charlie Battles actually made money," says McCoy). The younger woman had ambitions beyond the classroom: On weekends, while her cowboy was off riding bulls, she was singing her songs in local bars.

The two women kept in touch after graduation, through the breakup of McCoy's marriage and the rise of McEntire's career. In April 1986 McEntire called McCoy, by then teaching in Bartlesville, Oklahoma. The singer had finally got her first record deal, she was out on the road and feeling desperately alone. "I need a friend," she told McCoy. "Won't you please think about working on the road with me?"

It was a wild idea, but McCoy was ready for a change. She had just broken up with her boyfriend, and after three years of teaching emotionally disturbed children, she was drained. "I was," she said, "looking for a new life." She sold her furniture, put a few things in storage, and in mid-June stepped onto McEntire's bus in Washington, D.C. She became the singer's all-purpose assistant, a paid companion.

The adjustment wasn't easy. "There I am in this bunk, no wheels of my own, being told where to eat. At the time Reba was very isolated, and I was on twenty-four-hour call."

Within a season or so, though, she fell into the life, and as McEntire became one of the first Nashville stars to develop a stage show, complete with choreography and costume changes, McCoy was one of the people who made it happen. The singer had always liked McCoy's taste in clothing; when she upgraded her show, she put McCoy in charge of her wardrobe. "I really got to love the road," says McCoy. "I liked not being tied down, I loved the shows. There were three clothes changes, and I was in charge."

Then, over Christmas in 1988, McCoy's car hit a patch of ice, and flipped, crushing her right arm. She needed months of physical therapy. Life on the road was an impossibility. She needed to make money, and she had an idea: Why couldn't she do for other singers what she had done for McIntire: hone their image, work on their hair, their makeup, their clothes. Within the month, RCA's Joe Galante had hired her to work with an up-and-comer named Jo-El Sonnier on his first album cover. By the time she got the call from MCA to work with Yearwood, she had done over a hundred album covers.

The cover of *Trisha Yearwood*, the result of McCoy's efforts, showed the singer with her hair in ringlets, fresh from the curling iron. She was wearing an oversize denim shirt; a gold wedding band glistened from her ring finger. Perfect shots for an album she dedicated to "her husband and best friend" and the Suches Seven, her college roommates; perfect shots for a young woman whose lyrics were about beat-up Chevy trucks, drive-ins, and the Tastee-Freez. But while it was the ideal image for Yearwood's first album, it wasn't one that could or would last long. It said everything about where Trisha Yearwood came from, and nothing about where she intended to go.

Country music has had a woman problem since the days when it was little more than a string of fiddle contests across the Southeast. Women rarely appeared on stage. It wasn't that they didn't play the banjo or the fiddle, it was just that they were encouraged to keep their talents noncompetitive and at home.

The first women to record were Samantha Bumgarner and Eva Davis, who did a few banjo and fiddle duets in 1924 for Columbia Records. They were followed by a few minor solo acts, Roba Stanley and cowgirl singer Billie Maxwell. Still, until Sara and Maybelle Carter came along, most women appeared in public only as accompanists or background singers in family bands. The Carters, according to Sara's estimation, recorded over three hundred sides. Sara's husband, Alvin Pleasant Carter (Maybelle was married to A. P.'s brother Ezra), wrote most of their music and managed their business affairs. None of their records were million-sellers, but the Carter Family songs—"Homestead on the Farm," "Little Village Church Yard"—have become part of the standard repertoire for country and bluegrass singers, relics of a fast-disappearing rural Elysium.

Their popularity came from their records and their radio broadcasts on the high-wattage stations operating just south of the

Mexican border. Despite their success, A. P. never allowed the sisters-in-law to travel much. Most of their appearances were confined to schoolhouses, churches, and little movie houses not far from their home. It wasn't considered seemly for a woman to be on the road.

When a woman finally made it to the top of the country charts in 1952, her husband was not far from her side. Nashville-born Muriel Deason was given her stage name, Kitty Wells, by her husband, Johnnie Wright, after an old parlor song—"I Could Marry Kitty Wells"—that had been sung on the Grand Ole Opry by the Pickard Family.

Wells started out as a harmony singer for her husband and his brother-in-law, and when RCA signed them in 1949 she came as part of the package. She recorded a couple of sides solo; sales were dismal. Three years later, though, at Wright's urging, Decca signed Wells to her own deal, and at her first session, she recorded that pioneering number one song—"It Wasn't God Who Made Honky Tonk Angels," a retort to Hank Thompson's "The Wild Side of Life." But while Wells may have been breaking tradition with her honky-tonk laments, Nashville propriety dictated a demeanor that was strictly "sunbonnet sweetheart," all gingham and rickrack. Her promotional material described her as "an active church worker and a true daughter of the South," and her cookbooks were sold after each performance.

Demure as her comportment was, though, the Opry establishment still wouldn't approve her material. Wells made scores of appearances on the Ryman stage, but she was never permitted to sing her biggest hit. Opry officials thought it too outspoken.

Kitty Wells may have been the first to sing sass and independence; Patsy Cline was the first to live it. She had a stevedore's vocabulary and a taste for liquor. Her husband, Charles Dick, worked nights at Nashville Newspaper Printing, so Cline hit the road on her own, traveling without chaperones. She held her own during recording sessions, battling her producer, Owen Bradley, to make the music that she wanted. Gordon Stoker, leader of the Jordanaires, recounted their sessions for Ellis Nassour, Cline's biographer. "Owen would tell her he was running the show, and Patsy would say, 'Well damn it, I don't guess there'll be a show if there ain't a star on stage.' Then Owen would crack, 'I should have known you were the star with that light following you around the room,' and Patsy would answer, 'Well, at least it ain't no damn halo.' "

She wore form-fitting cocktail dresses and mules instead of gingham and boots and was one of the first country performers, male or female, to actually move on stage. The Opry refused to let her appear one night when she turned up in a pantsuit. It was deemed inappropriate stage attire.

Cline pushed not just personal boundaries but musical ones as well. When Owen Bradley backed her with string arrangements and the hushed harmonies of the Jordanaires, her records started being played on pop radio stations. "I Fall to Pieces" and "Crazy" made it to the top of pop charts.

Since Cline, a slow, steady parade of women have cautiously ventured away from the roles deemed "appropriate" for female singers. It has been the most tentative of revolutions. Even Dolly Parton, who was the first to flaunt her sexuality, did it with an improbable wig, a more improbable figure, and a wink, all told, a persona more comic than erotic.

k. d. lang, with her studied androgyny, never had a chance in Nashville. Tanya Tucker is still the only woman in country music who can get away with a beaded suede G-string and fringed bikini top (her license plate once read "MS. BAD ASS"), but that's probably because she'd been sold as a Laredo Lolita from the start. At fourteen, Tucker turned up on stage in a skintight pantsuit singing "Would You Lay with Me (in a Field of Stone)" and a decade and a half later had two children out of wedlock, no apologies offered. "That's just Tanya," is how one Nashville songwriter explained it. "She's just a good ol' girl. Everyone's just used to it by now."

But Yearwood had made her debut as the girl next door, the nice girl with a pretty voice who did what her daddy told her to do. It left her on somewhat uncertain ground as to where she would be permitted to go.

* * *

It wasn't that Ken Kragen was unaware of the country market's essential conservatism. Perhaps because he was based in Los Angeles and not Nashville, he just didn't worry about it. All he knew was that Yearwood had potential, that she needed work, and that he wanted to get it started as soon as possible.

In that memo he sent her in October 1991, there were fifteen items. The first: "Get into best possible physical shape through proper eating and regular exercise." She didn't just need to be skinnier, he told her she needed to be healthier in order to endure life on the road. In January, Yearwood hired a full-time trainer, another Belmont graduate named Jarrah Herter. She spent two hours a day with Yearwood while she was in Nashville, and traveled with her as well, making sure she exercised and monitoring her meals—special orders of broiled chicken and baked potato.

Then there was the matter of photographs. The photos from that first album cover were only eight months old in October 1991, but the image hadn't worn well. "I have yet to see a photo of you that truly does you justice," Kragen wrote. "You are frankly more attractive in person than your photographs show. We need to engage two or three of the top photographers in order to get some really outstanding photos of you for use in publicity, merchandising and recorded product."

The goal was the right image and an abundance of public recognition. According to the Kragen school, the latter would be achieved by garnering a mother lode of award nominations. "Such nominations are critical because they bring with them potential exposure on the awards shows, media attention and a hook around which we and MCA can do advertising and various other promotions. Ultimately our goal is the Horizon Award," he wrote, referring to the trophy offered up each fall by the Country Music Association to the performer whose career has seen the most growth in the past year, "as well as nominations in the female vocalist, single, album and video categories. . . . We need to begin immediately to lay out an advertising and promotion campaign geared toward your being nominated and ultimately winning some of these key awards."

The Kragen agenda did not come cheap: New photography, choreography, a trainer, and those various promotions would add up to over two hundred thousand dollars for the year. By November of 1991, Yearwood's first record had already gone gold, which, after production fees and the cost of videos and the like were deducted, would appear to have left her with considerably more than that. But that's a bit of an illusion. MCA is entitled to withhold as much as 40 percent of royalties to cover returns—albums shipped but not sold and eventually returned to the distributor. The distributors usually have two years to reconcile their books, two years to hold onto royalties before they have to disburse them to the performer. Then there was the Garth Brooks tour, a marketing coup but a fiscal disaster. She was paid just twenty-five hundred dollars per performance, less than half of her cost to put on the show. "It's the kind of exposure people are willing to pay for," said Kragen, and that's precisely what Yearwood was doing. In fact, the coffers of Trisha Yearwood, Inc., were virtually empty.

At first, she considered taking out a bank loan to finance the Kragen agenda. But MCA understood the benefits to be gained from the plan. Malcolm Mimms approached Bruce Hinton about accelerating payments, and he was amenable.

Nearly fifteen thousand dollars of that advance went to cover new photographs. The session had first been set for mid-December, but Yearwood had canceled at the last minute, pleading illness. She rescheduled for the first day of March, the day after her first Opry appearance. On that stellar Sunday morning, the singer arrived at the photo studio, on a deserted block in downtown Nashville, with a considerable entourage: a makeup woman; a hairdresser; three photographer's assistants; Sheri McCoy; who had just dissolved her business to work for Yearwood full-time; and Nancy Russell, the publicist.

Russell, who had been hired through Ken Kragen, had been working with Yearwood for just over a month. She had grown up mostly in southern California, only tangentially involved with country music. Her style was more New Wave than Nashville— black dresses, black bicycle shorts, black berets, rarely without sunglasses, even after dark.

Russell deplored the media's image of country music. "We are not a bunch of small-town hicks," she often insisted, making it clear the description was a personal affront.

Russell had followed a singer to town four years earlier. And though the two split up after a yearlong marriage, Russell had stayed in Nashville, working her way from room service at the Hyatt Regency to factotum at *The Nashville Network* to her current position as a publicist at Evelyn Shriver Public Relations, a seven-year-old firm founded by a onetime New Yorker with one of the glossier rosters in town. Russell started out with George Lindsey, the actor who had played Goober on *The Andy Griffith Show*. Six months into the job, she sufficiently impressed Shriver to land Ken Kragen's young client, Travis Tritt, and when Kra-

gen went looking for a publicist for Yearwood, he turned happily
to Russell.

Handling Tritt and Yearwood was Russell's first serious job,
and she took none of it for granted: Were Travis and Trisha
getting enough exposure, was it the right exposure, were the
photographs sufficiently flattering? She fussed over every detail,
living from one crisis to the next. "I get real territorial when I'm
representing people. I will go to the wall, take the bullet for them
if I have to. No other artist is as good—it's that simple."

Russell believed that her manic diligence had its roots in her
upbringing. Both of her parents died when she was seven, and
she passed through a series of foster homes before she was finally
adopted. She came of age as an indefatigable survivor, all elbows
and determination. When it came to her clients, she was a lioness
with young cubs, fiercely loyal, territorial, occasionally beyond
reason.

"Basically I'm insecure," she said. "But that's what makes me
good at this job. Insecure people are the best at publicity, we're
always trying to gain approval, we just redirect all that to the
client."

The photographer, Randee St. Nicholas, met Russell's image
of what country could be. Barely off the plane from L.A., St.
Nicholas had arrived in the studio in green denim jeans and a
tight white undershirt (no bra) under a fifties jeweled cardigan.
Her shoes, green suede Beatle boots, were Claude Montana.
"This is as country as I get," she announced as she walked in the
door.

St. Nicholas fussed with her camera and lights while Yearwood
was made up. In all, it took just under two hours to turn Trisha
Yearwood into a star. Mary Beth Felts started with her face.
First came concealer, then a light foundation, which highlighted
an already perfect complexion. She shaded taupe along her cheekbones, then moved on to the eyes. The false eyelashes required
a full ten minutes, eight segments on each eyelid, one painstaking
clump at a time. Lipstick came last—first outline, then color.

After Felts finished her face, Maria Smoot moved on to her
hair, a half-hour comb and pouffe job. Perfection was achieved
just before eleven.

Yearwood surveyed the result in the mirror, batted her eyes,
and pursed her lips into a sex-kitten pout. "I'm a babe, and I

didn't even know it. I feel like singing happy birthday to JFK," she said, and in a breathy little girl voice, she did. "Happy birthday to you, happy birthday to you, happy birthday Mr. President, happy birthday to you," she trilled, an entirely passable Madison Square Garden Marilyn Monroe.

It was a considerable departure from the young woman pictured on that first album cover, but it wasn't so far from the songs inside. "That's What I Like About You," the third single released from the album, was a honky-tonk personal ad: "I like a man who will lay down beside me/I like a man who will stand up to me too." And "You Done Me Wrong (and That Ain't Right)" made it abundantly clear that Yearwood wasn't the sort to stand by her cheating man. She might have been betrayed, but she was far from forlorn. Yearwood's new handlers wanted to play up that swagger. "The idea here," explained Russell, "is that she can be sensual and sexy without being slutty."

As Prince's newest album blared from the cassette player, Yearwood put on a black bustier under a faded denim shirt. St. Nicholas pushed the shirt down around Yearwood's shoulders. "Now just lean down, into the camera, just get comfortable on your elbows. . . . You're going to love that. You look so beautiful."

St. Nicholas took a couple of Polaroid test shots and brought them over to Yearwood. They could have been pinup shots, the singer all "come hither" and cleavage, a ringer for Claudia Schiffer, the Guess? jeans model who was supposed to look like Brigitte Bardot. It was a long way from Kitty Wells in her gingham and sunbonnets—or even Patsy Cline's lamé.

"What are we doing to country music?" she asked, nodding her approval. "They are going to kick us out."

"Nah," said Russell. "They'll just have to move out of the way."

They broke for lunch just after one. Yearwood started to explain why she had broken that first date for a photo shoot. Yearwood may have been awkward on stage, but she played well with small groups. A charming woman with a gift for easy intimacy, she turned almost anyone into a friend, if only for an hour or two.

She had just ended a very bad relationship, she explained to St. Nicholas, her first since her marriage had broken up. The boyfriend had traveled with her, and she had, for a few months, handed her life over to him.

"We were playing Chicago, and he came in and looked at me," she said. "I was wearing a black jacket over a black bustier.

" 'You're not going on stage dressed like that,' he told me. I told him that no one is going to tell me how to dress. He walked out, and I pinned my jacket together," she said, pulling her shirt together as she spoke. "I can't believe I let someone tell me what to do. . . . But I'd just broken up with my husband, just gotten my first gold record. . . ."

When he wasn't out on the road, matters only got worse. He would call, demanding to know whom she was with, making nightly accusations of infidelity. "And somehow," she said, "I thought this was normal."

Then, in December, just before that first photo shoot had been scheduled, she had found out that he was still dating an old girlfriend who was ostensibly long since gone. "It was as bad as finding out someone had died," she said. "I felt like I should be on *Oprah* or something. 'Women who survive self-destructive relationships.' Men," she concluded, "are scum."

One of the photographer's assistants gathered up the paper lunch plates, and St. Nicholas gestured Yearwood off into a side room. She had picked two more sites for shooting, an old church and a graveyard, and she wanted to make sure Yearwood approved. ("This is the Bible Belt," St. Nicholas explained. "You never know.")

Yearwood had no qualms. She changed into a black spaghetti-strapped dress, draped a motorcycle jacket over her shoulder, and together with St. Nicholas and entourage, headed over to the church, a run-down affair about two blocks from the studio.

As St. Nicholas shot on the church's stairwell, a rusted-out Chevy Nova pulled into a parking lot across the street. A mustachioed man, a Jesus tattoo on one forearm, a Virgin Mary on the other, got out of the driver's side and walked toward the church. "Can I help you?" one of St. Nicholas's assistants asked, intercepting him before he got to the church.

"Who is she?"

"Trisha Yearwood," the assistant replied.

"Can I talk to her?" he asked, and handed over his card. Inscribed in the middle, in bright red script, was "Los Lonely

Boys/Music For All Occasions." "This is me," said the man, pointing to the name in the upper left corner: "Ringo Garza, Rhythm and Singer, Father." Ringo junior, Henry, and Joey, ten, fourteen, and twelve, were, respectively, drums, bass, and leadman.

Garza explained that he was a truck driver—eighteen wheelers—who had just moved to Nashville from San Angelo, Texas, with his sons. They'd played a few bars in Texas, but he wanted a chance at the big time. "I made a video, and I've been sending it around to lounges," he said. "Haven't gotten much though. It's like going around in circles. We just haven't met the right people yet. Is there anything you can do to help us out?"

An hour passed. Finally, as the crew were folding down the light diffusers and rolling away the camera dolly, Garza approached the assistant again. "We really just need someone who will listen to our music," he said. "Can I have your card? We're fixing to make it to the top, and I want to know who I'm talking to."

CHAPTER 6

*T*HREE DAYS AFTER THAT PHOTO SHOOT, A SEMI-SCHIFFERIZED Yearwood (moderate makeup, no visible cleavage) appeared for what is called the Artist Radio Taping Session, the kickoff event of the 1992 Country Radio Seminar. Along with Fan Fair, the annual convention at the Tennessee State fairgrounds, and the five days surrounding the CMA Awards, Seminar, as it's called, is one of the three holy weeks of the Nashville year. Regular business comes to a screeching halt as the minions who make country music possible in the hinterlands are wined and dined and sufficiently indulged to insure that they will continue to do more of the same.

At 3:45 P.M., the radio executives, some one thousand strong, started gathering outside the velvet cordons of the Knoxville Ballroom in the Opryland Hotel. The battalion came armed: tape recorders and fill-in-the-blank scripts (Hi, this is _____ [Star's Name] and mornings sure got easier when I started listening to WXYZ), guitars, hats, and pens to sign them, to prove they had been touched by the stars.

Inside the ballroom, each record label had set up a station for its stars, a lineup of folding chairs and banquet tables, each divided into two-and-a-half- by three-and-a-half-foot cubicles lined with sound-absorbent foam so radio spots could be recorded cleanly. A sign posted near the front door listed a single regulation: "FIVE MINUTE MAXIMUM PER ARTIST."

At four o'clock sharp a security guard dropped the cord. The race was on.

They queued forty strong for Vince Gill and Marty Stuart; even at five minutes an interview they wouldn't be gone until nearly dinnertime. "I'm shooting to get fifteen of them," said Larry O'Brien, a cowboy-hatted program director from KVOX in Moorehead, Minnesota, number twelve of twenty-five waiting for Yearwood. "I already got two before this, B. B. Watson and the Remingtons, but those really weren't much of a wait. You have to know how to pace it."

At the front of the line, Yearwood smiled, taped, hugged, and signed. This was Yearwood's inaugural taping session, her first year of this three-hour sound-bite marathon, but she handled it with the poise of a pro. "The first time I saw my name on the charts it freaked me out," she told a program director from North Carolina. "I had no idea I'd go top forty," she said to the next, Mike Carta, of KVET in Austin.

"We have this chant: 'Roo, roo, roo,' " said a burly middle-aged man in a bright red shirt. "Could you just do that? And if you could do happy birthday, that would be great."

"Happy birthday to Roo," she sang, "Happy birthday to Roo, happy birthday from Trisha and the Roo Crew, happy birthday to you. Roo, roo, roo. This is Trisha Yearwood on the New Rooster Country." The tape recorder snapped off, and he moved out of earshot. "Well that's a great way to make a complete idiot of yourself in five minutes," she said.

Over the next three hours, she performed this routine scores of times.

For a blonde woman from Pennsylvania: "Please use extra caution driving during the holiday season. This is Trisha Yearwood for WZPR in Meadville."

For a program director from Florida: "This is Trisha Yearwood. Can you believe they have me making coffee at GC101 Gator Country?"

For a heavyset woman from Georgia, who handed her a T-shirt with a Holstein on the front: "Hi, this is Trisha Yearwood for WCOW. This cow leads the herd. Hi, this is Trisha Yearwood. For cow-powered country listen to WCOW. This cow don't draw flies."

For Doug Peterson of KOEL, Oelwein, Iowa: "Hi, northeast Iowa, I'm really looking forward to seeing you at the Jones County Fair."

For a deejay from Corpus Christi: "Hi, this is Trisha Yearwood with Rich Edwards on K99, the only country . . . The only? Is there another country station there? I shouldn't say that. I've gotten into trouble for that before." She quickly edited her lines. "Hi, this is Trisha Yearwood. Thanks for listening to country music on K99."

Rock acts are fairly well insulated from the men and women who play their songs. Country singers, especially newer, less established acts, are expected to embrace those radio employees like long-lost second cousins. They expect an occasional phone call, a visit if the singer is passing through town. Even the most established stars make an effort to court country radio. Whenever Reba McEntire makes an appearance, she calls the local radio stations, just to thank them for playing her music.

Not only can such attentiveness make a career, it provides insurance for the time when a singer hits the inevitable weak streak. It doesn't matter if a performer produces hit after hit, but come the weak song, the weak album (and every singer has one), the program directors will support the acts they know, the acts who have taken the time to talk to them, to call, to make personal appearances at their stations.

The Knoxville Ballroom was one of the better maps for charting the stars. There were fewer people waiting in line to see Prairie Oyster, a Canadian band, than there were in the group. Cleve Francis, the black cardiologist turned country singer, spent some twenty minutes talking to a gray-haired man who didn't even appear to have his tape recorder running. Emmylou Harris was sitting alone in her booth, under the Warner Brothers logo. She may be a legend, but radio was simply not interested. Just across the hall, the line for Garth Brooks was already out the door—and he hadn't even shown up yet.

Father Heffernan, a Catholic priest from Ontario, was on his seventh pilgrimage to Nashville. The reverend was the unlikely host of a two-hour country gospel show. "I'm sort of a religious Ed Sullivan," he explained as he surveyed the room from an empty table by the water cooler. "There are so many newcomers, so many lines. It never used to be this big. I feel sorry for the ones where there's nobody's waiting. The radio people, well, most of them just pour through here like it's the Judgment Day."

By Father Heffernan's measure, Trisha Yearwood had cleared the pearly gates. Her line remained about twenty deep until the room closed at seven.

Father Heffernan's apocalyptic assessment of the proceedings runs fairly close to the mark. While a top-ten hit doesn't guarantee sales, a performer who is shunned by radio can just about forget having a career. People don't buy what they haven't heard.

It has been thus almost from the beginning. Country radio got its start in earnest on September 9, 1922, when Fiddlin' Jack Carson made his first radio appearance on WSB in Atlanta. But while WSB was probably the first station to feature live country performances, the Grand Ole Opry—the big top of country radio—traces its origins to WBAP out of Austin. In January 1923, the Texas station broadcast the first barn dance, a ninety-minute program of square-dance music directed by an old-time fiddler and Confederate veteran named Captain M. J. Bonner.

Those were the early, unregulated days of American broadcasting, and WBAP's signal could be picked up from New York to Haiti. Listeners tuned in to the Austin show by the tens of thousands, a fact that so impressed a radio man named George Hay that he resolved to bring the barn-dance format to the new Nashville station that had just hired him as its program director.

Unlike most radio stations, which were owned by newspapers, the Nashville station had been started in November 1925 by a local insurance company, National Life and Accident Corp., acting on some long-forgotten executive's inspired notion that radio would be the perfect tool for selling the company's policies. The station was named WSM, for "We Shield Millions."

National Life's executives, establishment Nashville to a man, were initially leery of Hay's proposal. They regarded fiddle music as crude and were reluctant to have any part of it, but their snobbery took a backseat to their business savvy. Most of their customers, working-class people who bought weekly policies, were the sort who listened to that backwoods music; sponsorship of a barn dance was the perfect marketing ploy. If they liked the music, the logic went, they'd be that much more likely to like the policy.

At 8:00 P.M. on November 28, 1925, Hay announced the first hour-long broadcast of the barn dance, along with its first performer, an eighty-year-old fiddler named Jimmy Thompson. Within two years, the people liked the music so much that WSM expanded the barn dance to three hours, triple the length of the preceding show, NBC's *Musical Appreciation Hour*, with Dr. Walter Damrosch.

On December 10, 1927, Dr. Damrosch opened his hour with a small concession to modernity: "While most artists realize that there is no place in the classics for realism, I am going to break one of my rules and present a composition by a young composer from Iowa. This young man has sent us his latest number, which depicts the onrush of a locomotive. . . ."

When the time came to announce the WSM barn dance, Hay announced that while there might be no room for realism in the classics, the following three hours would be nothing but realism. Hay then introduced Deford Bailey, the black harmonica virtuoso, who would play "Pan American Blues," inspired by the train that ran near his home. When Bailey finished, Hay took to the microphone. "For the past hour, we have been listening to music taken largely from the grand opera," he declared, "but from now on we will present the Grand Ole Opry!"

By the end of the 1950s, the Opry wasn't only the king of the barn dances, it was just about the last one still on the air. The show owed its longevity to two factors. Rural programming everywhere was being threatened by television; radio revenues were in a sorry state. But since WSM was owned by an insurance company, it didn't need to be a separate profit center. WSM also had the benefit of savvy programmers. Other barn dances stuck to older, established performers, but the Opry was quick to showcase newer, younger talent. The Opry elders may have had their problems with the new stars' wilder ways, but they apparently recognized that the only way to hold onto an audience was to make the Patsy Clines, Faron Youngs, Hank Snows, and Hank Williamses part of the show.

But while the Opry had survived the fifties intact, on the whole, the country music business was reeling. Radio stations that had been carrying country music were playing Elvis Presley instead. Battered on one side by television, on the other by rock and roll, sales of country records plunged, and Music Row worried for its future.

Unlike the rest of the music industry, which generally behaves like so many warring city-states, Nashville has always managed to present a united front. In 1958, just months after the Country Music Disc Jockey Association folded under the assault of rock and roll, the music publishers, record companies, and radio broadcasters joined forces to form the Country Music Association. Its mission was strictly commerce. As one brochure noted, "The 'c' in country music stands for Cash." Its arsenal currently includes detailed demographic studies of country music listeners (5 percent more likely than the general public to have checking accounts, 24 percent more likely to have home gym equipment, 13 percent more likely to own a microwave oven) provided to station owners as well as to the media. In all, the CMA has been a remarkably effective lobbyist. Since 1961, the first year anybody counted, the number of country stations has gone from 81 to 606 in 1969 to 2,203 in 1992.

• • •

Yearwood's next five days were a treadmill of cocktail parties and meetings. With Ken Kragen working the room at her side, she smiled, she charmed, she made every effort to convince each executive that he or she was more important than the one who had come before. Three days through, thanks to lobbying months before by Bruce Hinton, Yearwood performed at the luncheon sponsored by the American Society of Composers and Publishers (ASCAP). This was the debut of the new and improved Yearwood, and her songs were especially chosen for the radio crowd. She sang four songs off her first album, all of which had been released to radio. In addition, she sang "Wrong Side of Memphis," an up-tempo bluesy piece about a singer's trek to Music Row, chosen because she wanted it for her next album and she hoped it would be the first or second single.

Ken Kragen had arranged to have dinner that night with his newest client. They met back at the hotel, and he picked up his messages as he went to his car. Yearwood was in the passenger seat as he sorted through the pile. "This is interesting," he said. "Don Henley called. Looking for you."

The man who had played backup for Linda Ronstadt, the Texan turned Angeleno who had sung "Hotel California" and "Desperado," the man responsible for some of the cleanest vocals in the 1970s, the most eligible bachelor in rock, wanted to find her? Not quite Elvis risen from the grave, but for Yearwood, a close second.

Kragen waited until they were seated at Amerigo's, a local Italian spot, then returned the call from his portable phone. Henley, it turned out, had seen Yearwood on *The Tonight Show* in January and had since heard her on the radio. "This girl is good," he told Kragen. She reminded him of Ronstadt, he said, not just her voice, but also her songs. Henley was putting together yet another benefit for his Walden Woods Project, the latest and noisiest of the political causes he had taken on over the last dozen years. Would she be willing to appear? For Kragen, who considered support of what he called "good works" integral to a performer's career, the Walden project sounded perfect. He liked the idea, he told Henley, but it was up to Yearwood, who just happened to be there with him.

Kragen handed the phone to Yearwood. Henley repeated his request. Yearwood didn't know anything about Walden Woods. Henley explained that he was trying to save the acreage from a condominium development planned by Mortimer Zuckerman. Zuckerman had agreed to hand over the land if Henley and company would make him whole, and the singer was holding a series of concerts to raise the ten million dollars needed to buy him out. Would Yearwood be willing to appear March 30? He would cover transportation costs for her and her band if she would agree to donate their fees.

Yearwood wasn't sure of her schedule, but if there was any way she could manage it, she told him, she'd be there. At the end of the conversation, Henley asked where he could reach her. She gave him her number, promising to call as soon as she was sure of her schedule. "Don Henley has my home phone number," she shouted to the restaurant as she hung up the phone, "Don Henley has my home phone number."

On March 30, Yearwood flew to Los Angeles for the Walden Woods concert. Two hours after she landed, Kragen called. He needed her for a meeting later that afternoon with some cosmetics executives.

That meeting was pure serendipity, the result of a series of meetings Kragen had had on behalf of his other young country client, Travis Tritt, with Jay Coleman, a man who specialized in finding celebrities for product sponsorship. Kentucky Fried Chicken had wanted to use Garth Brooks as its spokesman, but had been turned down. Coleman wanted to talk to Kragen about the possibility of using Tritt instead.

Kragen, a perpetual promotion machine, used the occasion to send along some of Yearwood's photographs from the St. Nicholas shoot. Their favorite shot was a version of St. Nicholas's first portrait, a sultry pose in front of the makeup room mirror. Yearwood's hair was messy in a just-out-of-bed sort of way, and she was wearing a bustier and shirt, both pushed down to reveal an impressive expanse of cleavage. They agreed she had never looked better.

Jay Coleman was suitably impressed. He had been working for months with Revlon, trying to set a deal first with Gloria Estefan, then Mariah Carey. With each star came the same sticking point: They wanted seven figures to make a deal; Revlon was reluctant to foot the bill.

On March 25, Coleman had a meeting with Revlon's chairman, Ronald Perelman. He came armed with Yearwood's portfolio. "If you are only going to be willing to spend a relatively low sum for your advertising, you need an emerging artist, not an established star," he told Perelman. "What's attractive to a new artist is the five or ten million dollars you will spend in advertising. They'll do a deal for the exposure, not just the money." Coleman brought out Yearwood's picture, lectured Perelman about the exploding market in country music, and made his pitch: "She may not be a household name, but as a new artist she has come on like a bat out of hell—and she has one of the best managers in the business, one who knows how to build careers." Coleman suggested that the next time Perelman was in L.A. he visit with Kragen.

At first blush, it seemed like an odd marriage. While country singers had long been used to market products, they mostly tended to be aimed at the lower end of the market: Dolly Parton promoted Downy fabric softener; Randy Travis, Coca-Cola; and Barbara Mandrell, prunes and pantyhose. But two things were working in Coleman's favor. Not only were the country music demographics (provided, of course, by the Country Music Association) shifting upward, Revlon itself was looking for a new way to reach less affluent customers. The company had been conducting focus groups for months trying to find the right image for a new fragrance, and as it happened, Yearwood's name had already been mentioned. The cosmetics company was also among the sponsors for Henley's Walden Woods show.

Perelman called Coleman two days later. He was going out for the Academy Awards on March 30. Could a meeting be arranged?

The timing was perfect. Yearwood would be in town for the Walden Woods benefit; Kragen freed up his afternoon. Three hours before he was to escort the model Cindy Crawford to the Academy Awards, Perelman pulled into the circle drive of Kragen's Holmby Hills estate. Perelman, a small man given to large cigars, was puffing away as he walked through the door. Kragen, who usually does not allow smoking in his home, did not ask the billionaire to snuff it.

"She isn't here?" Perelman said when he was told Yearwood wasn't scheduled to arrive for another twenty minutes. "Well, what are we going to talk about until then?" Somehow they got through the next half hour. When the singer arrived, Kragen introduced her to Perelman, the chairman of Revlon, one of the last surviving eighties takeover artists, a man, by *Forbes*'s estimation, worth $2.9 billion. Yearwood had never heard of him.

What would she think about working on a product with Revlon? Perelman asked. "I think it would be great," she replied. "But I'm not a model. Besides, you already have Cindy Crawford."

That's not what they had in mind, Perelman told her. Revlon was thinking about reviving Charly Girl, finding a new image for the product. The other possibility, he said, was creating a new perfume.

They talked for a half hour or so; everything sounded tentative, and Yearwood, while intrigued, was dubious that anything would come of it. She had never considered herself a beauty. The notion that she would be used to sell a line of cosmetics seemed altogether improbable. In all, she was more concerned about the next day, about her performance and actually meeting Don Henley.

At eight the next night, Yearwood did her second turn on the stage of the Universal Amphitheater. It was a short set, and by all accounts it went well. Her band flew out early the next morning, but Yearwood stayed on. Don Henley had invited her to lunch.

He picked Yearwood up in his Porsche. Her tape was winding through his cassette player. His favorite song on the album, he said, was a mournful ballad titled "Lonesome Dove." It was, she replied, the song she wanted to be released as the next single. She reminded him of Ronstadt, he told her. Over Italian food, they got to talking about things southern. The thing he missed most about Texas, he told her, was biscuits and red-eye gravy. Her favorite food, she replied. Lunch went on for an hour and a half or so, and at two, he dropped her off with an open invitation: "If there's ever anything I can do to help, please feel free to call."

She was going into the studio in three weeks to record her next album, she told him. "I'd love if you could sing on it."

"I'll be there," he promised. Nice compliment, she figured, but she didn't really believe anything would come of it.

Twenty-four hours later, Yearwood was in Tampa, loading in her gear for an evening show. "So, how was it?" asked Tim Lauer, her keyboard player.

"Way past cool," Yearwood said, maneuvering her suitcase to the back of the bus. "But what's my daddy gonna say if I come home with a forty-five-year-old rock star?"

Part II
THE ROAD

I thought it was nothin' but just glamour—you get up there and you sing a few songs and that's it, and somebody waits on you hand and foot. I didn't dare think of ridin' two or three hundred miles with rollers in my hair, tryin' to sleep on the bus and gettin' out at truck stops and eatin' hot dogs and hamburgers. That didn't enter my mind.

—Tammy Wynette

CHAPTER 7

THERE'S NO TELLING HOW JACK YEARWOOD MIGHT DEAL WITH Don Henley, but he has managed to reconcile himself to his younger daughter's life, which resembles nothing he has ever known, or for that matter, ever wanted. As his daughter put it, Jack Yearwood does not travel well. He rarely takes airplanes, partly because he does not like flying, mostly because he is happiest at home, and home is middle Georgia. His is a tightly circumscribed life where even North Georgia is considered unfamiliar turf. A great aunt who settled there late in life was considered a stranger, as Jack explains it, "because she lived so far away."

Jack and Gwen Yearwood fought a losing battle to keep tabs on their gypsy daughter as she caravanned across the continent. On a cork bulletin board in their kitchen in Monticello, just beneath a photograph of their granddaughter, was a map of the United States. Clusters of pushpins obscured the type. "We tried to keep up with the cities she was in," Gwen Yearwood said, "but it just got to be too much."

* * *

A rock-and-roll tour is a Homeric journey, three or more months at a time, but it is an odyssey with a clearly defined end, a time when a performer can go home, build a life that lasts clear from one weekend to the next. Country singers live like truckers. They generally have three-, four-, five-, and six-day runs, with a few days off at home to get laundry done and return a few phone calls. Songwriters have lent lyrics to the journey, but they've never quite captured the relentlessness of it all: Arrive at the venue, set up, play, pack up, pile back into the bus and, sometime around two in the morning, head off to another motel, used less for sleeping than hygiene. The band, marooned together twelve, fourteen hours a day, has the sort of intimacy its members barely have with their families.

That peripatetic life is born of fiscal necessity. Of the $2 million Yearwood expected to bring in in 1992, nearly $1.3 million would come from the $10,000 to $20,000 she charged to perform. Tampa, Florida, was Yearwood's twenty-eighth stop in 1992, and it was only April 2, one of the slowest times of year. In the country music business, action doesn't really pick up until the summer and fall, when the singers are staple entertainment on the state and county fair circuit, playing bandstands and flatbed trucks from Tupelo to Toledo.

In some ways, road life isn't so different from the days when Roy Acuff got his start with Dr. Haver's traveling medicine show in the 1920s. Back then, those touring wagons, with their myriad liniments, were among the best entertainment offered in rural America. Before the "doctor" came on to sell his patent medicines, a performer—often in blackface—would show up to warm up the crowd. The man who would become the King of Country Music was one of those blackface performers, but at least he was one of the lucky few who actually made a living from music. Most of the early Opry stars held down day jobs during the week and got paid for their music only on Saturday nights.

All that changed in 1932, not long after WSM became a fifty-thousand-watt clear-channel station heard all over the southeastern United States. The people who listened to the Nashville players wanted to see them, and so the Opry formed the Artists' Service Bureau to handle bookings. Each Sunday and Monday an armada of cars and trailers would head out of Nashville, making two or three stops before turning back in time for the next Saturday night broadcast.

Stars and stagehands shared cramped sleeping quarters—the backseats of station wagons or the trailers bumping along behind them on backwoods highways. "Once or twice a week we might check into a little old dumpy motel," Loretta Lynn recalled, "though most of the time we'd go into a doggone filling station and take sponge baths."

These days a few singers on the country circuit—Glen Campbell, Kenny Rogers, Reba McEntire—travel by plane, but most take the bus. Buses make it easier to get to smaller cities where the nearest airport is dozens of miles away ("You finish a concert, the bus is only twelve feet away, so no waiting around," said Lynn). They also provide a piece of privacy from the pawing public. Unlike an airplane, parked on a distant airstrip, a bus can double as a fortress and a dressing room, a necessity when the only other mirror might be lining a latrine shared with a thousand other fairgoers.

The back of Yearwood's modified 1982 Silver Eagle was the first-class cabin, while the middle was lined with ten bunks for the rest of the entourage, each with its own air-conditioning vent, light, and vinyl curtain to close out the world. There was a tiny bathroom as well as a kitchen—microwave oven, refrigerator, trash compactor—in front, along with a small table and sofa. Both the stateroom and the front area had a television set, video-cassette player, and stereo. Hanging off the front curtain rods were two misshapen wire coat hangers, makeshift racks for the cowboy hats worn by Yearwood's road manager and guitar player.

Yearwood leased her bus from Hemphill Brothers Coach Company, an outfit based in Nashville. The Hemphills, Trent and Joey, buy the vehicles as shells—metal frames and motors—from Eagle Coach Corp., based in Brownsville, Texas, then outfit them to performers' specifications. (Yearwood chose her bus's interior design, but not the exterior paint job. She was faintly embarrassed by the lavender detailing, especially the "Fantasy" scrolled across the rear window.)

The Hemphills got into the bus business thirteen years ago. They know what people want from their buses, they say proudly, because they've lived that life. For two decades, Trent and Joey were the keyboard player and baritone, respectively, in the Hemphill Family, a traveling gospel troupe. "We know what it's like to be stuck on the side of the highway with traffic buzzing by," said Trent. "We know what it's like to try to navigate through the bunks in the middle of the night and have to dodge sharp corners. If you are on the road for forty weeks, four days a week, you don't want everything closing in on you." When Hemphill buys a bus, the cabin is seventy-eight inches high; the brothers literally saw the top off and reattach it in order to add another eight inches. "The guys," said Trent, "like to be able to leave their hats on."

The company charges about $10,000 a month for a bus like Yearwood's, with another $135 to $150 a day, paid by the performer, for the driver. Yearwood's driver, thirty-year-old Steve Hoker, was a pudgy born-again Christian who took to the road after being laid off as a baggage handler for Delta Air Lines. His first employer was a traveling Pentecostal preacher, a Jimmy Swaggart disciple who succeeded in converting him after two years or so. Though the job didn't last, the conversion did.

Hoker had started with Yearwood in February; his previous assignment had been with Ricky Skaggs, a country singer and born-again Christian who had been on the road for fifteen years. Skaggs didn't drink, he didn't smoke, and his band rode separately. It was the staidest tour of duty around.

This group, Hoker conceded, was a considerable departure. "They're still green," Hoker said, and he kept his distance. Even if he happened to be awake (he drove nights, slept days), Hoker never joined the band for dinner, and he waited on the bus during after-hours carousing.

You could say a country singer's road band is seen and not heard: The musicians seen on stage are rarely the same ones heard on the album. Nashville's studio musicians are an elite barely three-dozen strong; the army of road players numbers in the hundreds. The troops are young, few last past their fortieth birthdays. After a decade or two, even the rush of a crowd's applause wears thin, inadequate compensation for a job where the pay is generally mediocre—Yearwood's musicians make $200 to $250 a show, plus room and a $25 per diem—the meals are dicey, and the motels anybody's guess.

Theoretically, the road is supposed to be a way to break into the better jobs on Music Row, but it seldom works out that way. The problem is that getting studio work is basically a matter of being noticed, and the road just doesn't offer that many chances. For one thing, road players are essentially copyists, paid to recreate the licks recorded on the album. Impressing someone that they have the musical skills to do original work is not part of the job description. And the brutal schedule leaves little time to make the Music Row contacts critical to getting studio work. So while a singer's career accelerates, the road band's remains largely static. Given the close quarters and the sheer time on the road—over 130 days in 1992—things can get pretty tense.

In February 1992, there were five musicians in Yearwood's band: Tammy Rogers, who played fiddle and acoustic guitar; Johnny Garcia, the lead guitarist; Jay Hager on bass; Ric McClure on drums, and Tim Lauer on keyboards. Along with the road manager, Leonard Arnold, there were three other regulars on the bus: Jarrah Herter, Yearwood's physical trainer; Alan Haege, who handled the sound system; and Lisa McLaughlin, who took care of concessions, the photos, T-shirts, sweatshirts, and key chains that could bring in as much as four thousand dollars a night.

Lauer, who was twenty-four and a friend of Yearwood from college, was the bandleader, responsible for determining song lineups for each performance, arranging rehearsals, and holding auditions for new members. He was the first person Yearwood hired for her band. She lured him away from the Forester Sisters, a group that hoped to compete with the Judds but never quite rose to the task. Of the band members, he was the most serious about his churchgoing (he described himself as "a Godly man"), and, like the rest of the band, did no drugs and generally drank only in extreme moderation.

There might not have been much in the way of intoxicants, but the group could get rather giddy. Lauer, especially, was wont to play class cutup, parading through the bus with Victoria's Secret lingerie strapped over his jeans in a sophomoric burlesque.

That spring, Yearwood was still fresh to the road, still enthused by the adventure of it all. "I would never travel on my own bus," she said one day while the coach was rolling down the road. "If we ever got so big that we needed two, well, I guess we'd just draw lots to see who'd travel where." She barely used her stateroom, preferring to sleep in a bottom bunk. She shared her motel rooms with Jarrah Herter, and her exercise classes were a group affair, beds shoved aside, McLaughlin, Rogers, and Yearwood lined up on the wall-to-wall carpeting with Herter shouting instructions; it looked not unlike a girls' gym class. Yearwood was offhanded about her status, and her band loved her for it.

It doesn't take long for road players to get weary, for a certain hardness to set in. But this group, like its star, was still brimming over with enthusiasm. "The music is great, the people are great, the bus is great," Lauer said, "and we're an integral part of the whole thing. It's the best gig I've ever had." The constant chorus was "I love my job," piped up by Lauer, McClure, or Hager, apropos of absolutely nothing. "It's like traveling with the high school band," noted Leonard Arnold, who at age forty-nine was the resident grown-up.

Arnold, who has been in the music business a full quarter century, is a sort of professional Texan. He's a tall man, over six feet, with a mustache, beard, and thick graying ponytail. He wears pressed-felt cowboy hats (black in winter, white in summer, never white past Labor Day) and hand-made boots from the fabled M. L. Leddy in Fort Worth. He almost never buys boots off the rack, regardless of economic circumstance.

Arnold was born in north Texas, then moved south to a little town called Mercedes. "If Lonesome Dove really existed, it would have been Mercedes. . . . I always did figure I was Gus McCrae," Arnold said, referring to Larry McMurtry's retired Texas Ranger, your basic cowboy rake and rambler: fast gun, extraordinary courage, unfailing honor.

In truth, Arnold was the son of an air force sergeant, a mechanic by training. In a town of ranchers' boys, he considered himself a cowboy even if no one else did. His business card reads "Trail Boss," though the only thing he's ever rounded up is a herd of unruly musicians.

Arnold started out intending to be a schoolteacher. He spent seven years in and out of college, his degree detoured by rock and roll. He finally quit altogether and supported himself playing guitar in local bands. "These days guitar players are a dime a dozen, you can't make it unless you're the best," he said. "Back then, though, guys with a lot of emotion could pull it off. That was me." He was a fixture on the Texas rock circuit, and when it moved en masse to southern California in 1970, he got a house by the beach with a couple of the other emigrants, including a drummer named Don Henley.

Arnold lasted only six months in California. "I should have stayed," he says now. "I'd be a lot richer if I had. But then I've always had a way of taking a wrong turn." Back in Texas, he landed a job with Michael Martin Murphey, a singer-songwriter from Dallas, and became the inspiration for Murphey's song "Cosmic Cowboy."

In 1977, Arnold moved back to L.A. in earnest, and got a job in the backup band for a singer produced by Henley. Two years later, he started up his own band, Blue Steel, and things looked as if they were finally going to happen. The band got a record deal with a label called Infinity and signed on to open for the Eagles. "Infinity," says Arnold wryly, "isn't always forever. The label folded three months after our album was released. The record just died. Broke my heart."

The only good news that year was his marriage to a twenty-four-year-old country singer named Kristine Oliver who performed with her older sister, Janis. But neither the sisters nor Arnold had much success in L.A., and in 1984 Janis left for Nashville, where her husband, Vince Gill, had a record deal. Later that year the Arnolds decided they, too, wanted to get out of town. Arnold answered phones in Mattel's consumer complaints division to pay for the move.

The plan was to go back to Texas; then, at the last minute, they decided to join up with Janis in Nashville. That year the sisters won the Wrangler Talent Search (Arnold still drives the van they won) and landed a deal with Columbia Records. They christened themselves the Sweethearts of the Rodeo, after the Byrds' country rock classic, and, in 1986, released their first album.

Arnold, meanwhile, had gone to work as Emmylou Harris's road manager. Harris worked only from April to September, and when she stopped for the season, Arnold went out on the Sweethearts' first tour. He never went back.

Arnold worked with the Sweethearts until the beginning of 1989, when, after the birth of his second daughter, he decided to stay home and take care of the kids while his wife was on the road. For the next two years, he happily played househusband. Then the Sweethearts started to look a little shaky. Their third and fourth albums got abysmal reviews; worse, their singles never broke the top five. "I've been around long enough to sense these things," says Arnold. "Bands get five years, things slow down. I had to prepare."

He went back on the road, first with a difficult young singer named Shelby Lynne, then with Roger Miller. But Miller soon took ill (he died in October 1992) and canceled half his performances, leaving Arnold without much of a paycheck. He went looking for work in the fall of 1991, which is when Yearwood came along.

The job was everything he wanted: Not only was Yearwood easy to work with, but she did interviews when asked, let people on the bus to take pictures, showed up on time, and, besides, he liked her music, and her career was on the come. The near future, at least, was set. From Arnold's perspective, Yearwood was as good as it got.

The Tampa performance was Yearwood's eighteenth date opening for Randy Travis, who, until the coming of Garth Brooks, was the hottest thing to happen to country music since *Urban Cowboy.*

Travis—square jaw, lean body, Republican haircut—was one of the first marketable country singers to come around in the eighties. He was the first of the "new traditionalists," a phalanx of handsome young men in tight blue jeans determined to take country back to its roots.

Travis's road to stardom was blazed by a waitress from Charlotte, North Carolina, named Mary Elizabeth Hatcher. In 1977, Lib Hatcher, then in her thirties, bought into a local club called Country City, U.S.A. One of the first things she did was institute a talent contest, and one of the first contestants was a seventeen-year-old guitar player from Marshville, twenty miles away. The teenager had managed to get himself into all kinds of trouble. When he went on stage at Hatcher's club, he was awaiting sentencing on a breaking-and-entering charge.

His name was Randy Traywick, and after he won the contest, Hatcher offered him a job. She also talked the judge into giving her custody and moved the teenager in with her and her husband. Eventually the husband moved out.

Traywick and Hatcher moved to Nashville in 1980, into a house on Sixteenth Avenue, skirting the outer edges of Music Row. Randy Ray, as he called himself, worked as a dishwasher (and part-time singer) at the Nashville Palace, a tatty club just across from the Opryland Hotel where Hatcher had got herself hired as manager.

Hatcher tried to get Randy Ray a deal, but after every label turned them down twice, she paid for him to make his own album. They recorded it live at the Palace and sold it right next to the cash register. One night in 1984, a Warner Bros. scout heard Hatcher's prodigy at the Palace and, unlike all the others before her, was convinced he could be a star. She renamed him Randy Travis and convinced Warner to release two singles. The first single, "On the Other Hand," didn't fare particularly well.

But after the second, "1982," went to number six, Warner released "On the Other Hand." This time, it went to number one. Travis's first album, *Storms of Life*, was expected to sell twenty thousand copies. It sold three million.

With Travis's success came the attendant curiosity about his private life. For the first few years, he and Hatcher, twenty-odd years between them, refused to discuss their relationship. They were "best friends" was all Travis would say. There were no other women in his life. In March 1991 the *National Examiner* charged that Travis was gay. Homosexuality is not acceptable on Music Row, and the report created quite a stir. First Travis strongly denied the charge, then, two months later, he and Hatcher got married.

By the time he and Yearwood played Tampa in April 1992, Travis's popularity had declined somewhat (his most recent album had gone gold, while the one before it had gone platinum), but he was still big enough to be the main act in a tour sponsored by the truck division of General Motors Corp.

The GMC performances are the best kind of setups: no flatbed trucks, no dusty ball fields, no plastic overhangs that provide little protection in a downpour. Travis and Yearwood played enclosed arenas, auditoriums with standard sound and lighting systems and audiences that numbered in the tens of thousands. This is big, corporate business; there's never any worry that the promoter won't come up with the check at the end of the show.

It had been two months since Joe Layton worked over Yearwood's stage show, and as Kragen says, he might have been expensive, but he was worth it. Gold record and two number one singles notwithstanding, Yearwood was still a novice on stage, and before Layton came to tinker, it showed. She wore little makeup; her long hair wisped, unstyled, halfway down her back. On her album cover, that homespun look made her seem accessible; on stage it made her look like a sixties folk singer who had wandered into the wrong crowd.

She copied her moves from Garth Brooks, venturing to the edge of the stage, pointing out at the audience and smiling. But unlike Brooks, she didn't know how to work a crowd. There was little patter with the audience; "Can y'all hear? Y'all doing okay?" she would ask before beginning the next song. The band members each seemed to be playing on their own stages, intently watching their instruments, paying little attention to the crowd and even less to the singer they were supposed to be supporting. "She was legendarily awful," said Timothy White of *Billboard*, "a monstrous distraction from what was good about her record."

By Tampa, though, that had changed. Even though Yearwood had had no sleep in two days, she looked better than she had on her best days on the Garth Brooks tour. Her hair had been cut to shoulder length, teased up slightly in front, a single wave cutting back, just past her right cheekbone. The month before, she had hired a professional to teach her how to do makeup, and spent about a thousand dollars for a two-tier makeup case and its contents. Her eyes were lined, her cheeks highlighted, her lips painted deep pink. She didn't look like an overly coiffed country music queen; she simply looked professionally pretty.

She opened her forty-minute set with "Who Turned Out the Lights," a torchy ballad about the end of a love affair. She stayed close to the center-stage microphone, but where before she simply looked as if she didn't know where else to go, now it was deliberate, not desperate. At the end, after the long last wail, she turned her face off to the side, away from the audience, leaving the light to outline her in sad, lonely profile. She had hopes of using her second number, "You Say You Will," on her next album. She shimmied through the sassy, upbeat song about a woman who's tired of putting up with a recalcitrant mate ("I keep forgiving/I keep forgetting/I keep expecting you to change/ You say you will but you never do"). The little waves that used to punctuate each lyric had been replaced by smoother moves, left arm folded, hand behind her back, right arm in front, her walk turned into a strut.

She introduced the next song with a bit of clearly canned, but still greatly improved, patter. "Did any of you see the video for our last single, 'That's What I Like About You'?" she asked the audience, to enthusiastic applause. "We did a video for that single. And in case you missed it, here's the story. We hired a brainless hunk, and he did his job real well, prancing around all day, spraying water on his body so it looked like he'd been working out. Well, I got real tired of him looking better than me, so in the last scene, when he's in this hammock, I dumped him out. I just want you to know . . . that wasn't in the script. It was my idea." As the audience applauded, Garcia, Rogers, Yearwood, and Hager moved to center stage, lining up for a bit of corny but effective kick-up-your-heels choreography. Yearwood gave up the limelight to each of the instrumentalists in turn, slinking down Garcia's back as he worked his guitar solo, hovering over Rogers's shoulder as she danced into her fiddle. As Yearwood finished the song, she retook center stage, and closed with a flourishing curtsy.

In addition to the songs from her album, Yearwood generally "covers" one or two standards. Her repertoire includes James Taylor, Merle Haggard, and Dolly Parton. That night she did a wrenching version of Taylor's "Bartender's Blues," then another cut off her album. Finally, she shouted, "I'm gonna leave you with the one that did it," and launched into "She's in Love with the Boy," ("the only teenybopper country record I know of," as Jay Phillips, a radio programmer in Oklahoma, put it). As Yearwood sang about Katie and Tommy, a parade of little girls in oversize Trisha Yearwood T-shirts, hand in hand with their parents, approached the stage, and each handed Yearwood a single red rose. By evening's end, she would have two dozen.

Yearwood was permitted one encore when the crowd earned it, which, in Tampa, it did. She went out with Elvis Presley's "Trying to Get to You."

Usually there were postperformance obligations. Yearwood either met with the local General Motors dealers or sat behind the concession stand and signed autographs for an hour or so (a boost to sales as well as fan loyalty). But tonight there was no "meet and greet" scheduled, and Yearwood was too exhausted from the California trip to put in time behind the T-shirt stand. Most unusual of all, she and her band would actually sleep in their motel. Country bands generally travel by night, but with no performance the next day, Friday, April 3 was what Lauer called the WPS, "worst possible scenario": no performance, no pay, and not enough time to get home.

Come the next day, half the group taxied to a guitar shop in town while Yearwood, McLaughlin, and Herter went to the mall across the street. Yearwood made virtually all the purchases: a new suitcase, new sneakers, and a new set of plastic steps for her aerobics workouts. After two hours of shopping, Yearwood returned to find a message to call Russell.

The news was not good: MCA hated the photo shoot.

* * *

What would come to be known as "the cleavage controversy" began with a phone call from Nancy Russell to Susan Levy, head of publicity at MCA. Almost as an afterthought, Russell mentioned that she had just received the singer's new publicity photos.

"What pictures?" Levy wanted to know. No one, apparently, had told her there was going to be a new shoot. No one, for that matter, had talked to her about whether it was time for a new image. "I didn't want to be in the position of having Bruce Hinton come in, throw the photos on my desk, and say, 'Why are we doing this?' and have to say, 'I don't know anything about them.' "

Russell had never encountered that kind of concern from a record label before. With Travis Tritt, Warner Brothers had permitted her and Ken Kragen to operate fairly autonomously. Still, when a performer's record label is worried, it is up to the publicist to respond, so Russell arranged to meet with Levy and her boss, Janet Rickman, bringing both the new publicity photo as well as a swatch of shots from the entire shoot.

Rickman is a handsome woman, with an angular face and curly waist-length gray hair. By background, she is a bit of an odd woman out on Music Row. Her father was in the air force; her mother grew up in society Nashville. Her legacy was a certain vestigial primness.

Rickman's first job had been at an advertising agency, before she graduated from college. After she finished school, she worked as a probation counselor with teenage girls but left after three years, frustrated with her inability to affect their lives. She went from there into a job as an assistant in the promotion department at Mercury Records, eventually moving over to public relations. She was hired by MCA in 1987 as vice president of publicity and artist development, a rough marriage of her previous jobs.

When she saw the photos, it brought out her most protective instincts. She was quietly concerned, Levy, who tended to be considerably more voluble than her boss, noisily so. "I think it's crazy to send pictures of Trisha with her cleavage hanging out when the last time people saw her she looked like Rebecca of Sunnybrook Farm," she said. "People are going to say she's been through the cookie cutter, she's been Kragenized."

"It's too much change too quickly," was how Rickman put it when she called Kragen in Los Angeles to tell him MCA didn't want the photographs used. Kragen called Russell, who, in turn, called Yearwood. Russell was beside herself. This was, to her mind, the Nashville establishment at its worst. "This would never," she said, "ever happen in pop."

"I don't get it," Yearwood told her. "First they want me to get skinny, then they get pissed off when I show it."

Russell told her that she still wasn't sure what would happen, that Kragen had told her he wanted to talk to Bruce Hinton. Yearwood hung up and called Los Angeles, but Kragen was not in the office, and she was heading out for the evening. There was nothing to do but try again the next day.

At noon Saturday the bus loaded for its next stop. It was a short ride, just three hours, arrival signaled by a banner waving over the sign marking the city limits:

> Welcome to Daytona Beach
> Spring Break Capital of the World.

Yearwood left the bus in search of a phone. This time, she reached Kragen. He had finally talked to Bruce Hinton about the photographs, he told her, and they had reached a compromise. Which, knowing Bruce Hinton, was inevitable.

On Music Row, they call him the Senator. With his patrician features and full head of white hair, he looks not unlike the actor John Forsythe, a statesman out of central casting. But he wasn't given the name just for his looks. In a business filled with board-room warriors, Hinton is a diplomat, able to balance the interests of the various lobbyists he deals with in the course of a day.

The fifty-six-year-old executive was born in Indiana, promoted an Erroll Garner concert when he was still in college, and, in 1960, went to work for Warner Bros. Records in New York. He spent the early sixties in a variety of corporate positions, then, in 1967, joined Jimmy Bowen, who was forming his own record company in Los Angeles. When Bowen's operation folded, Hinton formed his own independent promotion firm, the first to focus on country records. In 1984 he moved to Nashville to work for Bowen at MCA. Five years later, he took over.

While Bowen made waves in the calmest of seas, Hinton prided himself on his tact. He eliminated the fractiousness that had surrounded the previous regime, and pared down the label's roster, from forty-six acts to twenty. "He got on the wave at the right time," said Al Teller, the head of all of MCA Records. But Teller did not dispute Hinton's skill at riding its crest. In 1992 MCA Nashville's revenues of about $110 million accounted for nearly one third of the total revenues of MCA's entire record division.

Unlike most of his music business brethren in Los Angeles, Hinton was neither braggart nor vulgarian. He hewed to his midwestern roots, insistent but never loud. It was a demeanor that made him the ideal conciliator. Now, it was his job to make peace with Ken Kragen, convince him to change the photographs without slighting the manager or his client.

Hinton explained to Kragen that he realized it was just a little bit of cleavage—"We're not talking *Playboy* material here"—but he wanted to be sure the critics focused on her music, not on the fact that she had been working out. He was especially worried because it was just her second album. He wanted to do everything possible to keep Yearwood from being dismissed as a one-album wonder.

"What are the alternatives?" Yearwood asked after Kragen had explained the executive's concerns.

"Crop the cleavage. It is the one easy thing we can do to make MCA happy, and it won't affect the image. There are times to fight the label. This is not one of them."

Yearwood listened, considered his logic, and decided that sacrificing the bottom 15 percent of her new publicity shot made a lot more sense than alienating her record label. "Let's just do it. How fast can we get the new pictures made?"

With a spare hour before sound check, Yearwood, Jarrah Herter, and Ric McClure wandered down to the beach, where the annual bacchanal was going strong. Two long processions of cars cruised the sand, while a few yards away dozens of kiosks sold memories of spring break '92. Two of the more popular items: a T-shirt emblazoned "Party Till She's Cute" and a plastic funnel labeled "Beer Bong."

Off in the distance, the Bungee jumpers were screaming.

"We've made an executive decision," Yearwood announced. "We're going to crop the cleavage. Half the people buying those pictures are little girls. Their moms probably wouldn't want their kids to buy pictures of me with my chest hanging out. I don't exactly want to be signing across my cleavage."

The night's performance was a little bumpy. Hager's bass went dead halfway through "That's What I Like About You"; the instrumentals on "The Woman Before Me," the new single, were a little weak. "I want to talk about this performance when we're back on the bus," Yearwood said to Hager and Lauer as she headed back to her dressing room, a mirrored cubicle that smelled of Lysol. The door read, "Visiting Team."

Yearwood had an hour to kill before she and Travis had to meet the local car dealers. As she flipped through an old copy of *Vogue*, Jeff Davis, Travis's road manager, wandered in. "Kragen told me some Revlon executives are going to be flying in from Palm Beach for the show in Miami," she said. "Can you make sure they have passes? Kragen is worried that there's going to be a problem, and I'd be grateful if you could cater to his paranoia."

• • •

Corporate sponsorship has been part of country music since the musicians took to the road. First there were the medicine shows, then, during World War II, R. J. Reynolds sponsored the Camel Caravan, an Opry-star tour of army bases; more recently, everyone from Budweiser to Wrangler jeans has paid to lift their logos above the stage. General Motors pays several million dollars in promotion and fees to underwrite these performances. In return, performers agree to stay on and meet local sellers and buyers, presumably making a Chevy truck that much more appealing than a Dodge.

Half an hour later, Travis appeared at Yearwood's door to escort her to meet the truck dealers. As they walked into the hallway behind the auditorium, there was a loud squeal. "Who killed the cat?" Travis asked.

The "meet and greet" was more like a meet and shoot. The two singers stood behind a desk, and the V.I.P. guests filed through one by one. Each, in turn, stood between the singers, put his or her arms around them, and had a Polaroid taken by a trio of photographers. No autographs allowed.

After the last photograph of an overweight, mustachioed truck dealer, Davis went to Travis's side, Arnold to Yearwood's, and they made a flying wedge through the crowd. Yearwood and Arnold were pretty much on their own; Travis was tailed by a small, peculiar posse. Hatcher, a tiny white-haired woman, was about four feet behind, and she, in turn, was trailed by a squat crew-cut woman known simply as Suwanna—a Thai masseuse whom they had met in Los Angeles. (Unlike the Yearwood group, who travel together in a single bus, Travis, Hatcher, and the masseuse were the only occupants of their silver coach, one of a half dozen in the Travis caravan. The rest carry lights, sound, sets, and the band.)

The procession split off as it headed into the parking lot, Yearwood off to her bus, Suwanna, Hatcher, and Travis to theirs. The sign just above their windshield, the one that usually contains the vehicle's destination, read "HOME SWEET HOME."

A small crowd had gathered just beyond the fence. "Trisha, over here," called a man holding a pigtailed blonde on his shoulders, his camera flashing as the singer turned and smiled before she headed onto her bus. "I guess I should go out," Yearwood said. "I didn't sign tonight." Arnold escorted her to the near side of the fence, where she signed T-shirts, photos, tickets, scraps of paper proffered by the crowd.

"She still likes this stuff," Arnold said. "She'll get over it."

The various band members, who had been getting ready for the bus to pull out, dispersed. Hager and Lauer headed back into the auditorium to call their girlfriends. Lauer was dating a senior at Ward Belmont; Hager, a dental hygienist. For both, those pay phones were the lifeline for love on the run.

Of the two, Hager was the more assiduous. There were calls upon arrival, after sound check, after dinner, a pause for the performance, and, if time allowed, another call afterward. His phone bills had run to four figures in the four months since he had been smitten while sitting in the dentist's chair. He ended up going back for hundreds of dollars of dental work he couldn't really afford, finally getting up the nerve to ask her out after he had a five-hundred-dollar tooth bonding. "It was worth it," he said, "much whiter," running his finger over his front teeth for effect.

Hager, another Ward Belmont alumnus, fancies himself a hipster, though the exact vintage is a little unclear. His hair is cut in sort of a ducktail, his preferred shoes a pair of black patent-leather loafers. His last job was with a struggling young singer named Davis Daniels, a considerably lower-rent production. He not only played in the band, he drove the van, subsisting on four hours sleep a night. "This gig is so good I feel like I'm in the *Partridge Family*," he'd say, reflecting on his good fortune. And if asked, he would specify the episode.

This night, though, he would have cause to reconsider.

CHAPTER 8

Aᴦᴛᴇʀ ᴀʙᴏᴜᴛ ꜰᴏʀᴛʏ ᴍɪɴᴜᴛᴇs ᴏꜰ sɪɢɴɪɴɢ ᴀᴜᴛᴏɢʀᴀᴘʜs, Yearwood climbed back onto the bus, and Hoker pulled out, bound for Miami. It was just past twelve-thirty, and except for Alan Haege, the sound man, Leonard Arnold, Yearwood, and Ric McClure, the drummer, everyone had retired to their bunks. At about two in the morning, McClure headed back to bed.

McClure had the bottom bunk in the back row; Hager occupied the slot just above his. As he got ready to climb in, McClure noticed that the curtain on the middle slot was open and there was no one inside. The implication was clear. Just to make sure, McClure checked the stateroom. It was empty. He headed back up front and reported the bass player AWOL.

"We left the Hage [pronounced with a hard *g*, as in *egg*] in Daytona," he told the others.

"We're not going back," Arnold announced. Arnold had never approved of the marathon phone sessions, and this, he hoped, would put an end to them. In any event, the situation wasn't all that dire. Arnold figured Hager would be able to hitch a ride later with Travis's entourage.

Yearwood's bus pulled into the parking lot of the Miami Sheraton at about six. Arnold was the only one who unloaded immediately. He was back on in ten minutes, leaving a list of room numbers and keys on the front table. It was another three hours or so before the rest of the band ventured out into the humid Miami morning. McLaughlin, the first to go in, ran into Hager almost immediately. "Did you get here okay?"

"No problem, man," he said, managing studied cool even at nine in the morning. "Pulled in hours before you did." Later it came out that he had spent the night on the van carrying the video equipment, which compares favorably to traveling by bus in rural Burma.

Yearwood spent much of the afternoon agonizing over extracurricular activities. Her plans were dependent on someone she referred to only as the Maverick; they traded a half dozen phone calls (Should we meet for lunch? Should we meet before the show? Oh, let's just get together afterward) before settling on an agenda. Yearwood hadn't dated anyone in months. She had tried to convince herself, and anyone who asked, that she had soured on romance. "It's hard to have a relationship with this life except with another musician," she said, "and that's a disaster. Right now I'm just focusing on my career." But three weeks before, at the end of the Country Radio Seminar in Nashville, she had met the Maverick.

Robert Reynolds played bass for the Mavericks (hence the handle), a new country band that had just signed with MCA. The Mavericks weren't your usual country band: The lead singer was the son of Cuban émigrés, and the group was based in Miami, not exactly a hotbed of country-music activity.

Yearwood had discovered the group playing in one of the hospitality suites at the Opryland Hotel. Yearwood and Reynolds had spent just one day together, four weeks before, but they'd spoken every few days or so since. She had three days off between Miami and the next show, and Reynolds invited her to stay. She was, she said, "intrigued."

On the bus over to the venue, Yearwood, who was not just the star but also the boss, announced that she was less than happy with some of the band's recent performances. "We've been missing licks; Jay and Tim have been hitting some clunkers. That shouldn't be happening. Let's listen to this," she said, and brought out a cassette of her album. "I forgot about this album. It's pretty good.

"We need to slow 'Woman Before Me' down. We need to go back to the way it is on the record. Last night it was feeling like it was about to fall apart any second. Let's all just watch Ric. Ric is never off."

McClure is the band's ballast, musically and temperamentally. He was born in Morgan County, Kentucky, not far from Keith Whitley. As teenagers the two faced off in local talent contests. They shared a certain look: slender build, full head of straw-colored hair, a pale complexion that turned crimson under the slightest bit of sun.

At thirty-five, McClure had been playing professionally longer than anyone else in the band. He had spent most of his career working for Jerry Reed, the singer responsible for one of the more memorable song titles in country: "She Got the Goldmine (I Got the Shaft)." As road gigs went, it was a good one: Reed had him play on two of his albums, and he even got a cameo in one of Reed's movies, *What Comes Around*.

After nearly eight years, though, Reed's career was starting to slip, and it was time to move on. McClure eventually landed with the Forester Sisters, and when Lauer invited him to join Yearwood's band, he jumped. A dozen years on the road had taken care of any illusions of stardom. He just wanted steady work with someone he respected, and Yearwood fit the bill.

McClure has a marked stutter. Though it disappears when he sings, offstage it has left him a cautious speaker who listens intently to the conversation, only occasionally joining in. He adored Yearwood, and she returned the affection; he was the one she turned to in distress, the only one she spent much time with off the road. Not long before, Yearwood had told him she was hoping to use him on her next album. It was a compliment that he didn't want to count on. For McClure, the most important thing was Yearwood's success. If she did well enough, he reasoned, they could have their own major tour. After all those years on the road, he wanted this to be his last season of county fairs.

Tammy Rogers, the twenty-eight-year-old fiddle player, shared none of McClure's caution. This was only her second year in a Nashville band, and of all the band members, she seemed the most pained by the limits of road musicianship. "Do we have to play it just like it is on the record?" she asked after Yearwood's admonition about tempo.

Rogers had been playing fiddle since she was a girl in Texas. Her family had a bluegrass band, and at eleven she had started going out with them on weekends, using the money she earned to buy her own instruments.

Like Lauer and Hager, Rogers had graduated from Ward Belmont, where she had been a stand partner in orchestra with Chris Latham, Yearwood's ex-husband. Though she had lost touch with him after college, she had run into Yearwood and Latham at a Nashville record store about a year and a half before. Yearwood had just got her record deal. Rogers had just got her first road gig with Patty Loveless. "When I get rich and famous, you can be in my band," Yearwood told her. When Yearwood needed a fiddle player, she called Rogers.

While she was glad to be there, she wasn't shy about her ambition. "It's frustrating to be the first to work up songs on the road and then have someone else play on the album," she said. "Either they end up taking your performance, or else they change it and you have to learn the song all over again."

Rogers was a good player and a better performer, dancing into her fiddle as she played her solo on "That's What I Like About You," kicking up her inevitably short skirt as she took her licks. Of the players, she always got the biggest applause, and when she moved to center stage during the two numbers that featured her fiddle, she came close to stealing Yearwood's show.

Yearwood didn't mind Rogers's flamboyance, but she had only limited patience with her drive. "If it's a single, yes, you have to play it like the record," Yearwood told her. "The licks were put there for a reason. Especially if it's a single. People want to hear what they hear on the radio."

Rogers was silent.

"I really want people to be blown away by our music," Yearwood said as the bus pulled up to the auditorium. "We are good musicians, and there is no excuse for not getting it right."

They went on stage at seven. "The Woman Before Me" came halfway through the show. McClure slowed it down by a full beat. Rogers played gamely, the light catching her hair as it flew over her fiddle. The audience, as always, went wild.

After the show, Yearwood retreated to the bus. She was expecting guests, and she wanted to change into something more comfortable.

Kragen's concern about the Revlon representatives from New York proved unwarranted. A pair of women soon turned up in Yearwood's dressing room. Cecil Kanale—black silk shirt, black slacks, black Chanel bag—was in charge. This was, she confessed, her first country concert.

Yearwood walked in looking commensurately coutured, wearing a white Donna Karan jacket over a black catsuit. "Did you like the show?" she asked.

"I had a hard time hearing," Kanale replied. "People come to concerts, then scream so loud you can't hear the music. Call me silly. I don't get it."

Kanale proceeded to matters at hand. She surveyed Yearwood's outfit.

"I have that jacket. . . . So what do you think about all this?"

Yearwood repeated her lines from the meeting at Kragen's house. "You already have Cindy Crawford. I'm not a model. It would be a great opportunity, but I'm not going to pretend to be something I'm not. If it's right for you, fine. If it's not, something else will come along."

"So how did they leave it when you met Ron Perelman?" Kanale asked.

"Basically it was, 'You're pretty, we'll call you.' "

"If we were to do this, would you want your own scent or an existing product?"

"I liked the idea of Charly Girl,"

"Do you have any ideas for a new scent? Nashville?"

"Not," Yearwood was emphatic. "People like me are trying to change the image of what country music is. We want to make sure that just because it's country, people don't think *Hee Haw*."

"Your hair is pretty," said Kanale, making it clear that wasn't what she had expected.

Yearwood replied with her usual mantra. "I don't have big hair, and I don't wear fringe. Music that used to be rock now is considered country. I used to listen to Bob Seger and Linda Ronstadt along with George Jones and Tammy Wynette. That's what I'm trying to get across. There's an opportunity here to not make it look like hay bales and cow herds. We're just not that way anymore."

Kanale looked impressed. "We've been trying to revive Charly Girl for a new market. Charly is now a woman. We're looking for a new market, we need young girls. Who is your market?"

"I'm sort of the den mother of country music. I sell to a lot of twelve-year-olds. It's a good group. A twelve-year-old fan is hopefully going to buy records for awhile."

It all sounded good, but it was still too soon to commit. "I guess we've gotten to everything for now," Kanale said and, assistant in tow, left to find the car that would get her to the airport for a late-night flight back to New York.

"We'll see what happens," Yearwood told Arnold, then moved on to more pressing matters. "Have you seen the Mavericks?"

Reynolds appeared at the door moments later with two of the other Mavericks. They looked considerably more rock than country. Raul Malo wore his hair in a thick black braid. Paul Deakin, the drummer, cultivated a downtown New York look, short hair, white shirt, blue jeans, white socks, and thick black oxfords. Reynolds had brown hair past shoulder length, and a silver hoop piercing his left ear.

"Wanna see the bus?" Yearwood asked, and escorted the trio back to meet her band. She showed them through the bunks and stateroom. Malo and Deakin wandered, and Reynolds stayed behind, sitting with Yearwood on the front banquette, holding hands, sandwiched between McClure and Rogers.

Arnold surveyed the scene from the driver's seat. "Boy's too good-looking," he said, out of Yearwood's hearing. "Besides, neither of them has any business getting involved. He's going out on the road for the first time—the girls will be throwing themselves at him. And Trisha . . . I want to get her rich and famous, and then we can worry about finding a boyfriend."

Yearwood, though, had not asked for Arnold's opinion, and he did not volunteer. An hour later, she stepped off the bus with her suitcase, headed to a Holiday Inn for three days at the beach, her first time off in three months.

On Wednesday morning, Reynolds drove Yearwood to the airport for a flight to Atlanta, where her parents would be waiting to drive her back to Monticello. She had no idea when she'd get a chance to see Reynolds again, didn't really have any idea if she wanted to get involved, but she wasn't really thinking about him much. Thursday night she would be playing in her hometown, her first performance there since she had hit the big time.

CHAPTER 9

*I*N THE LAST ROOM BEFORE THE EXIT OF THE COUNTRY MUSIC
Hall of Fame—after Elvis Presley's solid gold Cadillac, Patsy
Cline's cigarette lighter (decorated with the Stars and Bars, plays
"Battle Hymn of the Republic," found in the plane wreck that
killed her), Minnie Pearl's hat, and Stringbean's banjo—is the
last painting Thomas Hart Benton finished before he died. *The
Origins of Country Music* is dedicated to Tex Ritter, one of the only
men in both the Country Music and the Cowboy Halls of Fame.
It is an epic canvas: guitar-playing cowboy, barefoot dulcimer
player, preacher in a waistcoat coaxing hymns out of sunbon-
neted choristers, fiddler in overalls calling out a square dance.
The backdrop is a broad-planked front porch, that mythic cabin
in the hills every country singer claims, rightfully or not, as his or
her beginnings. "We are still a nation trying to go home, not really satisfied with the way we are," says the country music histo-
rian Bill Malone. "We eagerly embrace modern changes; at the
same time we are a little worried and anxious about the loss of the
familiar. Country music is a way of recovering roots, the most
non-threatening way you can do it."

That halcyon barn dance, of course, is even more a fantasy for
the singers than for their audiences. For those who have turned
song into salary, those country towns that made their lives possible are an evanescent paradise. They can visit, but they can
never, not as long as they have their careers, really return.

* * *

General Sherman missed Monticello when he blazed his way through Georgia, so the town still has a half dozen antebellum homes. They aren't especially notable specimens. Monticello never had that kind of money, then or now, which helps explain why Sam Walton bypassed Monticello on his mercantile mission a century later. Since the nearest Wal-Mart is thirty miles away, most of the dozen-odd shops bordering Monticello's town square are still open for business. Joe's Department Store—"JOE'S" is spelled out in blue tile in the pavement out front—is among the biggest establishments. Joe Gasses owns the place and runs it with his wife. He inherited it from his father, who had the pavement tiled forty years before. The display is a homely affair: There are a half dozen rows of dress, shirt, and slacks racks. The shoe department consists of three fold-down chairs and a dozen rows of cardboard boxes where customers can fetch their sizes out of the inventory. Like everything else on the square, Joe's is holdout small-town America.

Trisha Yearwood's homecoming was the biggest thing to happen in Monticello since Joe Pesci came to town to film *My Cousin Vinny* —and he wasn't local. The city fathers even repainted the city limits sign to read:

> Welcome to Monticello, Georgia.
> Home of Recording Artist Trisha Yearwood.

Thursday had become, at least unofficially, Trisha Yearwood day. The beauty shop on Confederate Square had a "WELCOME HOME TRISHA " sign in the window, as did the dry cleaner next door. Down the street, at her father's bank, the tellers were all wearing Trisha T-shirts. "It's just so exciting," said Kim Camp, one of the cashiers and a Piedmont classmate of the singer. "We've never had a celebrity from Monticello before."

Small-town girl returns home. It made for terrific copy, and Nancy Russell had driven down from Nashville to oversee the event. By eleven o'clock she and her charge, a producer from "Crook and Chase," TNN's answer to "Regis and Kathie Lee," were trailing Yearwood as she walked the town square. Joe Gas-

ses was on a ladder, paintbrush in hand, as Yearwood walked
by. "I heard you was coming home, so I was getting my store
painted."

"Kind of slow, aren't you?" she said.

"I didn't know you were coming home so fast."

Gasses's wife observed the proceedings from behind the sales
counter, where clip-on ties were for sale next to the register.
"We're just crazy about her," she said. "The Yearwoods are a
good family, so it makes it worth a lot more."

Cameras followed as she headed into the Tillman House for
lunch. The Tillman House is the only restaurant in town except
for a Hardee's, and lunch is cafeteria-style, meat loaf, liver, and
vegetables—turnip greens or macaroni and cheese. There are
two beverage options: sweet tea and unsweet tea. "Do I simulate
eating, or do I get to do the real thing?" Yearwood asked.

After lunch (nonsimulated), as she walked back out into the
streets of town, a tiny woman, dwarfed by her white bouffant,
passed by. "Miss Emmy, Miss Emmy," Yearwood called, and
walked over and hugged her.

"We're all just so proud of you," the older woman said,
beaming.

"Tell Mr. Emmet I said hey," Yearwood said, climbing back
into the car. "She played organ in church for years and years,"
she explained. "I used to think Mr. Emmet owned the church."

Over at the Yearwoods', the big event of the afternoon was the
appearance of Uncle Wilson, Gwen's brother, on their father's
white Harley. His wife, concerned for his safety, arrived simultaneously in her Chevy. "I don't know why I do it, but I cry every
time I see you on TV," she said as she hugged her niece.

Two hours later, everyone headed over to Piedmont Academy,
Trisha's alma mater and the site of the concert. The parking lot
was still empty, except for a single pickup truck with a bumper
sticker that said, "God, guns and guts made America free. Let's
fight to keep all that."

In the back of the school Jack Yearwood supervised a massive
iron barbecue emblazoned, "We are cooking with the Bank of
Monticello." There would be no limp baked chicken this night;
Yearwood had sprung for sirloin.

Inside the auditorium, a banner hung above the stage: "WE ♥
TRISHA."

The crowd started arriving at around six. Hard Smith didn't really like country music, he said, but his wife had insisted they come. "She goes to church with Gwen. Thinks Trisha just hung the moon."

Eight-year-old Katlin Toller was there with her aunt, who taught school with Gwen Yearwood. "I want to grow up and be like her," Katlin said. "I think she's pretty, I like country music, and she sings it so good."

At 7:00 P.M. sharp, Rhubarb Jones, deejay from WYAI in Atlanta, came on to introduce Monticello's homegrown country music queen. "Only one thing can keep me from going to a Braves opener. And that's a pretty woman. We have one here with us tonight. . . . Miss Trisha Yearwood."

She walked down the center aisle, then up the side stairs of the stage. "It's okay to yell and holler," she told the crowd. "You'd better, or I'll feel like you didn't want me to come home."

There was a wolf whistle from one of the side bleachers. "Did I ever date you?" Yearwood asked. "Bet you wish I did." For the first time in months she was playing to a crowd that was there to see her, not just killing time before the main attraction.

"You know," she said, midway through the show, "The last time I was down this aisle is when I graduated. I think it's real important for all you youngsters to get your education. I just want you to know that mine was real important to me, and I'm really grateful to Piedmont for providing me with the tools to get started."

An encore was obligatory. "I know Elvis is in this building," she said, "so this is for him." She did her usual, "Trying to Get to You."

There was a second hour-long performance and then two hours of autographs. The line made it perfectly clear just who listened to Yearwood and why. There were the little girls who revered her, and the teenagers who wanted to be her, small-town girls like Becky Joslin, a sophomore from Wesleyan College in Macon, who grew up in Lula, Georgia, a town of just under a thousand. "She talks about what people are feeling," Joslin said. "That means a lot to us. We are plain folks who dream of hitting it big—we can live that out through someone like Trisha. You look at her and say, 'Maybe I could do it, too.' "

What those girls did not understand was that once you do live the dream, you can only sing about how plain folks live their lives. Celebrity sucks up everything in its wake. Jimmy Bowen put it best: "If you want to be a star, you have to want it more than you want anything else in your life, because your competition does. If you don't go for it in that manner, you will not get it." Fame occupies every vacant corner of one's life.

Trisha Yearwood, sitting at a table in small-town Georgia, was closing in on the center of that cyclone. "Ohmygod, I can't believe you're here," she cried as three young women her age got to the front of the autograph line after a twenty-minute wait. The woman were Yearwood's college roommates, three of the Suches Seven who got a dedication on her album. They looked not unlike the Yearwood of that first album portrait, sweaters over blue jeans, scrubbed-face pretty. "I'm sorry I haven't called," she said. "It's just been so crazy. . . . I met Don Henley," she said, and did a wide-mouthed teen scream. They laughed, took pictures arm in arm. "Come out to the house," she said. "I'm going to be there with my folks all day tomorrow."

There were pledges to keep in closer touch, promises to show up the next day. With another hour of autographs to sign, there just wasn't time for much more.

The next day was an off day, and Yearwood and the band spent it out at her parents' house, where there was an unending supply of pork barbecue, iced tea, and, courtesy of Jack Yearwood, home-baked bread. Midway through the afternoon Ken Kragen called.

"What's happening with Revlon?" she wanted to know.

"It looks good, but there's a hitch. They want to call it 'Nashville'."

"If they call it 'Nashville,' they can find someone else."

Kragen asked her for alternatives. She suggested "Blue Guitar," after the song she thought was going to be the title cut on her new album. Kragen promised to present it to Revlon. There would be no deal, they agreed, without a suitable name.

There were two more stops on the Randy Travis tour before the band headed back to Nashville—Pensacola, Florida, and Montgomery, Alabama. In Montgomery, the highlight of the day was a visit to Hank and Audrey Williams's side-by-side graves. There was a marble cowboy hat on his tomb, cowboy boots chiseled into hers, and, across the headstones, small square replicas of each of his hit records.

For Yearwood, the main event was still eight days away. On April 21 she would be going back into the studio to record her second album.

Part III

THE RECORD

Making Hearts in Armor

I've been asked what the Nashville Sound is a thousand times, and I've given a thousand different answers. And I think I've been right every time. It's a song that's our kind of song and a bunch of musicians who can put it over.

—Owen Bradley

CHAPTER 10

NASHVILLE LIKES TO CALL ITSELF MUSIC CITY, U.S.A., BUT the recording industry actually came to town relatively late. Ralph Peer stopped off in the fall of 1928 to record a few Opry acts, but that was pretty much it until 1945, when Decca's Paul Cohen recorded Red Foley in the WSM studios. That enterprise, too, was short-lived; after a session or two the station's management informed its engineers that they didn't want WSM's quarters used for extracurricular activities. Within months, those underlings departed to found Nashville's first recording operation, Castle Studio, in the Tulane Hotel, just blocks from the Ryman.

With most Ryman stars living within a ten-minute drive, Castle became a sort of house studio for the Grand Ole Opry, used by virtually every recording company until 1953, when Owen Bradley opened his Quonset Hut on Sixteenth Avenue, the first studio on what would become Music Row. (Thus began Nashville's notoriously tangled mix of personal and corporate interests. Bradley was still with Decca when he opened his studio. No one, apparently, had any problems with him both managing a label and running a studio on the side.)

Today there are roughly three hundred recording studios in Nashville. Like virtually all the studios, the Sound Emporium, where Yearwood would be working, was an independent operation, booked by the day. Actually it was two studios; the larger one cost $1,300 for the day, the smaller one $600. Last year with

84 percent of the weekdays filled, the Sound Emporium pulled in over $300,000.

Keeping a studio booked requires giving producers what they want—technology that will enable them to make the best possible music. The equipment in Studio A, where Fundis would be working with Yearwood, was valued at nearly $500,000 and included two kinds of taping equipment, analog and digital. Neither is a particularly complicated process: Musicians create a sound, the microphones pick it up and turn it into electronic impulses that are channeled through a control board and transferred onto magnetic tape.

Even though the digital equipment costs three hundred dollars more a day to use, producers generally consider it money well spent. Analog reproduction is essentially a continuous copy—an analogy, that is—of the real thing. It cannot distinguish between sound and background noise, which means that every time an analog tape is copied, that noise increases and the reproduction becomes more distorted.

Digital reproduction converts each sound into a number, billions of them, each of which is then converted back into sound. No matter how many times it is rerecorded, that number stays the same, so the recording never changes; the only distortions come from the original conversion of sound into numbers. With digital recording the producer and engineer can more precisely control the sound—in this case, the music—they are receiving from the instruments in the studio. There is no worry about distortion each time they rerecord a part, making their results that much more accurate.

The studio costs do not include fees for the sound engineer and his assistant ($40 to $50 an hour) or the cost of tape reels ($155 apiece). Seven reels would be used to make Yearwood's album.

The gadgetry in Studio A can do as much as can be done to enhance an individual sound. It can increase volume, make a tone last longer, alter its timbre, adjust it so that its volume remains consistent. Yearwood and the band record ensemble, but each voice and each instrument is recorded onto one of thirty-two individual channels, so that any player's mistakes can be isolated and fixed without everyone having to record the song over again. Those separate tracks have another purpose: They make it possible for new instrumentalists and vocalists to be added to songs recorded weeks before.

At the Sound Emporium, the console, the locus of any recording studio, was manufactured by the Neve Corporation. It is a twelve-by four-foot wedge of dials, levers, and dancing light meters that anchors the control room. This is where the sound engineer pushes the buttons that weave the individual musicians' parts into a whole. Perched on an aluminum ledge over the board were two Sound Emporium additions to the gadgetry: a plastic cactus and a Statue of Liberty. Thanks to a computer chip, each gyrated whenever music came through the speakers—a sort of visual analogue for the audio process going on inside the huge machine.

Technology plays a large role in deciding where to record, but the recording equipment was only one reason Fundis chose the Sound Emporium. "Making music requires a delicate psychological balance," he explained, hands shifting as if trying to support a fragile load. "If something works, you stick with it."

Not only had he recorded Yearwood, Williams, and Whitley at the Sound Emporium, he had swept its floor some twenty years before as a twenty-four-year-old in 1972.

The Sound Emporium is about a five-minute drive from Music Row and a half dozen blocks up from Ward Belmont's campus, in the midst of one of Nashville's older residential neighborhoods. Next door is a small white building labeled Sun Records, the corpse of the Memphis label made legend by Elvis Presley. These days it exists mostly for tour groups, a place where its owner, Shelby Singleton, can make a few dollars selling records from the original Sun catalog.

For Garth Fundis, sentimentality, and a sense that you don't fix something that's not broken, more than made up for the fact that up-to-date technology notwithstanding, the Sound Emporium, too, was somewhat past its prime. The Sound Emporium had begun life as the Jack Clement Recording Studios in 1969; the name changed after bankers forced the Cowboy to sell in 1975, in order to make good on the loans from his motion-picture fiasco, *Dear Dead Delilah*. The current owner was Roy Clark, the banjo-playing host of *Hee Haw*. Clark had lost interest to the point that he hadn't been on the premises for over a year and had had the operation on the market for even longer. At best, its future was precarious.

Back in the Clement era, the place had been a monument

to whimsy. Clement put Jim Tilton, the New York theatrical designer responsible for *Oh, Calcutta*, in charge of decor. He turned the drummer's alcove in the smaller studio into a mock Victorian gazebo, complete with gingerbread detailing around the mock roof and windows. The furnishings included an assortment of antiques, an intricately carved Indian chaise longue, a marble fireplace, and a gas chandelier among them. Crushed velvet covered the walls, and there were reproduction Oriental rugs on the floors.

Jack Clement wouldn't have recognized the place anymore. Those rugs were the only remnant of his vision. Outside, on the front wall, an unknown gang member had spray-painted "Rio Lives." Inside, the walls had been repaneled with rough raw barn wood, with glass cubicles for the acoustic guitar player and drummer. The effect was an odd combination of chemistry lab and county fair.

Other studios take great pains to keep their clientele comfortable: Some have kitchens, others ersatz living rooms with widescreen television sets. The Emerald Studios, right on Music Row, had its own pool table. The Sound Emporium, though, had few of those amenities. The waiting-room sofas were getting a little threadbare. A small portable television with a static-filled picture was propped next to an aging Coke machine, which, if you hit the lever just right, delivered soft drinks free. There was a bowl of fresh fruit that didn't quite live up to the name.

A few blocks down from the Sound Emporium, in a large rambling wreck of a house, Jack Clement toiled away on his latest folly. On his office wall was a small stringed instrument, a Clement ukulele, created in a factory in his basement. "Nobody else was making a serious ukulele," he explained. "No one ever did. And if you give me five grand, I'll put you right into one of these." The ukulele factory, he allowed, was currently on hold, as were his plans to have the house converted into a college. "It is zoned for a school from here to the end of the block, and one of these days I want to get it chartered, have regular classes and stuff. But first," he said, "I'm going to change the whole way people make movies."

Undaunted by his failure with *Dear Dead Delilah*, he had turned the attic into a video production facility, complete with sets. One room had a fake window, flowers blooming out of the window box, another an exterior view, gray clouds painted on blue sky.

He had just started his first production. "Tex Cobb is up there filming a martial-arts video. It's basic self-defense, combined with an aerobics workout."

• • •

Fundis had blocked out just seven days for actual session work. Unlike rock recording in New York and Los Angeles, where bands take over studios for months, making an album in Nashville is more of a nine-to-five, or, more precisely, a two-to-nine, enterprise. And where that rock record will probably cost a quarter of a million dollars to record, the country album will cost half that. The difference? "In Nashville, the songs are ready before they get to the studio," says Irving Azoff, who heads Giant Records out in Los Angeles. "These people come in prepared."

Yearwood's first album cost $102,558.24 to produce, almost $23,000 under budget. Fundis projected the second would cost $140,000, with most of the money going for studio time, which he projected would cost about $10,000 more this around. He had also increased the amount of his own advance, from $25,000 to $32,500 (in addition to his fee, Fundis receives 3 percent of record royalties).

Yearwood received just about the same advance ($20,000) that she had for her first album. Her second album would have to sell over 200,000 copies for her to receive any royalties. But as she knew, she had to do more than make a meager profit. She needed to have this album sell as least as well as her first one. That would be no easy task, and Yearwood was feeling the pressure.

"I was nervous making the last record," she said, "but it's worse this time. Before it was because I never made a record before, now it's because I made one and it sold a million records and I have to do it again." Which was one reason why she had ended up out with the Mavericks, in town en masse from Miami, until two o'clock the night before.

"So, how's Trisha handling all her success?" Eddie Bayers, a drummer given to loud T-shirts who had known Yearwood since her demo days, asked as he walked in the door. Bayers, the first to arrive, had seen the singer just once, in passing, since their last recording session over a year before. "You'll see," Fundis replied. "Mostly, she's about three feet off the ground."

Bayers was one of six players who would be doing the session work that day. The others were Matt Rollings, the piano player;

Brent Mason (who wrote "Heartbreak Highway" for Keith Whitley) on electric guitar; Dave Pomeroy on bass; an acoustic guitar player named Don Potter; and Weldon Myrick on pedal steel.

They and their fellow sidemen are, quite simply, the best in the business. For years, Nashville players were the nameless instrumentalists who made country songs fly. It took Bob Dylan to turn them into demicelebrities. He put the names of the Nashville sideman on the jacket for one of the albums he recorded there: *Nashville Skyline*. With that imprimatur, they became less of a local find than a national treasure, a thirty-man squadron that could be counted on to get the song right in three hours or so, certainly no more than six. (John Sebastian immortalized them in song: "Nashville Cats been playin' since they's babies/Nashville Cats work before they're two"). Some constellation of those thirty players can be found on virtually every record out of Nashville, scores upon scores of all-star specials.

Using the Sound Emporium wasn't Fundis's only concession to sentiment. The producer had first assembled this group when he was working with Whitley, and with two exceptions (the original steel player, Paul Franklin, had taken a berth with Dire Straits, and Mac McAnally, the guitar player, had his own deal and was out on tour), they were the same group that had played on Yearwood's first album.

Yearwood bounded into the studio at about a quarter past two. Wearing little makeup, an oversize T-shirt lettered "NEWS CAFE" over black leggings and high-topped white Keds, she looked like an improved, but altogether recognizable, version of the woman they had recorded with fourteen months before. Yearwood walked over to a large gift basket on the control-room desk containing an astonishing assortment of snacks and candies, and took out an envelope as Bayers grabbed a small box of peppermints labeled "Reception Sticks." "Sounds like something from a proctologist's office," he said. Yearwood opened the card. "From Mac [McAnally]" she announced, as Fundis motioned her off to a pile of tapes at the corner of the console.

"I've got six or seven of the things we talked about set aside here," he said. "How would you feel about starting with 'Move That Mountain'?"

"Cool," she nodded.

"I'll be back in a minute," he told her, and headed toward the phone.

That two-minute conversation was the culmination of months of planning. Within weeks of finishing the first album, Fundis had started culling through the scores of demo tapes (he logged over two thousand in 1991 alone) sent to him by local music publishers. The first album had debuted Yearwood as a talented singer with an interesting, if uneven, choice of material. The songs that Fundis and Yearwood were considering for her second album were considerably more demanding. They were looking for songs that, lyrically, moved Yearwood beyond the cheeky ingenue of her first album. Musically, they wanted to push the limits as well, with songs that were not simply straight-ahead country, compositions that would allow the singer to explore her considerable range.

• • •

The songwriters on Music Row are the last incarnation of Tin Pan Alley. The Brill Building tunesmiths have long since decamped, but while songwriting on the coasts has turned solitary, Music Row remains a tight fraternity. Publishing companies still clutter the buildings along Sixteenth and Seventeenth Avenues, each of them chockablock with cubicles furnished with a sofa, a guitar, and a keyboard, laboratories for composition.

Like the old Victorians that house many of Nashville's publishers, the very word *publisher* dates from another era, when a song's popularity was measured largely by the sale of its sheet music. At first, along with everyone else in the music business, none of the music publishers paid much attention to the hillbilly songs. It took a couple of Nashvillians to realize there was money to be made. In 1942, Roy Acuff and a songwriter and pianist for WSM named Fred Rose formed the first publishing house that focused exclusively on country music. It would eventually make both men millionaires.

By the time Acuff and Rose got into the business, the phonograph record had supplanted the actual printed sheet. Congress recognized that change in 1909, when it passed a law that once a publisher granted anyone the right to make a commercial recording of one of its properties, anyone else could legally record it by filing the basic informational forms required by the law. The fee for that mechanical reproduction was two cents a song, to be paid to the publisher for every recording sold. That fee remained the same until January 1, 1978, when it was keyed to the consumer price index. Today, there is a statutory rate of 6.25

cents for any song up to five minutes, with a penny and a half more for each additional minute. According to most contracts, the publisher owns the copyright to the song and is entitled to 50 percent of its royalties (with the songwriter getting the remainder), which explains why Jimmy Bowen, or any of the other producers who own publishing companies on the side, might be particularly eager for a singer to record songs that he or she owns. If a record sells only 100,000 copies, a song's publisher is entitled to $3,125. If an album goes platinum, the money becomes quite meaningful: $31,250 per tune, not counting the money that comes in if the piece is performed on radio or television.

The American Society of Composers, Authors, and Publishers (ASCAP) was the first organization to monitor broadcasting rights. Founded in 1914, ASCAP was designed to protect composers from unwarranted use of their material. Anyone using music was required to pay a fee to the not-for-profit organization, which, in turn, dispersed those moneys to its members. For its first few decades, ASCAP primarily serviced Tin Pan Alley. The organization had little interest in getting involved with hillbilly music.

ASCAP had a virtual monopoly on the licensing business until 1940. But on December 31 of that year, the organization's contracts with the radio networks were due to expire. ASCAP wanted to double its fee. The radio networks prepared for a fight, establishing a rival organization, Broadcast Music, Inc. (BMI), in the fall of 1940. Since ASCAP already controlled most of the popular music, BMI went after the ethnic and hillbilly composers ASCAP disdained.

Radio broadcasters battled ASCAP for the first ten months of 1941, boycotting ASCAP songs. By the time an agreement was reached, BMI had 36,000 copyrights from 52 publishers, and the hillbilly music that had been played for so long without compensation for its composers achieved fiscal legitimacy.

ASCAP has long since eliminated its bias against country composers (Garth Brooks and Trisha Yearwood are covered by ASCAP, along with the Gershwin brothers, ZZ Top, and Aaron Copland). Today, Music Row is equally split between the two, with a small number of songwriters handled by Selected Editions of Standard American Catalogues (SESAC).

All three organizations essentially track radio play of their members' songs. Though the methods of calculation vary, the disbursements should be roughly equivalent. If a song makes it to the top twenty, it should earn anywhere from $30,000 to $50,000. If it hits top five, as virtually all Yearwood's do, the publisher and writer can generally count on splitting $75,000 to $125,000. Two or three of those a year, and it's quite a comfortable living.

Though Yearwood had written a few songs (Kenny Rogers recorded one, a Canadian singer named Michelle Wright another), she had relied on others for her first album and intended to do so again for the second. "I'm a stronger singer than I am a songwriter," she said, and she was smart enough to play to her strengths. Given the sales of her first album, and her success in getting radio play, it also meant that she would be on the top of every publisher's roster.

Unless the material was coming from a publisher or a writer Fundis knew, there were generally three hurdles to getting a song recorded by Trisha Yearwood. First, the song had to clear Scott Paschall, Fundis's assistant, his first and only employee. Paschall had come to Nashville straight out of the University of Kansas and had spent three fruitless months looking for a job on Music Row before he was forced to take a gas-station job to support himself. A mutual friend had suggested he look up Fundis (they were from nearby towns in Kansas), and the producer took him on as an unpaid intern for three months before finally paying him a salary. He was twenty-eight and ambitious. He loved working with Fundis, but he was also contemplating breaking out on his own. He was learning a lot, but the pay was dismal— just fifteen thousand dollars a year.

Paschall shared Fundis's flat midwestern accent (callers had a hard time distinguishing their voices) as well as his taste in music; he was the one who had first spotted "The Woman Before Me." He edited out about 75 percent of the tapes they received.

Fundis, in turn, winnowed the pile further. Of the hundred or so songs he had sent her over the year, Yearwood had approved fifteen. The plan was to record all of them, then select the best ten for the album.

"Move That Mountain" had not gone the usual route. Keith Whitley had written the song when he was in his teens. Fundis had already recorded it with a bluegrass singer named Tim O'Brien, but O'Brien's record label, RCA, had decided against releasing the record. Several months before, Fundis had been sitting in his office listening to the stillborn album, and it had occurred to him that the song might work for Yearwood. He had sent the tape to her out on the road; she had loved it.

Fundis had two reasons for wanting to start with the Whitley song. The first was the song itself; he thought its edgy bluegrass, almost gospel, sound would get the musicians' energy flowing. The primary appeal, though, was emotional. "Most of these guys played on Keith's stuff," Fundis explained. "It sort of reestablishes the bond between them and me as producer. Besides, they've got a soft spot for his stuff. . . . I'm guilty of playing on that."

Fundis himself shared that soft spot. The phone call he went off to make was to Faye Whitley, Keith's mother, to tell her that he was about to record one of her son's songs. "I'm still not sure it's going to make it to the album," he told her, "but I just wanted you to know."

While Fundis was on the phone, the band milled around the control room. Tim Lauer, the keyboard player from Yearwood's road band, walked in with his girlfriend, Angela Peters, a pretty blond college senior in a broad-brimmed straw hat. Yearwood introduced Lauer around, and he politely shook Matt Rollings's hand. It was the first and only time he would meet the man whose music he would end up replicating.

Yearwood, Lauer, and Peters moved to the sofa in the waiting room. Peters pulled out a calendar. "We want to set a date," Lauer said, skittering over just what the date was for. "I want to figure out when the best time is, around September or October, when I can take a couple days off. For a honeymoon."

"So you kids are gonna tie the knot. I want to be there for this." Yearwood pulled out her own calendar, and they kicked around a couple of possibilities, finally circling the second Friday in September. "Can't wait," she called out as Lauer and Peters headed out the door.

Fundis motioned her into the control room. "All right, folks," he said, "time to get to work." It was two-thirty. As the musicians filed into the room, Dave Pomeroy, the bass player and appointed band leader, handed each a sheet of paper from a pile he was guarding atop the control board.

Pomeroy, thirty-six, had been in Nashville fifteen years. For the last seven, he had been one of Fundis's most regular players. He generally worked with four different instruments, his favorite being a ten-year-old electric upright bass, one of only four ever made. It is a cross between an acoustic string bass and an electric bass guitar. Like the acoustic instrument, it has a bridge, but it also has electronic pickups. The combination creates a deeper and richer sound than either of the instruments from which it's derived.

Pomeroy is as idiosyncratic as his hybrid instrument. He plays in a jazz band and dresses early Woodstock—tie-dyed outfits (blue, pink, purple) with high-top sneakers to match. Fundis selected the bass player as bandleader for these sessions not only for his musicianship, but because he was the only one in the group who didn't command double the scale set by the American Federation of Musicians. As bandleader, he would be paid commensurate with the others, and would be required to perform one additional duty. Before each session, he had to listen to demo tapes of the songs and transcribe the chords into what's called the Nashville Number System.

The number system is essentially a crib sheet for making music. The chart for "Move That Mountain" is twenty-one rows of numbers down the middle and a lineup of *V*'s and *C*'s down the side.

The numbers stand for the chords in a given key; the *V*'s and *C*'s for verse and chorus. The first five lines look like this:

```
        F
      1 1 1 1
  C 1 1 4 1

      1 1 4 1 1
  V 1 1 4 1 1
```

Translation: The song is in the key of F. There is a one-line intro (four bars of an F chord); a two-line chorus (two bars of an F chord, then B flat, back to F, an additional F on the second line); then a two-line verse, structured the same way as the chorus. Roman numerals have been used to represent chords since the

Middle Ages, and in the thirties and forties gospel groups used different shapes for each note of the major scale. But it wasn't until about 1957 that Neal Matthews, a member of the Jordanaires, started writing out song sheets with Arabic numbers. The Jordanaires were working two or three sessions a day, and Matthews needed a way to write down vocals so that they wouldn't have to commit tremendous amounts of material to memory. In the early sixties, Charlie McCoy, Wayne Moss, and David Briggs, three session musicians, caught on to Matthews's system, and by the mid-sixties it became the approved method of charting music in Nashville, where many musicians couldn't read standard musical notation.

One of the advantages of the number chart is that since the numbers simply represent the relationship between chords, regardless of key, a song can be played in any key without rewriting the chart. For example, if the Whitley song were shifted to A, the musicians would know to switch the progression to A and D. If it were C, 1 would represent C, 4 would be F.

The system lacks the precision of standard notation, but that rough limner has its advantages. It demands improvisation, allowing Nashville's sidemen to shine. There's an oft-told story in Nashville: An out-of-town producer asks a session player if he can read music. "Not enough to ruin the song," he replies.

As the musicians eyed the chart for "Move That Mountain," Fundis put on the tape of the O'Brien version. After the first few lines, a few bars of fast-paced steel and acoustic guitar, Don Potter, the acoustic player, piped up, "I got a feeling it ain't a ballad."

About thirty seconds later, a flash of recognition passed over Brent Mason's face. The guitarist pointed his thumb at his chest and smiled. "You overdubbed on this one," Pomeroy told him.

It was the first time the musicians had heard what they would be playing that day, which was the way they preferred it. "Rehearsals tend to make the music sound too programmed," said Bayers. "This way, you hear songs and you know what to do, you get the music and you go."

There is no script for making this music. There is a demo tape and a chart, but that's not much more than a starting point. For the next three hours there would be endless tinkering, a sort of aural anarchy over which Fundis, as producer, would preside.

Though Yearwood had heard the song before, this was the first time she had focused on how she was going to sing it. "This needs to be a little higher," she said, "but not much. Let's try C. I need to go in and check it out."

She and Rollings headed into the studio and sat down together on the piano bench. She sang a few bars. "I think it can go up even further," she said. "Maybe E-flat, like 'She's in Love with the Boy.' " She tried it, but still wasn't quite happy. "Maybe B. We'll know it when we hear it."

As Yearwood and Rollins fussed with the key, Pomeroy noodled with his hybrid bass. "I'm having problems with the weather," he said. "The humidity changes the wood, the neck moves, and it alters the height of the strings from the neck of the bass." It took about two minutes for him to tighten the four strings to get them back in key. Fundis, meanwhile, hovered over Rollins and Yearwood, trying to figure out where the key should be. "Why don't you try A?" he asked.

"It might be a little easier," said Yearwood. "The question is whether it sounds good. Besides," she said, elbowing the piano player beside her, "Matt can't play in this key anyway."

"I can, too," he replied, and launched into a riff that sounded like a piano accompaniment to a silent horror picture.

"I want to try A," said Yearwood. "That's it," she said, after she sang the first line.

With the key decided on, Yearwood and the band ran through the song for the first time, without the tape running, then again with it on. Fundis turned on the talk-back, an intercom that allowed him to speak into the studio. He was concerned about a section about a third of the way through. "Instead of ending your solo with a chord, Matt, can you try it with a single note?"

Gary Laney, the sound engineer, rewound the tape, erasing their first run-through, and then the band started up again. "I'm not getting Brent in here," said Laney. It was a major problem— Mason's guitar was not coming into the control board—but Laney approached it with his usual equanimity.

Laney had been working at the Emporium for twelve years. He started by doing carpentry for minimum wage, and, as Fundis had before him, worked his way up to the control board. He wore a baseball cap of brightly colored Guatemalan cotton, but it was less fashion than camouflage for the five-inch scar welting up the back of his scalp.

This was Laney's first session in four months. In December, after months of mysterious headaches, he was found to have a malignant tumor. The good news was it was outside his skull, but he still had to have radiation. His nubbly pate was the result of the treatment. "You just do your best to get through these things," was all he had to say about the ordeal, which was pretty much the way he handled the daily fiascos of running a sound studio.

As the players ran through their parts separately, it took Dave Sinko, the assistant sound engineer, about ten minutes to find the patch cord needed for the guitar track.

"All right guys, time to go," said Fundis. Then, instead of Bayers's usual "One, two" that started the song, the sound of a pack of barking dogs filled the studio, and the band broke up in raucous laughter. "Eddie," Fundis chided, "what are you doing?"

What Bayers was doing was playing with his drum samples. Until about 1980, Bayers's instruments were responsible for every sound he made. Computers changed all that. It is now possible to program hundreds, if not thousands, of different sounds, push a button, and hear snares, maracas, or, as in Bayers's case, a pack of wild hounds, several variations on the theme of flatulence, and Bugs Bunny.

For Bayers, those drum samples were more than a musical enhancement or comedic relief. They literally saved his career. Riding his motorcycle in 1986, he was hit by a driver who had run a red light. The impact crushed the main bone in his left wrist, the one that controls the mobility between the hand and wrist. He was in and out of casts for eight months, and the doctors didn't think he would ever have the strength to go back to the drums.

Despite his injuries, the performers who had worked with him—Rodney Crowell, Rosanne Cash, the Judds, among them —still wanted him, and he agreed to try. "They figured feel and groove was the bottom line, and they knew I would never lose that," he said. At first, Bayers made it easier on his left hand by programming high-hat parts and playing everything else with his right. As his left hand healed, he started using it sparingly, but instead of playing the traditional way, with right hand riding the high-hat and left hitting the snare, Bayers played open-handed, left on high-hat and right on snare. His hand had mostly recovered, and these days he used samples for about 30 percent of his parts, about as much as before the accident.

Fundis realized that Bayers's levity helped the musicians stay loose and maintain their spontaneity. Still, there was a job to get done. The producer pushed the button on the talk-back microphone again. "Eddie, put the dogs away," he said. And the drummer was back to the standard downbeat.

After another run-through, Fundis called everyone into the control room. He played the tape back; no one was quite satisfied. "Can we play the demo again?" Yearwood asked Fundis.

"I want it like that," she said after they had heard the recording. "Let's move it down. I don't need to blow it out and prove I can belt. I can do that later."

By 3:35, Yearwood was back in her makeshift booth—a stool and a microphone enclosed by three acoustic panels, one with a scrawled sign: "TRISHA'S WORLD." Fundis had once again assumed his control-room stance: back to studio, elbows resting on the top of the control panel ledge (the best acoustical spot in the room, to his mind), chin resting on intertwined fingers. His two index fingers were pointed up, steeple style, fingering his beard as the band played yet another take.

"It's feeling good, boys. Let's hang onto that and do another. Don, could you play it more solid, commit to it. The thing I'm concerned about is at the end of the first chorus. It has to happen kind of cool like and not just fall in there. It needs fewer notes."

And then it all came together. They ran clean through the first chorus, into the second verse. Then, out of nowhere, silence.

"What the hell . . ." Fundis said. He did not push the talk-back button.

"My earphones fell out," said Pomeroy. "I guess they were actually listening to me. I stopped playing, and by the time I got back everyone stopped."

"Let's save what we've got," Fundis said to Laney.

The band tried one more, but Fundis wasn't happy. "I want to go back and play the front of the one Dave stopped on," he said, talk-back switched on. "Then we'll just punch in at the top of the chorus and take it to the end." Pomeroy let out a Bronx cheer, then mimed hara-kiri.

Finally, just after four, they completed the take. Fundis called them back into the control room to listen. "This one's got the edge," he said.

"But it's still got that deep pocket," added Pomeroy. "If I could just do the two bars before, and after we punch in it will be smooth."

"Fine," said Fundis. "I think this one is a keeper."

But they were far from finished. For the next hour and a half, each of the instrumentalists would shuttle back into the studio and spend fifteen minutes or more polishing his part. Yearwood's "scratch" vocal stayed on for now. Her first-round efforts make it to the final cut far more often than most singers'. On her first album nearly half of the vocals were the ones she recorded with the band.

Potter worked over three bars for about fifteen minutes, then Fundis called Myrick in. "I want to try the steel in the solo," he said, and Myrick moved into the studio to work on the two-line instrumental.

Myrick was born in West Texas in 1938 and got his start playing steel at local socials while he was in high school. His big moment came when one of the better-known local bands asked him to join. They played live radio and made personal appearances with a lineup of teenage girls who formed themselves into a hula-dance troupe. During his first half dozen years out of high school, he worked in a grocery store, playing steel on the side. A local disc jockey convinced the steel player to move to Big Spring, where he got work as a cameraman on a local television show. It still wasn't enough to make a living, though, so Myrick took a day job on the local police force. "Whenever anyone needed me for recording sessions, I'd get a replacement for myself on the force," said Myrick. Finally, in 1963, he made the move to Nashville.

Myrick worked three years on the road before joining the house band at the Opry. These days he's one of only two Opry players who work regular sessions. "Most of those older guys don't work sessions," Fundis explained. "They tend to be automatic pilot—the spontaneity just isn't there. And sometimes they can get paranoid about the younger players moving in."

Myrick, though, was fairly laid-back. He played through the two lines, fingers flying over the strings. He looked up while he played, creating a sense of detachment heightened by the fact that you can't even hear the instrument in the studio; electronic pickups feed the tones directly into the console.

"I just love the sound of this," said Yearwood as she listened to the wail of Myrick's pedal steel. "I love to find spots to put him in."

The pedal steel guitar is another curious construction, essentially two bodyless guitars set side by side, with the strings raised and lowered by foot pedals. In one incarnation or another, steel puts the twang in country. Even before commercialization and electrification, musicians had often tried to get that wailing effect by running a knife blade or broken bottle along the neck of a guitar. The instrument's commercial popularity dates to the Hawaiian bands that toured the U.S. around World War I, who turned the guitar sideways. Those early instruments had only one neck; today's have two with ten strings apiece. Changing chords used to be fairly laborious; improved mechanics now give players the flexibility to change notes more quickly.

In Fundis's opinion, Myrick had taken a bit too much advantage of that range. "There's one place in the middle where it gets a little loosey-goosey," the producer told him. "I know I'm nit-picking, but can we try it again?"

As Myrick played his last run-through, the caterers set up in the next room. The food, like the pay, was a considerable improvement on the subsistence fare found on the road. There were steam tables of barbecued steak and chicken, squash casserole, and black-eyed peas. Dessert was a dense chocolate cake with a pecan frosting. Yearwood, her trainer out of sight, cut herself a very small slice. At about six-thirty Fundis finished with the last player and actually had dinner himself.

One of the badges of Music Row success has always been a fancy pair of cowboy boots; the more kinds of leather, the more successful the star. At the end of the meal, a curly-haired man with multicolored cowboy boots walked in the door. Judging by his footwear—tricolor lizard and ostrich—his career was doing just fine. His name was Tim Mensy, and he was born in Mechanicsville, Virginia, ten miles north of Richmond. His mother was a member of the Old Dominion Barn Dance, where her son had debuted at age three. Mensy spent his childhood playing mandolin and singing in the family band (parents and four siblings). They played up and down the East Coast, opening for Dolly Parton, Loretta Lynn, and Merle Haggard. Just after high school, he moved to Nashville, playing clubs and writing. Early on, one of his songs was recorded by John Conlee; more recently Randy Travis and Doug Stone had used his material.

Mensy had cowritten the next song on the Fundis-Yearwood agenda, "Nearest Distant Shore"—a ballad about self-preservation, pulling out of a relationship that threatens to destroy one's very being.

As soon as Mensy and his cowriter, Gary Harrison, finished the song, they had asked the owner of their publishing house, Pat Higdon, to send it to Fundis. Actually, they had it sent over for another of Fundis's charges, Collin Raye, a singer from Greenville, Texas, whose first record had gone gold. But while Fundis didn't think it was right for Raye, he knew it was perfect for Yearwood.

Mensy was here not just to observe but to play. After Fundis played the demo tape twice for the band, Mensy joined Potter in the acoustic cubicle.

Yearwood did a run-through, and she sounded fantastic. Her voice was solid, powerful, loaded with emotion. "Holy shit," Fundis said to Laney. "This is going to be great."

They did two run-throughs, experimented with keys, and decided to stick with the original, E.

Sinko turned to Fundis. "We're going to lengthen the dk on the reverb," he told him. "It's at one-point-five seconds, now it's at two." What that meant, quite simply, was that her vocals would trail off a little longer, making the music sound a little richer.

At 7:45 they taped the first take, and Fundis asked for another. At 8:05 he summoned them back in to listen. Fundis gestured to Mensy, giving him the prized listening position atop the console. Yearwood was nothing short of spectacular.

"There shouldn't be any new females allowed this year," said Mensy. "Play this for them. . . . Then, if you still think you can sing after you've heard it, maybe then we will give you a shot."

"Okay," said Fundis, "anybody got any fixes?"

"I think I did," said Mensy. "I need to hear it again, though. It's tough to hear something that lays back that far."

"Several times I thought we were at the previous bar," said Rollins.

"I thought I was back at dinner," said Potter.

Pomeroy wanted to go back and fix a string buzz, a couple of chords at the end where his fingers didn't go down quite far enough on the string. Potter had a problem as well. As they listened to the tape again, there was an insistent tap tap tap—Bayers's click-track, an electronic metronome that sets the beat of the song. Potter had the click-track's volume turned up so high that the beat had come in through his microphone. Fundis tried to figure out if there was a way he could cover it up with a cymbal, but when they tried that, the tapping was still there. Finally he had Potter rerecord those few bars, and that pretty much completed the track on that song. It was still only ten. Since they had started late, there was time to begin a new song. Fundis, though, decided not to push it. "Oh, let's just quit on a good one," he said, and everyone was out the door before eleven.

CHAPTER 11

*F*OURTEEN AND A HALF HOURS LATER, EVERYONE WAS BACK IN the studio. Everyone, that is, except Yearwood, who was running late because of an optometrist's appointment. She turned up at 2:35, and as she walked in the door, she pulled an envelope from her purse. "You're not gonna believe what Henley faxed Bruce Hinton," she said, and passed it to Fundis.

Yearwood wasn't the first beneficiary of Don Henley's facsimile machine, merely the most recent. Henley, "the Mad Faxer," as the producer John Boylan calls him, has spent years perfecting his weapon, firing off scores of missives to a vast array of correspondents. On April 21 he deployed his arsenal on Yearwood's behalf in a fax to the head of MCA's Nashville office. Again, he compared her to Ronstadt, again he praised her "song sense." But he wasn't simply lauding Yearwood, he was lobbying for her as well, trying to convince Hinton that even though MCA had already released several singles off her first album, he should consider one more: "Lonesome Dove." To his ears, Henley wrote, it sounded like a "smash."

"Maybe this will convince them to release 'Lonesome Dove,' " said Yearwood, after Fundis finished reading the fax.

"Don't count on it," the producer replied.

Just how many singles were to be released from the first album was something of a sore spot with the producer. Back in the fall, Tony Brown had told Fundis that they were going to release two more singles from the album. There had already been three:

"She's in Love with the Boy," "Like We Never Had a Broken Heart," and "That's What I Like About You." "The Woman Before Me" was sent out in March and would stay on the airwaves at least until June. The plan, thought Fundis, was to release one more single, preferably "Lonesome Dove," in June or July, with the first single from the second album going on the radio in the fall. With that schedule, he would have had until August or September to work on the new album.

Then, in February, the executives at MCA informed him that they wanted to accelerate the process. Because Yearwood was doing so well, they told him, they wanted to whet the public's appetite by releasing the first single from the new album in June. That meant Fundis had to be ready two months before he had originally thought, and even Don Henley probably couldn't change that.

Fundis was already getting worried. He had hoped to record at least three songs at that first session—as they had on the first album—but they had finished only two. At that rate he would either have to get all ten right the first time or schedule more sessions. Neither alternative was particularly appealing. He decided to attribute the slowness to first-day jitters and assumed the pace would pick up. Still, there was no time to waste. After giving Yearwood a minute or two to crow over the Henley letter, he pulled Pomeroy aside and asked him to hand out the first set of song sheets.

"Blue Guitar," the song they were planning as the title cut, was a departure from Yearwood's previous material—a hard-driving blues about a lonely visit to a tatty café on the edge of a nameless town.

"Boy, this really rocks," Yearwood said, after a particularly raucous guitar lick on the demo tape.

"I thought we were supposed to be doing country," said Potter.

"We did country yesterday," the singer replied, and with that, they filed into the studio.

They jammed for twenty minutes, and at 3:10 Fundis ordered the first taped run-through. It was so rough that he didn't even call the band in to listen. As Laney rewound, Fundis pushed the talk-back. "Can we get a little more drums into the intro please," he said. Fundis summoned them back to the control room after the next take, but he was still not happy.

"We're ending it with this huge roar," he said. "I just don't feel anything distinctive."

Everyone was working in the lower registers. Rollins was mostly playing on the bass end of the piano. Pomeroy, playing "a boogie thing," as he put it, could barely be distinguished from the keyboard.

"It's sounding muddy," said the bass player. "Everything is coming from the same place. We need to get the nose hairs out of there."

Rollins and Pomeroy went back into the studio to work out their parts. Since there really aren't any options on the bass, Rollins moved his part up an octave. They played it again, and this time it worked, the instruments distinct, but still deep, almost like something from Creedence Clearwater Revival. Fundis ordered up another take.

"That's it boys," he said into the talk-back, after they had played the song, and the band filed back into the control room.

"You're giving Bonnie Raitt a run for her money," said Pomeroy after the tape ended.

"I guess that's the idea," said Yearwood, although she did not sound terribly convinced.

It was not yet five o'clock, early enough to get started on a second song before dinner. "You Were Right from Your Side" is by Jim Rushing, a writer Fundis had known since the days when both worked for Jack Clement. On the top right-hand side of the lyric sheet the single word "FEMALE" was printed in capital letters. The label did not please Yearwood. "I don't like wimpy lyrics," was how she put it, "or most songs that are written especially for women. . . . Back when I was singing demos, I would hear all the time, 'We've got to change this lyric because a woman wouldn't say that.' That bothers me. Women cheat, too. They do the same things men do; they go out drinking, but they don't sing about it." Yearwood, who had put Merle Haggard's "I Think I'll Just Stay Here and Drink" into her stage show ("not the usual kind of thing you hear a chick singer do"), had cleared this song without knowing there were two versions.

They played the song twice in the studio with the lines in their original form ("You were a slave to freedom/To the highway and the song/My idea of freedom/Was wanting to belong"), taped the third, then trooped back into the control room to hear the results.

"The percussion sounds heavy," said Yearwood.

"It doesn't feel heavy," replied Bayers.

"She says it sounds heavy," said Fundis.

"Well, then what the hell am I saying?" said Bayers, laughing.

It was a neat turn by Fundis, and everyone chuckled through it. But the producer had made it clear that Yearwood was a force to be dealt with in these sessions. It was not simply his show.

The drums weren't Yearwood's only concern.

"This song just isn't me," she said, after hearing the tape a second time. "I was the one who was on the road, he was the one at home. That's my perspective. I'm not some poor little wuss. We need to try this again from the bitch perspective."

"Your call," said Fundis. "But I think we should have one of each version and decide later."

Yearwood grabbed a pencil off the console and reworked the chorus, reversing the first- and second-person pronouns (new version: "I was a slave to freedom/To the highway and the song/ Your idea of freedom/Was wanting to belong").

She headed back to her microphone and sang the first verse a cappella. By the third line, she was loose, rejiggering the lyrics. "Standin by the airport window," she trilled, "watchin' a big Delta Burke [it's supposed to be Bird] taxi through the sky." The band broke up.

"All right, boys and girls, let's get this done," said Fundis. And, just after 5:40, it was.

As the caterer came in to set up dinner (Mexican this time), Yearwood and Fundis talked song. There were two ballads in contention for the next session—"Who Turned Out the Lights," the elegy for fading love that Yearwood regularly performed live, and "Down on My Knees," a stark song of desperation by Beth Nielsen Chapman. Of all the songs she was considering for the album, "Who Turned Out the Lights" was the only one supplied by MCA. Like virtually every other record label, MCA has an artists and repertoire department that sorts through songs for its acts. But unlike some other labels, MCA acts as adviser, not arbiter. Yearwood and Fundis are not required to have their songs approved before they go into the studio.

"Hey, I found one song she liked, and even if she didn't record it that makes me feel like I'm part of the process," said Tony Brown, who came up with "Who Turned Out the Lights." "If an act hasn't been successful, yes, I might want to be more involved, but these guys have worked together before, and they've proved they know what they're doing. I'm available if they need me, but other than that I leave them alone. This is not the session police."

"MCA lets us make the record we want, not the record they want," said Yearwood. And as quickly became clear, the record she wanted did not include the MCA song. " 'Who Turned Out the Lights' is melodically solid," said the singer. "But 'Down on My Knees' kicks ass melodically and lyrically."

"So let's do it," said Fundis, and headed over to the tacos.

Fundis had known about "Down on My Knees" for several years. In 1987, he had briefly worked with Nielsen Chapman, then a songwriter (Tanya Tucker took her "Strong Enough to Bend" to the top of the charts) looking for a record deal of her own. But when she ended up at Warner Bros., the head of the Nashville office, Jim Ed Norman, asked to produce her himself, and she took him up on his offer. Still, Fundis had held onto her songs in hopes of finding a singer who could use them. Three years later, he had found Yearwood.

Nielsen Chapman wrote "Down on My Knees" in the mid-eighties, a time, as she put it, when she was preoccupied with her own life and had almost let her husband slip away. "It's about priorities," she explained, rather understating the case she makes in song, "remembering what's important." In Nashville parlance, the song is a "power ballad," a pull-out-all-the-stops, don't-leave-an-emotion-untapped cri de coeur:

> *If I had to live without you loving me*
> *I'd be down on my knees*
> *Ready to pray, darlin'*
> *Down on my knees*
> *Making you stay (whatever it takes)*
> *I'd be begging you please*
> *Don't take your love from me. . . .*

On the demo, Nielsen Chapman belted out the lyrics herself, running through the last line of the song, the title lyric, twice, once more than was indicated on the song sheet.

"Repeat if desired," said Fundis.

"That works with sex, too," piped up Bayers.

"Not if you're married," Yearwood retorted. And they headed out to the studio.

By 8:20, Fundis was sufficiently satisfied to summon them in to hear the recording. After Yearwood's last "down on my knees," Fundis dropped to his. "I'll stay, I'll stay," he said, and she smiled.

"It sounded gorgeous, guys," said Fundis.

"What about me?" said Yearwood.

"I told you I'd stay."

"You'd stay anyway."

"Well, I do have a contract."

Yearwood's vocal might have been perfection, but its strength demanded certain accommodations. "At the bridge there's such an enormous peak, everyone needs to get out of there," Fundis said, and ordered the musicians back in to try again. They went over the last section. Fundis listened as they waited in the studio. "Nope," he said into the talk-back. "I know it's deliberate, but it sounds like everyone has simply forgotten to play."

"Why don't we just do this?" asked Rollins, bounding in with the theme from Disney's *Snow White* ("Hi-ho, hi-ho, it's off to work we go . . .").

"Matt, why don't we try it with just you in there at the end," said Fundis. As Rollins played against Yearwood's vocals, Fundis smiled. "You wanna hear it?" he said. And the piano player rejoined the others in the control room.

"Sounds like a crossover to me," said Bayers.

"It's country," said Fundis.

"And why is that?"

"Because we're making it in Nashville," he answered. "Maybe we should put in a pair of twin fiddles. That'll convince them."

But even Fundis knew it was a reach to call this song country. He had considered using it on Yearwood's first album, but had decided that it went too far. "It just wasn't the time," he said. "We had to prove we could make it in the genre, now we can do what we want. One million albums later, we proved we know what we're doing." Still, he had not quite convinced himself he would be able to pull it off. "I just hope they let us put this on the album," he muttered, almost to himself.

Crossover used to be the promised land. No matter how well a country record did, there was always more money to be made in pop. Back in the midseventies, when single records were still available, even the hottest song would sell no more than three hundred thousand copies in the country market. If the same song hit the pop charts, it could sell millions. Which goes a long way toward explaining why Dolly Parton figured she could do a lot better if she left Nashville behind. Kenny Rogers turned himself into the king of that particular hill. As the rock-and-roll critic Chet Flippo described him in *Rolling Stone* back in 1979, "[Rogers] knows he has an average voice, but he also knows what to do with it. . . . For [him] music is . . . something that will sell records. If the music has to change, well, that's what you do." By the end of the seventies, the faintly Falstaffian former bass player had worked his way from jazz to rock to folk-rock to pop. He transformed himself into a crooner complete with big band and dinner jackets, altogether suitable for center stage at the Mirage.

Crossover was why Rogers could afford to fly when every other star in the country flotilla was busing around the nation, why he didn't have to spend an extra hour or two after every show signing ticket stubs, T-shirts, and eight-by-ten photos.

Rogers, Parton, et al., weren't the first, of course. Country performers had been crossing over since Vernon Dalhart's "The Prisoner's Song" sold a million copies in 1925. Owen Bradley turned Patsy Cline into a pop princess in the early sixties. But Bradley was simply making the music he wanted to make. He wasn't obsessed with taking Cline to the top of the pop charts. "There was never an attempt to cross 'em over," wrote Flippo. "If it happened it happened and praise God for the extra gravy."

But by the end of the seventies and early eighties, any singer who didn't want to cross over, who didn't want to be played on pop radio, was more or less consigning his or her career to the county fair circuit. *Urban Cowboy* came custom-made for commuter cowpokes. Eddie Rabbitt was Barry Manilow in Tony Lamas. A ticket out was a ticket up: Forget the pedal steel and Dobro, bring on the string (not fiddle) section and capture every market you can. No one talked much about integrity, artistic or otherwise.

"A lot of the established country stars and record producers are making records by formula," was how the Nashville manager Bill Carter described the situation in 1985. "They are so caught up in conforming to what used to sell and what radio stations will play, the new records don't have any life to them." When the urban cowboys left their Luccheses to collect dust in the closet and traded in their Chevy trucks for Volvos, those saccharine soundalike ballads stopped selling. While total record company sales grew 13 percent between 1980 and 1984 to $4.3 billion, country music revenues dropped 6 percent to $430 million. "The fabled Nashville sound . . . may soon sound as dated as the ukelele," wrote Robert Palmer in *The New York Times*.

Palmer wasn't so much sounding the death knell for Music City as for the soft-cornered music designed to appeal to the pop crowd. Within months of Palmer's obituary, Warner Bros. Records signed Randy Travis, and country started getting back to its roots.

In the early 1990s, country music might have been pulling in listeners from every conceivable genre, but *crossover* had become a dirty word on Music Row, akin to asking a light-skinned black person to pass in white society. Garth Brooks may sing his version of Billy Joel's "Shameless," but he was aggressively uninterested in courting pop radio. "Country music has made a home for me," he said, "and this is where I'd like to stay. As far as the pop world goes, well, I've seen what they can do to acts who try to go over; that's not what I want. I'm flattered by getting airplay from other formats, but I am not asking for it." The attitude was, "Let them come to us," and by and large it worked.

For his part, Fundis knew he couldn't have Yearwood singing music that made her appear to be kowtowing to the pop market. He knew "Down on My Knees" was a good song, and he knew quality was his only motivation, but he worried about the marketplace. For now, though, he didn't have the luxury of letting himself get consumed with anxiety. There was an album to finish, and that was still at least five songs away.

The last fixes were put on "Down on My Knees" by a quarter past nine, but that was not the end of the evening. Fundis had scheduled an extra session for one more song, one he wasn't even sure he wanted for the album.

A couple of weeks before, Fundis had got a call from a movie composer named Peter Afterman wanting to know if Yearwood would be willing to do a song for a new summer movie. *Honeymoon in Vegas*, a romantic comedy about a couple who elope to Nevada in the middle of a convention of Elvis impersonators, was to have a soundtrack of Presley standards, split between country and rock performers. He signed up Billy Joel to do "All Shook Up" and Willie Nelson for "Blue Hawaii." Afterman figured Yearwood would be perfect: He had heard her on *Hot Country Nights*, a short-lived NBC variety program, and found out from her newsclips that she was an Elvis fan. But the executives at the record label producing the soundtrack, Sony in L.A., had never heard of Yearwood, and they were reluctant to use unknowns. They were swayed not by her talent but by her management. Once they found out she was handled by Kragen, she was suddenly credible.

In mid-March Afterman contacted Kragen, who passed him along to Malcolm Mimms, and they struck a deal for just under fifty thousand dollars. His next call was to Fundis, to figure out which song she should do. Yearwood wanted to do "Love Me Tender," but Amy Grant already had dibs on it. Her second choice was "Devil in Disguise," and that was fine by everyone.

There was only a chart for "Devil." Yearwood had known the lyrics for years. At 9:40, Fundis put a tape on.

"Who's that demo singer?" asked Rollings as Presley belted out the song.

They headed out into the studio and played through it once.

"Let's get in tune, Dave," said Fundis. "Oops, I mean everyone."

Two takes later and it was over. Yearwood, though, wasn't happy with her vocal. "I think I can hold the last 'like,' and 'oh yes you are' longer," she said, and went back to rework it just after midnight. The effort was not memorable. "It's hard when you get tired," she said. "You think you're doing it, you hope you're doing it, and you're just too exhausted to tell."

"This isn't getting us anywhere," said Fundis. "I've got to ship this thing out on Monday. Where are you going to be?"

"I'm flying to Texas tomorrow, I've got a club date Friday, and a fair on Saturday. Monday I go to L.A."

"I think it's okay," said Fundis, "but why don't you fly back on Sunday so we can go over it if we need to." She agreed to rework her schedule, and with that, Fundis walked her to her car.

CHAPTER 12

TWO NIGHTS LATER, JUST PAST TEN, YEARWOOD LISTENED TO a cassette tape of the first two sessions as she sat in her bus, lined up against a curb in a parking lot in Fort Worth, Texas. She was fairly content with everything, except for "Blue Guitar." "It's like I'm trying to sound like someone else," she said, like Bonnie Raitt, or, more precisely, Nashville's answer to Raitt, Wynonna Judd. Judd's first album had come out two months before, debuting at number 4 on the *Billboard* 200, ahead of any number of pop and rock albums. It wasn't that Yearwood didn't like the song, she just didn't want it to look like she was mimicking the biggest thing to come out of Nashville since, well, Trisha Yearwood.

For the moment, though, there wasn't time for too much contemplation. She had five minutes to get on her eyeliner and lipstick. Then she was due center stage at the world's largest honky-tonk.

Billy Bob's, a sprawling structure in the midst of the Fort Worth Stockyards, only ever had one real rival, Gilley's, where John Travolta rode the mechanical bull back in 1980. But the Houston dance hall closed in 1986 and burned to the ground a year ago, leaving clear Billy Bob's claim as the biggest honky-tonk in America. Billy Bob's has a hundred thousand square feet of dance floor built over a complex of cattle pens once used during the annual stock show. The auction ring is now a bull-riding arena; on weekend nights they bring steers in for a few rough rides. "Real balls, not steel balls," said Billy Minick, a part-time rancher partial to freshly creased jeans, who is married to a former Miss Rodeo America.

Minick, who had been managing Billy Bob's since 1981, had scheduled Yearwood against his better judgment. She had performed at Billy Bob's just seven months before, and Minick had not been impressed. "She was real green," he said. "The girl could sing like a canary, but she stood up there on stage grabbing the microphone like she was wearing her first pair of high heels." As far as Minick was concerned, Yearwood wasn't ready to be working his public.

"Garth [Brooks] paid his goddamn dues, Travis [Tritt] worked crowds for years before he became a star," he complained. "Country is so hot right now that labels are throwing shit on the wall and hoping it sticks." Left on his own, Minick certainly hadn't been inclined to book Yearwood again so soon, but then she had switched managers. Minick had known Ken Kragen for years, and when the manager called to intercede on Yearwood's behalf, he was willing to listen.

Usually the work of cajoling club owners is left to booking agents. Yearwood was handled by one of the oldest outfits in Nashville, Buddy Lee Attractions. Buddy Lee, born Joseph Pinhal in 1932, still has the thick build of the professional wrestler he once was and the thick accent of his hometown, the Bronx. Lee started out as a rhythm-and-blues promoter (the Penguins, Jackie Wilson, Sam Cooke) in South Carolina in the midfifties. By happenstance, he landed a couple of country acts, Ernest Tubb and Marty Robbins, and when they brought in the crowds, he started looking for others. In 1961 Lee heard that Hank Williams's son had started to perform his father's tunes. He figured there was good business in it and contacted the youngster's mother, Audrey. Lee handled an East Coast tour for Hank junior, and the trip went so well that Audrey Williams and Lee ended up forming a partnership to handle other acts. Lee moved to Nashville and formed Aud-Lee Attractions. The agency lasted three years, until Hank junior had a falling out with his mother. He ended up with her share of the agency, and it was renamed Buddy Lee Attractions. When Lee bought out Hank junior's interest seven years later, the singer left the Buddy Lee fold.

These days Buddy Lee's agency handles bookings for Williams's illegitimate half sister, Jett, along with the World Wrestling Federation and over fifty country acts, including Garth Brooks, which was how Yearwood ended up there.

Day-to-day responsibility for Yearwood and Brooks fell to Joe Harris, a fifty-two-year-old South Carolinian who bears a certain resemblance to Orson Welles. Harris, the son of a traveling evangelist, flew in the air force in Vietnam. "Fourteen medals," he says when asked about his tour of duty. "Agent Orange and the hypertension that goes with it." He has been classified a disabled veteran and has a noticeable palsy. "You just do the best you can," he says, and gestures toward the New Testament front and center on his office desk.

Yearwood called Harris "Uncle Joe," and he reciprocated with avuncular protectiveness; he had seen Yearwood's new publicity photos, and he did not approve.

"There are certain things that are sacred between a man and a woman," Harris said. "I told Trisha this and I firmly believe it. 'Don't sell sex.' She's attractive, but it's keep-your-hands-to-yourself attractive. By having that quality, the ladies accept her also. They're not threatened. If you take her into the sex part, she will lose fans. Women won't buy a ticket to see another female, especially a sexy one, because they feel threatened. The ones that break out, like Dolly or Loretta Lynn or like Trisha, break out because women don't feel threatened. If she goes sexy, I think it would be her downfall. I think she looks good, and, as the saying goes, 'She's got it fine, don't flaunt it.' "

Harris, though, didn't have a lot of say when it came to Yearwood's image. "We can disagree and still go after the same goal," said Harris, the goal being the continued and increased success of Trisha Yearwood, Inc. If you think of Yearwood as a business, Kragen would be the chief executive, Fundis the chief operating officer, and Harris the head of distribution and sales, the man who figured out where and when she should appear.

Harris knew Yearwood needed extensive exposure in the Dallas–Fort Worth area—more country records are sold there than anywhere else in the U.S.—and Billy Bob's was the best place to get it. He also knew Minick was reluctant to book Yearwood again, which was why he asked Kragen to call Minick himself. If you book her, Kragen told Minick, I guarantee that she'll draw. If she doesn't bring in at least ten thousand dollars, I'll cover the difference. Minick figured he had little to lose.

* * *

As Yearwood emerged from her bus, Minick scanned her outfit, a low-cut velvet dress and bright red bolero. He did not approach her. "I don't mix with them," he said. "They're here to do their job, and I'm here to do mine. It's all business to me." And at first blush, Minick thought Yearwood would be better business this time. "She was in coal black the last time," he said, "buttoned up to here," gesturing at his throat. "She's looking better. Showing some cleavage. It works." As she made her way to the stage, he trailed behind her, hovering in a dark corner to gauge the audience response. "I don't know everything about country music," he said, "but I know what works for me."

There's a sort of broad-planked moat around the stage, then a dance floor, then a bar. Minick gestured over to a circle of blondes surrounding a tightly muscled young man in hat and denim shirt, sleeves rolled up just below his elbows. "If a guy can't get him a girlfriend in this place, he better just give it up," Minick said, then explained his first principle of star selection. "I can just look out on the dance floor and tell if an act is working. If it's full, we're onto something."

By that measure, Yearwood was doing just fine. The floor was crammed. Minick watched as Yearwood moved to center stage, standing tall and still for "Who Turned Out the Lights." The audience was still rustling. Next came "You Say You Will." Yearwood was all shimmy and sashay. "She should have been moving like that from the beginning. If she says, 'Hello, Fort Worth,' she'll have 'em." She did Minick one better, belting out the requisite greeting, then, before her next song, offering a paean to country music's current deity.

"There have been a lot of people over the last year who've helped me, but there's one person I'm especially grateful to. Last year he put me on his tour without ever having seen me perform. I'd just like to take a minute to thank Garth Brooks." The crowd started whooping.

"She's been coached," said Minick, finally satisfied that the show would sell. "Good for her," he said, as he walked off the stage, "good for us."

Yearwood was onstage until midnight. Afterward, she headed to a table to sign autographs for the next forty minutes. As she smiled and signed, Minick approached Arnold, standing guard off to Yearwood's right. "I just want you to know that in my eleven years in the business I've never seen a turnaround like that."

It rained all night as the bus cruised south 370 miles. At eleven the next morning, two hours late, Yearwood and her entourage pulled into the Freer Executive Inn, a twenty-five-room lineup of whitewashed bungalows on the outskirts of tiny Freer, Texas (pop. 3,271). Five and a half hours later, at four-thirty, Yearwood would be the headliner at the Twenty-seventh Annual Freer Rattlesnake Round Up.

Thousands of small towns across America have their own versions of the Freer fair, annual celebrations of civic chauvinism. In Vienna (pronounced Vye-enna), Georgia, it's the the Big Pig Jig (a barbecue competition). Dothan, Alabama, celebrates the peanut, Paintsville, Kentucky, the apple. The totems may differ, but the celebrations are much the same: Drink a couple of beers, eat a hot dog on a stick or two, head over to the Midway and ride to near nausea on the Tilt-A-Whirl, spend an hour or so listening to a country singer singing his or her heart out on the back of a flatbed truck. It is the biggest night of the year.

Other than the Round Up, there's not much to recommend this South Texas town. Rita Hayworth's father taught a couple of dancing classes here in the thirties. There's a barbecue joint named Headache's that has a pool table and a big-screen television, just about the only place to go on a Saturday night. The Rattlesnake Round Up got started as the Freer Oil-O-Rama in 1965, but no one was much interested in oil-field displays, so in the late sixties, the chamber of commerce invited the snake tanners to town and renamed the fair.

Snake hunting is a nocturnal sport, the kind of pastime that could only flourish in a place where the nearest movie theater is thirty-five miles away. Hunters ride up and down the highways looking for the snakes as they slither across the pavement, soaking up the warmth retained from the afternoon sun. The hunters' arsenal comes cheap: The snake catcher, as it's called, is a five-foot pole with a leather loop at one end and a lever at the other to make it cinch. The most common carriers are burlap bags (ill-advised since rattlers can bite through the fabric) or, preferably, wooden boxes with wire-mesh inserts. Mice or hamsters keep the rattlers plump until it's time to take them in.

* * *

It was eleven-thirty or so before Yearwood and company blearily tumbled out of their berths and congregated in the front of the bus. Arnold went to the motel office and returned clutching four Baggies containing keys and remote controls for the television sets. The band shared two rooms, split up by sex. Each had its own pile of peanut butter cookies, homemade by the motel staff.

Yearwood retired to the women's room to call Reynolds; the rest of the group headed down the street in search of breakfast. It was a fairly routine morning on the road—waking up in a town you've never been to before, trying to get fed and oriented in the hour or so before it's time to head over to the venue to set up, do sound check, and, finally, perform.

This morning East Riley Road was lined with ratty pickups, children on the hoods, legs dangling over dented radiators, watching a phalanx of patrol cars bleat their sirens. They were followed by a trailer holding the Freer High School automotive mechanics class—three teenagers revving up a series of truck motors, presumably refitted during class time.

The band had fifteen minutes for huevos rancheros, then it was back to the motel for a shower. Everyone was due on the bus by a quarter past twelve. At 12:30, Arnold took the steering wheel (Hoker was left to sleep at the motel) and headed into the single lane of traffic inching down the highway to the Round Up.

Yearwood played the roughs from her first sessions as the bus pulled into Rotary Park. The band was effusive in its praise, but Arnold wondered about the material. "I just hope she puts in some more of the up-tempo stuff," he said, "the pieces that those little girls love." For her part, Yearwood was becoming increasingly discontent with "Blue Guitar."

Just after one, Arnold parked behind the grandstand (actually a flatbed truck just behind home plate on the park's softball field), and the fair committee headed onto the bus with beers and fajitas. Yearwood was more interested in venturing out into the crowd. "You have to wander around," she said, "otherwise it all becomes the same. The great part of this is knowing where you've been, actually seeing stuff." As Arnold pointed out, this was her first fair this year.

The road manager guided her past the fair's other non-snake-related entertainment, a hypnotist named John Gardner. Gardner, according to his promotional material, specialized in turning audience members into celebrities, producing Maxwell Smarts, Tom Sellecks, and Willie Nelsons, as well as one man who thought he was a seat belt.

The main attraction was just past Gardner's show. Under a huge khaki tent, John Frank Shaddix, chief executive of Rare Skins, Inc., was paying $3.50 a pound for live rattlers. "The skin is for belts, boots, and hatbands," said Shaddix. "We use snake heads on key chains, rattles on earrings or hatbands. The gall-bladders are used in Japan for aphrodisiacs, the meat is sold. What's left goes to the rending companies for catfish food. My products are high quality. I don't sell to flea markets and gun shows. We don't sell product that's been pickled or antifreezed."

On top of the scales sat the brass trophy Shaddix had won in Sweetwater, Texas, site of the state's largest rattler round up. "I won the snake-eating contest," Shaddix explained. "Went through a third of a pound a minute—that's for fifteen and a half pounds of pure snake."

Yearwood eyed the three pens with faint horror. There were probably a thousand vipers in the pits, a mass of writhing, hissing, and rattling. Every few minutes, one of the larger snakes became sufficiently riled to bare its fangs, coil, and strike out toward the crowd, which was kept back by the four-inch-high wire mesh encircling the pits.

Alongside Shaddix's snake pits, another dealer sold bull snakes and baby pythons in empty liter-sized 7UP bottles. Not far away was a lineup of plastic cows, with retractable hindquarters so the aspiring cowboy could hone his roping skills in his own backyard.

Behind the tent, they were selling rattlesnake meat, three deep-fried pieces for a dollar. Arnold brought a selection back for the bus. The consensus: There wasn't enough meat to tell whether it really did taste like chicken. The only thing that made the meat even remotely palatable was a swig from one of the beers the fair committee had dropped off for the band.

Roger Corkill, MCA's Houston-based representative, seemed more interested in the beer than the rattlesnake meat as he watched the crowd gather for Yearwood. "You got cowboys who are horny, you got girls who want to screw 'em, and you have guys with babies on their shoulders," he said, "and every one of them is waiting for Trisha to come out and play them love songs."

At four-thirty, she did. There were about three thousand people standing in the rain, screaming as she walked onto the stage. Among them was Christopher Garcia, her guitar player's twelve-year-old son.

Johnny Garcia, medium height, handsome features, ebony hair worn in a ponytail, was born nearby in Weslaco, Texas. His father, Simon, owned a truck fleet that shipped workers up to farms in Alabama and Indiana during the harvest season, and he insisted that his son work on the crews during his summer vacations. But Simon Garcia didn't just teach his son to work; he bought the boy his first guitar and showed him how to play it.

Johnny Garcia played in a few bars in South Texas, but he never really considered making a living as a musician. He started up his own electrical contracting company in Weslaco when he was in his twenties and figured that was his future. Then, in the summer of 1991, he went to Nashville to visit a friend, a bass player. The friend was going to audition for Yearwood, who was putting together a band. Garcia went along—and ended up with a job. He folded up his business and moved to Nashville; his girlfriend joined him six months later. His son stayed behind in Weslaco with his mother. There was the occasional trip to Nashville, but what with his father's traveling schedule, the two hadn't seen each other in months.

The crowd, a riot of broad-brimmed cowboy hats, prompted a bit of improvisation when Yearwood introduced her third number. "This next song," she said, "was written about an imaginary man. But I'm starting to think he's somewhere in this crowd." The audience was hooting and hollering as she vaulted into "That's What I Like About You."

Yearwood had agreed to sign autographs after the show, and dignitaries got first dibs. Shaddix came onto the bus to present Yearwood with a snakeskin guitar strap; Arnold received a hatband, rattle intact. Just behind were Little Miss and Mr. Freer, resplendent in twin snakeskin vests. "Am I really going to meet her?" asked five-year-old Lisa Ann Rangel, the Little Miss. Yearwood stepped down from the bus and hugged the little girl, signing a photograph with her name. Behind Lisa Ann was Julie Devine, the teenage daughter of one of the live-snake salesmen. She was wearing a thirty-pound python around her neck. "Her name's Suzy," she said. "We keep her at home, feed her dead mice, wiggle them around so she thinks they're alive."

There was a snake show (death kiss with a cobra, escape from a rattler-filled sleeping bag) just behind the Shaddix pits, and Julie said she would be thrilled if Yearwood would come over. After an hour of signing autographs, including one on a patrolman's bulletproof vest, she did. Together with Herter and McLaughlin, she had a Polaroid taken with Suzy draped over her shoulders, a live, reptilian stole. "A real bonding thing," she said afterward.

At about eight, Yearwood and company finally pulled out of the fairgrounds. There was a last stop at the Executive Inn to pick up the driver, and at about ten o'clock the bus finally headed to the highway. Four and a half hours later, Hoker pulled into the driveway of a Rodeway Inn across from the Austin airport. Yearwood had two and a half hours to nap before her plane left for Nashville.

Yearwood got back to her apartment at ten the next morning. She slept for much of the day and headed to the studio to work on the vocal for "Devil in Disguise." On the way, she picked up Raul Malo, the lead singer from the Mavericks. Yearwood and Malo had improvised a couple of duets during one of the Mavericks' club dates in Miami, and she had been impressed by his pleading tenor. He was one of the few singers she had ever heard whose voice matched the power of her own. The week before, she had asked Fundis if he would consider using Malo for harmony vocals on "Devil in Disguise." It was the first time she had ever suggested a performer to Fundis, and she was unsure of herself. But Fundis trusted her judgment, and even though he had never heard Malo perform, he agreed to give him a shot.

The first few minutes left Fundis wondering what she could have been thinking. Malo was nervous, and his three-line harmony came out stiff and flat. "I know there's a trapdoor in here somewhere," Malo said as he stood in Yearwood's vocal booth. "Why doesn't someone just pull the rope?"

But after twenty minutes or so, he relaxed, and five takes later he worked out a short harmony, finally finishing just after nine. Afterward, Fundis and Yearwood listened to her vocals.

"It really does kick ass," he said.

"Maybe we should put it on the album," Yearwood said.

"Not a bad idea."

"I've been listening to 'Blue Guitar,'" Yearwood continued, her voice trailing off.

"It's not you," said the producer, finishing her thought.

"It sounds like I'm singing someone else's song."

"I know it. We've still got lots of time to fix it," he said, but both of them knew the song was not going to work.

They had just lost their title song, but for the moment it didn't matter. For the first time since they had started recording, both Fundis and Yearwood left the studio satisfied.

Yearwood and Fundis would have loved to grab hold of that momentum, head straight back into the studio, and get on with the album. But Yearwood, like most country singers, didn't have the luxury of uninterrupted studio time. On Monday morning at nine she was due at the airport to catch a flight to Los Angeles for the Academy of Country Music Awards, scheduled for April 29.

The Academy of Country Music was started in 1964 by the publisher of *Deejay Weekly* (since folded), and the owners of the Red Barn, a Long Beach, California, club (since burned to the ground). It was a good time to be setting up shop in California: Merle Haggard and Buck Owens were getting going in Bakersfield ("Buckersfield" to Nashvillians); Glen Campbell and Roger Miller were happening in Los Angeles. "California was cutting edge," explained Bill Boyd, one of the original directors of the academy. "It wasn't Earl Scruggs, but it was what was happening in country."

The Country Music Association may have been an effective lobbying outfit, but it had yet to occur to the Nashville elders to hand out statuettes. The California club owners, though, saw an opportunity for publicity, and they took it, in the form of the awards ceremony, a guitar and fiddle turn on the motion picture academy's extravaganza. (In 1966, the CMA responded with its own annual awards.)

For the last fifteen years, NBC has televised the academy's awards as a prime-time special—a compelling reason for virtually any star to go west to L.A. For Yearwood, whose manager's gospel was media exposure, a guaranteed two minutes in front of a prime-time network television audience was a command performance. Not only did she have a solo singing a verse and chorus of "The Woman Before Me," she was considered a shoo-in for top new female vocalist of the year. In addition, she and

Fundis were up for single of the year for "She's in Love with the Boy."

Yearwood spent the day and a half before the show with her sister and mother, who had flown out for the show. It was the first time either had been west, and Yearwood drove them around Los Angeles in a rented convertible: a little sight-seeing, a little shopping, two days free from work.

Fundis's primary purpose for the trip had nothing to do with picking up a gilded statuette. He wanted to meet the man who had commissioned "Devil in Disguise" and the woman who had written Yearwood's current single.

Peter Afterman had received the tape of "Devil in Disguise" not long before Fundis arrived. He loved the song, he told Fundis; he wanted to use it as the first single. sony, which was releasing it, would even put money up to make a video. There was only one hitch: Sony would be distributing the film and its soundtrack in August, just a month before MCA released Yearwood's second album. MCA had the right to keep Afterman from releasing Yearwood's song as a single, and Fundis knew the company probably would not want to give exposure to another label's product. The only way it might work was if the song was included on her album as well. "I'd love to do it," Afterman told Fundis. "I just hope politics don't get in the way."

The day of the awards show, Fundis had lunch with Jude Johnstone. The songwriter was new to Nashville—"The Woman Before Me" was the first song she had ever had recorded there— but she was an old hand at the music business; it was the only work she had ever done. She got started at eighteen in an improbable meeting with Clarence Clemmons, the saxophone player in Bruce Springsteen's E Street Band. They started talking on a flight to California; she told him she was a songwriter. "Send me a tape," he had told her, and a month or so later she did.

"Call me immediately," he telegrammed back. "Please call collect."

"Fly to New Jersey," he said when she called. "We'll figure out what to do with you." She went and stayed with Clemmons for two months while he and Springsteen recorded *The River*.

Later, Clemmons flew her to L.A. and introduced her to Springsteen's producer, Charlie Plotkin. Plotkin found her an apartment in Beachwood Canyon. With the unlikely luck that had started her career, she assumed she was destined for her own record deal. For the next five years she made dozens of demos, mostly piano vocals, but the charm never took. At twenty-four, she got a little more aggressive; she got her own band together and played once a week at the Bla Bla Cafe, still expecting an A&R talent scout to find her and offer her that deal. But Johnstone was trying to sell the blues in a world that was buying Blondie and the B-52's. Finally, in order to pay the rent, she took a seven-hundred-dollar-a-month publishing deal.

One of her first songs to be recorded was, "Cry Wolf," by Stevie Nicks. It was not the happiest of recording experiences. Nicks invited her to the studio to hear her version of the song. "That's good, that's real good," Johnstone told her, but privately she was horrified at what had happened to her song. Still, she knew, that recording would make back her advance and then some. "It was," she said later, "sort of what you expect."

Johnstone is a slow writer. "I have friends who work at this nine to five," she explained. "I don't know anything about that." By 1989, writing a song or two a year and having only limited luck with pop singers, Johnstone decided to try Nashville. Though she didn't know anyone there, she thought her material might work for Don Williams, so she sent a demo of a song called "The Fella Before Me" off to Fundis, cold. It made it through Scott Paschall, and the producer as well. It turned out there was another version of the song, one written for a woman. Yearwood ended up recording "The Woman Before Me" on her first album.

By the time Fundis and Johnstone met, she had already sent him a half dozen songs for Yearwood's second album. He liked them, he told her, but none of them quite worked. "I have one more," she said, "but I don't know if it's going to be ready on time."

"Girl, go home and get it finished," he told her.

Fundis, Yearwood, her sister, and her mother arrived at the Universal Amphitheater in a stretch white Lincoln at about five-thirty, half an hour before the show was to begin. Yearwood was wearing a sleeveless silver gown, reminiscent of the dress Marilyn Monroe had been sewn into for the Madison Square Garden show. Alan Jackson won for single of the year, but Yearwood, as predicted, got her award for new female vocalist.

Kragen, as always, had a plan. "I'm looking for an angle so we can have a photo tomorrow," he explained, "where she's not just one of eighteen people holding an award. I want it to be, 'Ohmygod, she got two awards at the same time.'" He wanted to take her to the press tent, where Bruce Hinton would present her with a plaque for going platinum. "Everybody gets an award," said Kragen. "This will make it an event, make her look different. Give people a reason to use this picture." There was only one hitch: Instead of going from the stage to the reporters' area, Yearwood was escorted back to her seat.

"Where is she?" Kragen asked the publicist running the show. "Why can't we get her back here?" Hinton trailed from behind, carrying a brown-wrapped package.

"I can't believe this is happening. Why can't she get out of the audience?" Russell said, puffing furiously on her ubiquitous cigarette. "I thought I felt an earthquake this afternoon, and there are riots all over the city. I want to get out of this town."

Finally, after ten minutes of pacing, one of the day's smaller disasters was averted. Yearwood appeared at the backstage door. Kragen took her arm. Sheri McCoy tried to grab her as she moved toward the press arena. "I want to get more lipstick on her," she said, but there wasn't time.

She went into the first press tent, set up for the photographers. "We have a surprise for you, Trisha," said Bruce Hinton. "I want to present you with an award for selling one million copies of your last record."

"Thanks, Bruce," she said, smiling as the light bulbs flashed.

"Tilt the thing forward, tilt it forward, we need them to see what you've got," Kragen whispered.

After the three-minute photo opportunity, Kragen escorted her to the print-press arena. She handed the plaque back to Hinton. "We'll do this again in there," Kragen told her. "Act surprised."

"I just love surprises," she said as they wandered through the alley between the tents.

McCoy stood at the back of the tent, watching as Yearwood was surprised for the second time. Her posture on the podium was beauty-pageant regal, right leg pushed forward through the slit in her dress. "That's my girl," said McCoy. "She knows just how to stand."

"What were you thinking before you won the award?" asked a reporter from a newspaper in Orange County.

"If I win, please don't let me trip on stage."

"Have you changed your look?" asked a man in an ill-fitting cowboy hat.

"I'm just trying to look as good as I can. I exercise now; I try not to eat at truck stops."

"What's it like to have your career move so quickly?" asked another.

"I try to see my family a lot. They tell me the things they think I need to hear, not what I want to hear. They tell me if they think I'm getting above my raising. . . . I'm enjoying the ride up, and I realize it's not always going to be like this. I just hope I can step aside gracefully when it's over."

With that, she was escorted back to the audience. Kragen's efforts worked; though the show would be preempted in Los Angeles by the first few frightening hours of the riots, that clip of Yearwood receiving her plaque for platinum made it onto CNN.

After the show, Yearwood, Kragen, and company headed over the Hollywood Hills to a small party at the Mondrian Hotel on Sunset Boulevard. It was an utterly disconnected affair, steam-table pizza and tortellini, crowd gathered at the wall of windows on the south side of the bar, watching as South Central Los Angeles went up in flames. Beth Yearwood, especially, was horrified. "I can't see how they came in with a not-guilty verdict," she said. "It just doesn't make any sense."

Kragen and his wife, nervous, headed home early. Yearwood and her mother and sister tried to go to Orso, down on Beverly Boulevard, but the maître d' had closed early. They tried three or four more restaurants in Hollywood, finally ending up in the San Fernando Valley, where Rodney King was only a story on the news.

They had been planning to fly out the next day all along. As they were chauffeured through the streets on the way to the airport, they could smell the char in the air and spot a few fires still flaming just east of the 405 freeway. The skies were filled with smoke.

The flight was delayed three hours, but Yearwood had to get home. On Saturday she had a performance in Cumming, Georgia, and two days after that she was due back at the Sound Emporium.

CHAPTER 13

As THE BAND GATHERED JUST BEFORE TWO IN THE ANTEROOM of the Sound Emporium on Monday, May 4, Matt Rollings collapsed, Camille-style, on the sofa. "I'm dying," he said. "Sinus infection." Illness was one of the few things capable of subduing the twenty-seven-year-old keyboard player. Rollings was the junior member not only of this group but of the fraternity of Nashville session players. With an abundance of freckles and a thatch of red hair the consistency of a freshly mowed lawn, he would show up at sessions and the other players would wonder if he was old enough to buy liquor. Then they heard him play. "He's a chameleon," said Bayers, who had been booked with Rollins six months after the keyboard player got to town five years before. "Never heard anything like it before." The drummer cosigned a loan so that Rollins could buy his first piano. By his second year he was playing on albums for everyone from Loretta Lynn to Lyle Lovett.

As Rollins moaned, Bayers asked after the awards show. Fundis answered with a mincing parody of an effeminate stagehand who, as each break ended, called out, "Seat fillers, it's time to take your places, seat fillers, please work with me." The riots went unmentioned.

There had been a slight switch in the composition of the band. Fundis had hired a new acoustic guitar player, Billy Joe Walker, Jr., a diminutive Texan with a quick, cackly laugh and a copious head of thick brown hair worn in a Nashville shag—short bangs, fringe over ears, back brushing down past shoulder blades. Walker had had his own radio show in Midland, Texas, by the time he was nine, moved into the Texas studios in his teens, and, at eighteen, had landed in Los Angeles, working with, among others, Kenny Rogers, Ray Charles, and the Beach Boys. He got to Nashville in 1985, doing session work and, eventually, releasing his own albums. His own music was more jazz than country; since Billy Joe sounded insufficiently urbane, he had just decided to drop his middle name. "Some people think you can't do this jazz-oriented music unless you're from a big city," he said.

That range (middle name or no) was precisely why Fundis had hired him. "Potter worked great on the other stuff," explained the producer, "but I wanted a different sound. We're moving from nice to gutsy."

Just how gutsy became apparent with the first song. At 2:15 Fundis put on a tape of "The Wrong Side of Memphis," and while the lyrics were country, the music was nothing short of raucous rhythm and blues.

"The Wrong Side of Memphis" owes its existence to Music Row, not just because of its theme (backwoods singer hits the road, destination: Opry) but also because of its very creation. That creative process had begun three years before in one of the Victorians along Music Row, at a publishing house called Patrick Joseph Music. Two of the songwriters hired by Pat Higdon, Patrick Joseph's proprietor, were getting acquainted over the kitchen sink. "Where are you from?" Matraca Berg, a twenty-six-year-old Nashville-born singer-songwriter, asked the other writer, Gary Harrison.

"Frayser, Tennessee," he answered. "The wrong side of Memphis."

"Sounds like a song title," said Berg. The two set up a songwriting appointment for several days hence in one of Patrick Joseph's guitar-and-piano-furnished cubicles. Most of the song came easily. The only hard part was coming up with that Tempest, the car that, in "Memphis," is driven to stardom.

"I knew it had to be a muscle car," said Harrison afterward. "When I was in high school, if you really had the bucks, you got a GTO. If you didn't quite have that much money, you got a LeMans. And if you just wanted something to ride and still had to have a Pontiac, it was a Tempest. . . . Besides, it rhymed with Memphis."

Yearwood had heard the song while she was still a demo singer.

After she was signed by MCA, she asked after the song, only to discover that Berg, who had her own record deal, at RCA, was planning it for her second album.

Berg recorded "Memphis," along with nine other songs, with entirely unhappy results. Together with her record label, she decided to shelve that second album. Not long afterward, Fundis ran into her at a party at Pat Higdon's. "How's the album going?" he asked.

"It's not," she replied. "Trisha can have 'Memphis' if she still wants it."

And she very much did.

Even before Yearwood knew she could record it, she had been using "Memphis" in her live act. It was a good, upbeat number, not to mention a variation on her own story. When it came to recording the piece, though, those performances were a liability. As Yearwood put it, "It's hard to hear when you get overly familiar."

Which helped explain why Fundis was urging her to consider using a Wurlitzer electric piano instead of the grand piano Rollings had used thus far. "It is the cheesiest of all keyboards," said Yearwood, when her producer suggested the switch.

"That's what's cool about it," Fundis replied.

But not cool enough. After three run-throughs, they agreed that the Wurlitzer didn't work, and they switched back to the grand piano. Thirty minutes later they had something Fundis wanted them to listen to.

Yearwood liked it, but wanted to rework the ending, to close with an extra chorus. "Maybe I could do one for every radio station—you know, like Clinton Gregory did with 'If It Weren't for Country Music, I'd Go Crazy.' " (The singer had customized the song, changing the last line: "If It Weren't for Station WXYZ, I'd Go Crazy.")

"I've been living on the wrong side of Dallas," she trilled. "I've been living on the wrong side of Houston."

"Why don't you try and get Poughkeepsie in there," said Pomeroy. "Or Altoona."

"Let's get serious, boys," said Fundis and the band headed back into the studio. At 5:15, they taped the version with the extra chorus (minus the regional variation). That, they decided, was the keeper.

Just before six, the band adjourned to dinner (blackened tuna, sliced steak), and Yearwood and Fundis started sorting through song sheets on the control board. The next three hours were still up for grabs. "I listened to 'Walkaway Joe' today," she said.

"We're going to do it," said Fundis, "but I want to wait." He had no reservations about the song, he said, but he wanted the band to be as loose as possible.

"This?" He gave her the lyrics for "Now She Knows," a ballad of love gone wrong, not dissimilar to "Nearest Distant Shore" and cowritten by one of the same writers, Tim Mensy. Pat Higdon had originally sent the song over for her first album. Yearwood had loved it, and Fundis had called to say he wanted it, only to be told that Reba McEntire had put it on hold a half hour before.

"On hold" is a sort of first come, first served option on a song. Whoever notifies the publisher first gets to keep it for the next album. There's a loose protocol to the process. If, after recording an album, a performer hasn't used a song, it is supposed to be put back into circulation, which is what happened with McEntire. As soon as she had finished her album, Higdon, who handled the song for Mensy and Gary Harrison, found out she had decided not to record it and called Fundis, who grabbed it.

The biggest problem in recording the song was figuring out the key. They did three takes in F before moving it up to F-sharp, which was, as Yearwood put it, "where it should have been all along." They called it a night at half past ten.

Nancy Russell was waiting when Yearwood arrived the next day at one. The publicist was there to referee an interview between Yearwood and a reporter from a Japanese airline magazine. Yearwood was at the point in her career where press—any credible press—was still important. The Japanese reporter, translator in tow, was working on a story on Elvis Presley. They talked for ten minutes, then went into the control room, where she played him "Devil in Disguise." Then, just after two, they exchanged gifts. She gave them signed copies of a CD; they gave her an alarm clock. For the next ten minutes, every possible permutation of the studio group (translator, Fundis, Yearwood, and the reporter) was photographed in the control room; the flashbulbs were still going off as the musicians congregated. Fundis had added one to their number, Sam Bush, a fiddle and mandolin player for the Nash Ramblers, Emmylou Harris's backup band and one of the most revered bluegrass musicians in the business.

At 2:20, Pomeroy, resplendent in pink T-shirt, pink tie-dyed jeans, and pink high-top sneakers, came in and handed out the sheet for "Oh Lonesome You" by the O'Kanes, a defunct duo that consisted of the Nashville songwriters Jamie O'Hara and Kieran Kane. The O'Kanes' first album had essentially been a series of demo records created in an attic studio. The production was minimal, the arrangements austere, the harmonies clear—straight-out neotraditionalist. The album produced two top-ten singles, and the O'Kanes' future, for a shining moment, looked infinite. But their success proved fragile. Two albums later, in 1991, Kane and O'Hara went their separate ways, and though Fundis had been working with O'Hara on a solo project, it had yet to find a taker.

"Oh Lonesome You" had been on the duo's first album, an up-tempo shuffle, about as country as you can get.

Yearwood looked wary as the demo played. "Don't worry," said Fundis. "It'll be cool."

They jammed for fifteen minutes, did two run-throughs and, at 3:10, Fundis said, "Roll 'em."

"I think it works," he said as they played, and fifteen minutes later they were in the control room, listening. By everyone's estimation, the song sounded fine.

Yearwood nodded as the song played, not at all displeased. "It's much cooler than I thought it would be."

"I told you not to worry," said Fundis.

"Well," said Bayers, "Is the food here yet?" It was not yet four o'clock.

The phone rang, and Fundis answered. "Trisha, Ken on line two." She headed out into the anteroom to talk to her manager. Moments into the conversation, Yearwood was frowning into the phone. A breeze broke her concentration. The front door had opened, and Leonard Arnold walked by, wearing a Sweethearts of the Rodeo sweatshirt. Arnold ambled into the control room, standing toward the back as Mason finished up the fixes on the guitar solo.

Yearwood, call finished, walked in, hugged Arnold, then joined Fundis, who was listening from behind the console as Mason worked on his part. "Ken have anything to say?" Fundis asked.

"I don't want to talk about it," she said, in a tone that made it clear he shouldn't press the issue.

Arnold caught the mood and figured to break it. He brought out a couple of pictures to show Yearwood, snapshots from the trip to Monticello. Yearwood, wearing a pair of black Ray-Bans, was straddling her grandfather's Harley. "Motorcycle mama," Mason called as he stepped into the control room.

"I'm trying to convince my uncle to give it to me," said Yearwood, finally smiling.

At 5:15 Pomeroy came in with the charts for the next song, an Emmylou Harris piece called "Woman Walk the Line." The song had been recorded twice before, by Highway 101 and by Harris herself. Not surprisingly, it was Harris's version that had sold Yearwood on the song.

The summer before, she had picked up a CD of one of Harris's older albums, *The Ballad of Sally Rose*, and discovered that the song that Highway 101 had cut as an up-tempo piece was, in fact, a ballad. "I had never heard Emmylou's version before," she said when she brought it to Fundis. "It sounds like something I could do." Her producer agreed.

Fundis used Harris's version as the demo. She sang the piece with an almost-nasal, bluegrassy back-of-the-throat twang. After a few bars of a particularly high-pitched whine, Rollins let loose with a loud meow.

"Matt," noted Pomeroy, "seems to have recovered."

"All right guys," said Fundis, "Let's work on this thing for twenty minutes, then break for dinner." As the band filed out of the control room, Yearwood cupped her hands and turned to the players. "Seat fillers, work with me. Seat fillers, work with me."

The band was playing as the most important guest of the day arrived: Tony Brown, who, unseen by Yearwood, appeared at the control-room door flanked by another A&R executive and his assistant. Fundis handed him the talk-back. "Sounding good, girl," said the executive. Fundis took the microphone back and announced, "Tony's here."

Fundis had invited Brown over earlier in the day. "We're having catering. Why don't you come by for dinner?" he said, knowing that Brown would probably come a little early to catch some of the session and hear a few cuts.

"Why don't you put on 'Memphis,' " he told Laney.

Brown listened, eyes closed, fingering his beard as the song played.

"I love it," he said. "I love the lyrics as a video."

Next came "Now She Knows." Brown lay back into his chair, his head resting on its back. "Great melody. Is that a track vocal?" Yearwood nodded yes. "Killer man, just a killer."

"We have to play you Elvis," said Yearwood, "then you can eat." Fundis mimed the keyboard while Brown did a silent, laughing sing-along with "Devil in Disguise."

"A killer," pronounced Brown again. "Who's the harmony vocal?"

"Raul from the Mavericks," said Fundis.

"What a great idea. That's a song I've always wanted to cut," said the only man in the room who had actually played with Elvis. "It's got to be a hit. Are you going to put it on the album?"

"We're thinking about it."

With that, they headed over to the steam table. As Brown and Fundis filled their plates, Sheri McCoy walked in, and Yearwood pulled her aside. "Kragen called," Yearwood told her. " 'I know you're close to Sheri,' he says, 'but I keep hearing bad comments about the dress you wore at the ACMs. It made you look heavier than you are.' I told him that I don't just listen to what people tell me. The dress design was both of our ideas. We looked at that book with pictures of Marilyn. Her arms looked heavier than mine do. . . . Why does he call me with this stuff when I'm in the studio?"

"What does he think you should wear?" McCoy asked.

"Just criticism, no ideas. I don't regret what I wore. I'm not coming from a place where I think I have to cover this up. If I cover it up, people will just say she has something to hide."

McCoy just listened as Yearwood vented spleen.

"Maybe we should go back to long sleeves," McCoy finally said. Yearwood nodded. "I should go talk to Tony."

She grabbed a plate and only the smallest portion of food (no dessert) and headed back to the control room, where Fundis and Brown were talking. "Who owns this place?" Brown asked.

"I'm about to," Fundis replied. It was the first time he had talked about it publicly, but for the last couple of months he had been negotiating to buy the studio. As the Emporium's biggest customer, he figured it made good business sense to own the place. Not only could he recoup some of what he paid for studio time, with a little attention, the place could be made much more appealing to other producers. Thanks to the money he had made from Yearwood's first album (and a bank loan), he had the money to invest. After two months of dickering, he and Clark had finally settled on a price of $550,000 (about half the appraised value of the real estate and the equipment); the lawyers were still working out the details.

"Congratulations," said Brown.

"Soon," Fundis replied. "Not just yet."

Yearwood joined Fundis and Brown in the control room. "I had this ridiculous conversation with Kragen," she said.

"I could tell something was wrong," replied Fundis.

"Women are always getting a hard time about what they wear," Brown said, after Yearwood had explained the criticism of her outfit. "With Vince [Gill], he turns up looking like he doesn't care, no one says anything. They put Reba on the cover of the paper wearing that *Gone with the Wind* number. A lot of people said it looked awful, but I saw that glint in her eye. She was having a good time. I just think you should wear whatever you're comfortable with."

Yearwood finally seemed to have found an answer she could live with, and coming from the number two man at her record label, it had credibility.

It took another hour to get back to "Woman Walk the Line." Fundis didn't have a version that he wanted to listen to until just before eight, and even then it was not quite right.

"We're just slamming the door on the ending," the producer said.

"What's the first line of the song, Trish?" asked Rollins.

"Don't bother sitting at my table," she sang from the booth.

"Why don't you try ending it with that?"

The result, everyone agreed, was inspired.

"You can stay," said Yearwood to Rollins.

The band finished just after nine, but Dave Pomeroy still had work to do. The bass and the bass drum were the pulse of the song, and they had to hit virtually the same notes, no error allowed. Of course, there were about a half dozen misses, and it was up to Pomeroy to fix them. "It's hard to fix one component of the drum set," said Pomeroy, but that was not the only reason. "Eddie Bayers is one of the greatest studio drummers in the world, and he was kind enough to let me say, 'Play it this way.' It was up to me to complete my half of that vision." The vision was completed a few minutes before eleven.

Fundis wasn't sure how many songs he had intended to get through that night, but he had hoped it would be more than two. Still, there was one more day left in this block of sessions, and he had another day scheduled just in case.

And Brown had liked what he heard. If MCA was happy, Fundis figured, it wouldn't hurt if they ran a little behind schedule. After all, they were the ones who had told him they would be releasing five singles back in the fall.

A bouquet of lilies was waiting for Yearwood when she got in on Wednesday afternoon for the last session scheduled with the band. As she walked through the studio door, she beelined to the envelope tucked in amid the stems. "From my new best friend," she announced, "Al Teller." Apparently Tony Brown had called the boss in Los Angeles to tell him the sessions were going well.

The day's first effort had absolutely nothing to do with the project at hand. Bruce Hinton belonged to a civic group for local executives, and the next day a passel of them would be coming through the Sound Emporium for a firsthand look inside a recording studio. The idea was to record the basic tracks, then let the executives add on their own vocals.

Pomeroy handed out chord charts for "Will the Circle Be Unbroken."

"I figure everyone should know this thing," Fundis said. "We'll do a verse, a chorus, and that'll be it."

They headed out into the studio, and did a quick run-through. Fundis pressed the talk-back button. "Not bad, guys, but it doesn't compare to Dale Evans singing 'Amazing Grace.' "

"Can I put on a fix?" Pomeroy asked. "I got it all backwards."

"Who fucking cares?" said Fundis. "This will be heard by nobody."

Pomeroy just stood there, waiting for another round. "Jesus," said Fundis. "One more. That's it."

Pomeroy did one take. "I'm still not happy," he said.

"Enough," said Fundis. And Pomeroy headed into the control room.

"They want me on *Geraldo* next Thursday," Yearwood said as Pomeroy walked in. "Nancy says its okay. Ken says it's okay."

"He's a greaseball," said the bass player.

"I really didn't want to do it."

"Let's vote on it," said Pomeroy. The tally was 6 to 0, against.

"Will you get me out of it?" Yearwood asked Fundis.

"What do you want me to do?"

"Tell Nancy you need me for another day of recording."

"You really should talk to Ken."

"But I already said okay."

"Later," said Fundis. "Let's get to work."

Yearwood had wanted "You Say You Will," cowritten by Verlon Thompson and Beth Nielsen Chapman, for her first album. But, as with "Down on My Knees," Fundis had been chary. The song was a little too bluesy, too close to crossover for comfort. Even though he didn't use the song, Fundis had told Chapman and her publisher, BMG, that he was committed to the song and wanted to keep it for the next album. It was an unusual state of affairs, but the publisher (and Chapman) had agreed.

The only problem was that BMG apparently hadn't made the situation clear to Thompson's publisher, EMI. EMI continued to pitch the song and, in January, found a taker: Holly Dunn, a Texas singer-songwriter who had had moderate success recording for Warner. The conflict became clear when the representative from EMI told the representative from BMG that the song had been taken.

"I thought, well, let's see how serious she is about cutting it," Dunn recalled. It took a single short phone call to discover that Yearwood was quite serious. "I wasn't going to jerk it out from under her," Dunn said, but she also refused to back off. After all, she insisted, "the publishing company is really under no obligation to hold a song for over a year." There was no legal way Yearwood and Fundis could claim title to the song. Nothing had been signed, no money had changed hands. Dunn had violated Nashville etiquette, but there wasn't a whole lot they could do about it.

Nashville, though, remains the kind of town where a certain

Jack and Gwen Yearwood with daughters Beth, age four
and a half, and Trisha, eighteen months

Jack Yearwood with daughters Trisha, age
three and a half, and Beth, age six and a half

Trisha Yearwood, age seventeen
TRISHA YEARWOOD FAN CLUB

Yearwood in *Little Mary Sunshine*
TRISHA YEARWOOD FAN CLUB

Beth, Jack, and Gwen Yearwood with George Jones
(second from right)
TRISHA YEARWOOD FAN CLUB

Ken Kragen
KEN KRAGEN

Nancy Russell
LISA ZHITO

Yearwood with Leonard Arnold
WILSON PAULK

Left to right: Johnny Garcia, Tammy Rogers,
Yearwood, Jay Hager
TRISHA YEARWOOD FAN CLUB

Tim Lauer
LISA GUBERNICK

Yearwood and Ric McClure

The Mavericks: *(left to right)* Paul Deakin, Raul Malo,
Robert Reynolds, David Lee Holt

Left to right: Katie Gillon, Ken Kragen, Scott Borchetta, Garth Fundis, Bruce Hinton, Yearwood, Al Teller, John Burns (president, Uni Distributing), Shelia Shipley, Walt Wilson

JACKY SALLOW

Tony Brown

PETER NASH

Jude Johnstone
BOB BURTON

Yearwood and
Don Henley
LISA McLAUGHLIN

amount of gentility is expected. So while Dunn intended to do the song, she wanted to avoid alienating Yearwood and Fundis completely. Was there anything she could do to keep them happy? she asked the BMG representative. The publisher told her that as long as her record label did not release the song as a single, Yearwood would be happy. And Dunn sent a letter to Warner asking just that.

"Did she send the letter?" Yearwood asked as Pomeroy handed out the song charts. Fundis nodded. "Is there anything we can do if she decides to release it anyway?"

"She won't."

At 2:30 Fundis put on the demo tape. Bayers and Rollins did a two-step to the music. By 3:15 they did their first taped take, and fifteen minutes later they were back in the control room. "It's the same problem I have with my band," said Yearwood. "It's too slick. We need to slow it down."

Bayers agreed to adjust the click-track down a beat, from 114 to 113 beats per minute. One more click-track adjustment later, and they had a version that pleased both the singer and the producer. For the next half hour, first Pomeroy and then Mason put final fixes on their parts. Yearwood had retreated to make a few phone calls, then, just after five, wandered back in, putting her arm around Fundis. "Will you call about *Geraldo*?" she asked. And Fundis picked up the phone.

"Nancy Russell, please. Nancy, this is Garth." He fiddled with the button on his shirt collar. "Timing-wise, I don't think *Geraldo* is going to work. We're on a deadline. . . . Is there another time that's good? Let me get back to you tomorrow. We're going to need more time to finish things up."

"Thanks," Yearwood said, hugging her producer as he hung up the phone. The singer had learned how to perform on stage, how to do make-up, how to work the camera, how to keep reporters amused. The one thing she had not learned was how to say no.

The dinner break, the last for this crew, lasted three quarters of an hour. As the waiter stacked up his last steam tray, the band stood and applauded.

By 6:40 they were back in the studio, listening to the last version of "Say You Will." The band started an impromptu line dance, each musician taking a turn at center stage. Billy Walker did the Pony, Bayers and Rollins repeated their two-step. Finally Mason, usually the most retiring of the lot, did a bump and grind that could only be described as a James Brown fandango. "Well, boys," said Fundis, "I guess we've got it."

Pomeroy had one more set of song sheets. He put the charts on the table, and Fundis asked Laney to play the next tape. "And now," he said, "for something completely different."

"Walkaway Joe" was Yearwood's story song—a sort of lyrical version of *Badlands*, the Terrence Malick film about a teenage boy and girl who shotgun their way across America after her father tells her she can't see him anymore. Midway through the demo, Yearwood looked up at Fundis. "Should we put Henley on the harmonies?" she asked. Fundis nodded, not at all convinced it was going to work out.

"Actually it's what happened to Katie and Tommy [the characters in 'She's in Love with the Boy']," Yearwood said after the song ended. "She gets pregnant, they were going to get married, then he robs a liquor store and leaves her."

Fundis had first heard the song more than a year before at a showcase at the Bluebird Cafe, a 110-seat club in a minimall that is the center of the Nashville songwriting scene. Amy Kurland is the Bluebird's school marm cum proprietor, holding quarterly auditions for new songwriters and grading them on their efforts. (Anyone who gets a B or above gets a three-song berth on a Sunday "Writer's Night." "I want no singular nouns rhyming with plural nouns," she says, "no *m*'s rhyming with *n*'s. And I am not a big fan of the rhymes 'me' and 'Tennessee' or 'arms' and 'charms.' If you've heard them once, you've heard them a trillion times."

Garth Brooks got his record deal after a showcase at the Bluebird; Kathy Mattea was discovered there as well. Every so often a publisher hires the place out for an evening, and has its songwriters perform their latest efforts. Producers attend because they know the pickings are good.

"Walkaway Joe" was performed that night at the Bluebird by Greg Barnhill, one of the two men who wrote it. Barnhill had six years in Nashville and one big hit ("Same Old Same Old Love" with Ricky Skaggs). The other writer, Vince Melamed was born in New York, grew up in L.A., and had done time playing with everyone from the Eagles to Bob Dylan. "I was at Woodstock," he said, when asked to detail his origins. He had moved to Nashville in 1985 to work with Rosanne Cash; he ending up staying for good.

The two men had been meeting two or three times a month for the last couple of years, but had yet to get one of their songs recorded. During one of their sessions in 1990, Barnhill had walked in with a phrase, a song title, he thought, that had come to him the night before. "I grew up listening to this story," Barnhill said, "where some girl would be wanting to marry some guy and the mother would be saying, 'Don't you do that honey.' And then the guy just disappears from the picture."

They wrote "Walkaway Joe" in two and a half hours. It took two and a half years to get it recorded. Fundis had wanted the song the moment he heard it at the Bluebird, but Wynonna Judd had already put it on hold. Judd didn't use it on her first album, though, and when Pat Higdon, Melamed's publisher, called, Fundis gratefully accepted his offer.

Still, Melamed wasn't expecting much. "It is about a guy who robs a gas station," he explained, "and most country record companies and radio stations don't want to know about that kind of thing."

Country radio is certainly the most prudish of musical formats, the only one with implicit (and occasionally explicit) moral guidelines. Country Music Television, Nashville's answer to MTV, refused to air Garth Brooks's video for "The Thunder Rolls" because it was deemed too violent. (By MTV standards, it would have been rated PG-13.) The main country station in Tucson still refuses to play any song that uses the word *damn*.

Even Yearwood had been wary of the stark lyrics of "Walkaway Joe" at first. She wasn't worried about whether radio would play the song, but she wasn't sure she would be able to summon the emotions required. It certainly wasn't a song she could have managed on her first album, but over the last year, she felt, her range had grown as she had been divorced and betrayed, as she had collided with the harder edges of life.

They finished the first run-through at 7:50. "I guess I'm going to be able to do this," Yearwood said.

The tape rolled at 8:05, then again at 8:20. Scott Paschall, meanwhile, was trying to figure out if he was supposed to be setting up another session, tentatively scheduled for May 11. "Matt can't come next time, neither can Billy," he worried. "It's hard to get people at the last minute."

Fundis sidled over to Paschall. "It remains to be seen if we need a next time," he said, then moved back behind the console. "I'd like to try just one more," Fundis said after they finished the fifth taping of the song. "I have an idea. Matt, Eddie, Trisha, why don't you go out and try it on your own." Without guitars and steel, and with Bayers using his hands instead of drumsticks, they got the best take of the evening.

"Do we have a session next week?" Mason asked.

"I don't think so," Fundis said. Counting "Devil in Disguise," which he was considering for the album, he already had eleven songs ("Blue Guitar" was officially out of contention), one more than the required ten. "I think we have enough—why make our job even harder? There's already stuff we won't be able to use."

"I guess that's it," said Fundis, turning his gaze to Yearwood. Yearwood, exhausted, said nothing.

"Thanks, everyone," said Fundis. And the musicians headed out into the night.

CHAPTER 14

FOR THE NEXT TWO WEEKS, FUNDIS TRIED TO CATCH UP ON TWO other albums, one with a songwriter named Dean Dillon, the other with Collin Raye. Dillon and Raye were recent additions to his roster, projects he had signed on only after he had lost his only other regular act, Don Williams, in mid-1991.

The parting with Williams had come quite unexpectedly. Williams's fifteenth album with Fundis had been released in 1990. The reviews had been merely serviceable and the sales middling. Still, Fundis had been expecting to start work on their next record in the fall.

One day in August, having been out of the office sick for the better part of a week, Fundis went in to go through his mail. Williams called while he was there. "I want to get together," Williams told him.

"Do you want me to come over right now?" Fundis asked, and Williams said that would be fine.

They barely exchanged greetings. "I've decided to have Allen [Reynolds] produce my next album," Williams announced.

Fundis was stunned. "Pal, I don't know how we could have made a better record. But if you need to do something else, I understand."

"I don't know, either," said Williams. And that, after seventeen years together, was it.

"There was just this empty feeling," recalled Fundis afterward. "If he had come to me and said, 'I think I might do something different on the next album,' that would have been one thing.

But this was all settled. It was a bit of a kick in the teeth. But Trisha was flying, I was just finishing an album with George Fox [Canada's answer to Randy Travis] along with *Kentucky Bluebird* [a posthumous Keith Whitley album]. I was busy. I was pretty upset for about a day."

He might not have been too upset, but he was pragmatic. Fox was a one-album deal; there would be no more music from Keith Whitley. He had seen tragedy and he had seen caprice, and he knew he couldn't have his future riding on a single performer, even one as promising as Yearwood. When Sony called in January to ask him to produce Collin Raye's next album, he said yes. And when Dillon, a successful songwriter, was proposing to record his second album for Atlantic Records, Fundis was his first choice. Yearwood, though, was the project closest to his heart. He was the one who had found her, who had worked with her from the beginning.

Yearwood spent just about all of those two weeks on the road, and on May 9 she had a gig at the Washington County Fair in Fayetteville, Arkansas. It was a show that nearly didn't happen.

Yearwood had already been paid half of her twenty-thousand-dollar fee. The minute he walked into the fairgrounds, Leonard Arnold began worrying that she would never see the rest of it. She was the fourth act of the day, which meant she would be the fourth act to get paid, and by Arnold's estimation it would take three times the two thousand people in the arena to cover Yearwood's fee.

Arnold went to talk to the road managers for two of the other acts, Bailey and the Boys and the Marshall Tucker Band, to see if they had been paid. They had, but it had taken hours. Worse than the delay were the denominations: lots of five- and ten-dollar bills, which, to Arnold, meant that the promoter was digging deep into his ticket receipts. Just after five, he went to talk to the promoter himself. There was a problem, the promoter conceded: His messenger had originally gone out to get a cashier's check but had discovered she couldn't get one on a Saturday. He was waiting for her to come back with the cash; she should be back any minute.

As afternoon turned to evening, the promoter grew increasingly evasive, and Arnold grew increasingly suspicious. The messenger should be back any minute, the promoter kept saying.

He couldn't understand what was happening. Finally, Arnold went back to talk to Yearwood, to discuss their options. She had two choices, he told her: She could simply refuse to go on, which would risk alienating the crowd, or she could go on, and, if she didn't get paid, sue for the payment later. Arnold recommended the second course of action ("We're already here; it's no skin off our backs") but advised her to check with higher authorities, that is, Joe Harris and Ken Kragen. She called her booking agent and manager. Both recommended that she play.

She went on stage, as scheduled, at six and played the requisite sixty minutes. Afterward she accompanied Arnold to collect her fee. They stood there as the promoter counted the money from ticket sales. It started out in twenties, then tens, then fives. After twenty minutes he was down to single dollar bills. To everyone's surprise—including, it seemed, the promoter's—there was enough to pay her.

When it was over, Yearwood started stuffing the bills into her shirt. "I want a record of this," she told Arnold. He went back to the bus, got her camera, and took a picture with the greenbacks overflowing her bra.

Yearwood got back to Nashville on Sunday and two days later flew to Miami for a few days with Reynolds. When she returned the following week, she began preparing to move. The apartment she had been living in was more hotel room than home, and though she was rarely in Nashville more than a dozen days a month, she had decided she wanted something larger, somewhere she would stay awhile.

Too many stars start spending money—buying cars, buses, houses, boats—as soon as their first record goes gold. It's not hard to fall fast and deep into debt. Yearwood, though, was a pragmatist. Her only indulgence had been a 1966 red convertible Mustang with the genuine pony interior. It cost fourteen thousand dollars, four thousand dollars less, she proudly noted, than the dealer's asking price. Except for that Mustang, Yearwood was reinvesting her money in her business; the life-style—and home ownership—could come later. She rented a modest two-bedroom ranch house in Green Hills, one of Nashville's nicer neighborhoods.

There wasn't much to move. All she really had was a fold-out sofa, a wrought-iron bed, and her grandmother's hand-sewn patchwork quilt (wedding-ring pattern), which she used as a bedspread.

On Tuesday night, the move completed, she reclaimed her dog, an exuberant husky-chow mix named Roseanne, who had been living with her ex-husband. Unfamiliar with the new surroundings, Roseanne barked into the empty night until just before dawn. Yearwood slept through her alarm clock, and she was twenty minutes late to the meeting where the men and women who would be selling her second album were to hear it for the first time.

• • •

Bruce Hinton didn't like to hear albums in progress, before all the harmonies and instrumental tracks were on. "I'd rather only hear the finished product," he explained. "Otherwise, frankly, it's just a waste of my time." By May 20, though, Fundis had only had time to finish one of the eleven songs. Still, the first single was due in two weeks, and Fundis needed to know which song they wanted.

The seven MCA executives left their offices at about a quarter to ten for the ten o'clock meeting at the Sound Emporium. Shelia Shipley, senior vice president of the Promotion Department, chauffeured Scott Borchetta, vice president of promotion, Walt Wilson, senior vice president of marketing, and Jim Kemp, the member of the marketing staff in charge of album design, in her green BMW. Tony Brown and Bruce Hinton shared Hinton's maroon BMW. Janet Rickman, the head of marketing and public relations, arrived alone in her Toyota.

Hinton took what was clearly the power seat, the swivel chair just behind the desk above the control board. Tony Brown occupied a smaller chair to his left, Rickman the one on his right. Wilson and Kemp settled into the sofa, and Borchetta and Shipley took up their positions just behind the control panel.

When record-label executives hear a recording for the first time, they usually get a full-out presentation: who wrote the songs, how and why they were chosen. This meeting was strictly barebones. Fundis handed out Xerox copies of a sheet listing the songs and their writers, "T.Y." scrawled across the top of the page. After a cursory round of greetings, he turned on the tape.

The reel began with "You Say You Will," followed by "Nearest Distant Shore" and "Oh Lonesome You." Yearwood (old version: denim shirt, jeans, white Keds) appeared halfway through the fourth song, "Woman Walk the Line," squeezed past Paschall, who was hovering in the doorway, and walked over to Fundis, in his usual position behind the console. She gave him a hug, and mouthed a silent "Sorry."

Brown looked over at Yearwood as the song ended. "Are you as good as what I'm thinking?" he asked, parroting the song's second lyric.

"I'm better," Yearwood replied. Then came "Walkaway Joe."

"That's got class all over it," Hinton said as the song faded. Hinton quietly dominated the conversation, his staff waiting for his response, then echoing it.

"I think so, too," said Fundis. "I've been hanging on to that for a year."

Hinton smiled and nodded through "Wrong Side of Memphis," tapping a Mark Cross pen against his thigh. Fundis played air fiddle. He wanted to put the genuine article on the album, but hadn't got to it yet. "I love the rhyme of Memphis and Tempest," said Hinton. "I would never have thought of that."

After "Now She Knows" Yearwood turned to Fundis. "Didn't you think it would be easier this time?" she asked. Fundis shook his head no.

"One, two, three, four," came over the loudspeaker. "Oh, God," said Yearwood. "It's Eddie." Fundis had decided to leave Bayers's downbeat on the finished version of "Devil in Disguise."

Hinton tapped his foot to the rhythm, lightly beating his Cross pen against his thigh. "I just love that," said Brown.

"It's just a little thing we thought we'd throw in," said Fundis.

After "Down on My Knees," Hinton looked over to Yearwood. "You going for vocal of the year with that one?" he asked.

Two more songs—"Move That Mountain" and "You Were Right from Your Side,"—and it would be over. Yearwood walked over and nuzzled in next to Walt Wilson. "I've got the watch on," she said, pushing up her sleeve to reveal the face of Elvis Presley. She had spotted the watch on his wrist the summer before, just after her album was finished. He had promised to give it to her if the album went gold. It did, and he did.

"Let's hear it again," ordered Hinton. After the second "Nearest Distant Shore," Brown said, "Great song."

"We still have a good bit to go," the producer replied.

"Should you ask about Elvis?" Yearwood said to Fundis.

"One of the things I wanted to do today is get your opinion on a song," Fundis began. "We did 'Devil in Disguise' for a movie soundtrack. We have kind of come to really like it."

"It feels to me like an extra song," said Hinton.

"It is the only one that's finished," Brown interjected.

"It's the only one with background vocals," Fundis added.

"I'm not talking about that," said Hinton. "I'm talking about it sounding different from the rest of the track."

"We do need one more up-tempo piece on the record," said Brown. "Do you want it on the record?" he asked, directing the question to Fundis.

Fundis, sensing Hinton's apprehension, demurred. "We didn't do it as though we were going to include it."

"Sony wants it to be a single," said Brown.

"So they'll throw a lot at it," added Fundis. It wasn't at all the sort of comment that was likely to persuade an executive from MCA.

"It gives you a dated sense because it's so known," said Hinton.

"It does stick out," Borchetta chimed in, his first comment of the morning.

"Sounds like it's kicked out to me," said Brown.

"I guess we'll need another up-tempo song," said Fundis.

"What's that Merle Haggard number she does," asked Hinton, "the drinking song? Maybe she could do that."

Yearwood rolled her eyes. "Don't you think that's so known and dated that it has the same problem as Elvis?"

"If you can't find anything else, I would love to see you do that," said Hinton. "It would certainly give the critics something to work with."

The conversation had clearly hit an impasse. The silence, but not the tension, was broken by Borchetta. Borchetta was second-generation promotion. His father, Mike Borchetta, had been head of the department at Curb Records out in Los Angeles, where his son had grown up. Borchetta had spent a couple of years traveling in road bands—rock and country both—before deciding that his future was on the phone. He had moved to Nashville and spent a couple of years working at MTM, back in the days when Yearwood was minding the record label's front desk. When MTM folded, he worked as an independent for a couple of years. Shipley had been sufficiently impressed that she put him on the MCA staff full-time in 1991.

"Well, I guess I'm going to go walk the line," he announced.

"I don't hear the first knockout single." Borchetta scanned the room for some show of support; no one said a thing. ("It was like someone dropped a large turd into the middle of the room," Fundis said later. "Everyone avoided it.")

"Well," said Fundis, ignoring Borchetta, "I guess we need to make a decision."

"It has to be up-tempo, since we're coming off a ballad," said Shipley.

"What do you want?" Borchetta asked Fundis.

"I think it's 'Say You Will' or 'Memphis.' "

"Is it possible for us to hear both finished?" asked Hinton.

"I can get them ready by the first of next week," said Fundis.

"You did 'Memphis' at the ASCAP lunch," said Shipley. "Radio guys have mentioned it back to me afterward."

"That's certainly the one I like best," said Brown.

Borchetta, though, pressed on. "I just don't hear another 'She's in Love with the Boy.' "

Finally Yearwood stepped in. "I don't want to try to do what I did last time," she said somewhat testily. "That's not what this is about. I'll be lucky if I find another one of those in my career. It is a great song, Garth liked it, I liked it, but nobody knew it would endear me to every little girl in America."

Brown moved in, trying to steer the discussion back to the next single. "The thing about 'Memphis' is that it has this young thing about it, short skirt, cowboy boots."

At Hinton's request, Fundis played both "Memphis" and "Say You Will" one more time.

"It really does smoke," Shipley said as "Memphis" finished.

"It really just paints a picture for me," said Brown.

"I'll start getting treatments for a video," said Rickman. "I want to get creative with this."

Moments later, Bruce Hinton declared the session over. "I've got to get back for a meeting. We'll talk again next week." With that, the MCA executives were out the door. It was half past eleven.

No one had questioned the quality of the album, but the surprise was that only Borchetta had voiced the obvious. Of the ten songs, only "Woman Walk the Line" and "Oh Lonesome You" were straight-out country. It wasn't that Yearwood was trying to cross over, but most of the album certainly didn't fit easily into the definitions of what country radio accepted as country music. It wasn't that she and Fundis had disregarded the market-place. They were simply following the lesson Jack Clement had taught Fundis so many years before. They did what they felt and kept their story intact. How that would sell was still a question mark.

"Shall we kneecap Borchetta?" asked Paschall as soon as the door closed behind the executives.

"I've got something special for him," said Yearwood. "I don't remember 'She's in Love with the Boy' wowing him last time." And they were off into a blow-by-blow rehash of the meeting.

"I was surprised at Bruce's reaction to 'Devil in Disguise,' " said Fundis. "Now what do we do?"

"I guess it's politics," said Yearwood. "I get the feeling Bruce had it in his head to say no before he got here. There's friction between Sony and MCA. Remember, Al [Teller, president of MCA Records] hates Sony, so Bruce doesn't want to do anything to help Sony out. The only way he can justify it is if he can see some benefit for MCA. But if it's on Sony and it's coming out at the same time, it's hard to see how that can happen."

"Well, I guess that's out. Should we record something else?"

"If we find something."

"What about Haggard?"

"There are songs that work live that don't work in the studio. The only way to do it is to blow it out. I would hate to cut it and then have them make us put it on the record. I think I made my point about the song being dated. Well, I guess we should call Ken."

She picked up the phone and handed it to Fundis. "I can never get through the codes here," she said. It was still not ten in L.A., and Kragen wasn't in. His secretary said she would call him at home, and within three minutes he was back to them.

"Let me try to turn this into a conference call," said Fundis.

He went to the phone in the anteroom, pushed a few buttons. But this man who could control hundreds of thousands of dollars worth of recording equipment was done in by his phone system. "Let's just talk to him separately," he told Yearwood.

She related her version of events—Borchetta's objections, Hinton's rejection of "Devil in Disguise"—then passed the phone over to Fundis.

"Everyone except Scott seemed to be into it," he said, and spent the next five minutes giving his version of the meeting.

"Let me call MCA," Kragen told the producer. "Let me talk to Trisha again."

"Garth doesn't seem to think it went badly," Kragen told her. "Except for Scott."

"Well, I guess I was a little negative," Yearwood conceded.

"Let me try to get hold of Bruce," Kragen said. "I'll be back to you as soon as I know more."

It took a half hour or so, but Kragen finally called back. "I talked to Walt," he told Yearwood. The marketing chief is regarded as the least political of the executives, someone who will tell you what's going on rather than what he thinks you want to hear—or what will serve his own purposes. "Walt thought the meeting went real well, and Hinton is unhappy with Scott. He took him aside afterward. Everyone really does think it's a great album."

She thanked him, assured him she wouldn't worry about it. In truth, she looked far from convinced.

Kragen had told Yearwood about a few other pieces of business. Revlon had a new name for the perfume: "Shameless," which was fine with her, as long as it was okay with Garth Brooks, who had taken the Billy Joel song to number one. Kragen also had another one of his fairly regular brainstorms. "How about a concert with you and Reba and Wynonna? RWT. Righteous Women Together."

She couldn't focus on it at the moment, she told him. She needed to get back to the album. Kragen promised to call as soon as he heard from Hinton, and Yearwood turned back to Paschall and Fundis.

"This has just been a great couple days. The dog barked all night, I got mascara all over my face this morning. When I went to get her last night, Chris was there with his new girlfriend. It was awful. I don't want him, but does he have to date someone else?"

"I know," said Fundis. "He's supposed to just shrivel up and die."

"Who does he think he is, going on with his life? Okay, I'm depressed enough. Why don't we work on 'Woman Walk the Line'?"

While some of her vocals were fine, there was still some fine-tuning to be done. A couple of lines had come off fast and flat. They spent an hour doing touch-ups. Kragen finally called back just after two.

Hinton really had been appalled at Borchetta's outburst. As far as he was concerned, the comments were out of line. Yes, Hinton liked the album, but he was very much against "Devil in Disguise." He insisted that the reasons were aesthetic, not political, but the result was the same. If Fundis and Yearwood were adamant, he would reconsider, but all in all he thought the song was inappropriate.

Whatever the status of "Devil in Disguise," they still had to think about harmony singers. Fundis and Yearwood knew they wanted Vince Gill. He had sung on her first album, and his tenor would work well on "Oh Lonesome You" and "Move That Mountain." On "Woman Walk the Line" they thought they'd try to get Emmylou Harris herself.

Did she want to include Garth Brooks on this album? She hadn't had much contact with him since the concert tour. And though she assumed their relationship was in good stead, she wasn't quite sure. If he was willing, if he was in town, she'd love him to do harmony vocals on "Nearest Distant Shore." Still, given that he had yet to ask her to sing on his new album, she was a little nervous that he might say no.

Then there was the matter of Don Henley. They had sent a tape of the two songs, "Walkaway Joe" and "Down on my Knees," to Kragen the week before, leaving it up to him to contact the singer. Yearwood was a little ambivalent. "I don't want this to look like 'Oh, she had Garth Brooks, and now she's got Don Henley,' like I'm dependent on some man for everything I do." That, though, had yet to become an issue. She was still waiting for him to get back to her.

The larger problem was what to include on the album, and whether to schedule another session. Without "Devil in Disguise" they still had the requisite ten cuts, three upbeat songs and seven slower pieces. It wasn't a balance that either was happy with. Paschall was assigned the job of calling publishers to drum up another upbeat song. It had to be done in a matter of days. Fundis and Yearwood were supposed to have their final song selection at MCA in two weeks.

* * *

Out in L.A., Jude Johnstone had no idea if Yearwood had finished her album. For the last three weeks, she had been frantically trying to finish the song she had told Fundis about.

It had been a tortuous birth, even for this slowest of songwriters. She had started working on the song in November of 1987, after her father's death. They had always had a strained relationship; there was love, but there was always distance between them. The month before, she had got a call that he was ill and in the hospital. She wanted to go home to Maine, but her mother counseled against it. She was sure he was going to recover; if Jude turned up, he might start thinking he was on his deathbed.

One morning Johnstone went to a coffee shop to meet a friend for breakfast. As she outlined the situation, she decided that she would go home, regardless of her mother's admonitions. As she was leaving, her husband walked in the door. He had just got the call, he said. Her father had died.

She wrote the last three lines and half of the first line of the chorus (". . . my heart's in armor/Though I meant to let you in/In an effort not to harm it/I have missed my chance again") in the days after his death; over the next years she filled out the three verses. She made it as much a song about lovers as parent and child: "It's about everything you ever meant to do and never quite managed," she explained. "It's about regret."

She had just about finished the song when she met Fundis. The only thing missing was half of that first line. When she played it, she would hum those first three bars, then slip into the second line. "I knew it was time passing, I knew it was a long *a*, but I just couldn't pull the words out of my brain."

But she had promised Fundis she would try. For two weeks she had worked on the song, to no avail. Finally, she asked her husband to take their two-year-old daughter away for the afternoon so she could have time on her own to think. As she sat there, on the piano bench, pencil in hand, the solution came. "One more day," she wrote down. "It was so simple," she said afterward, "I just couldn't find it before."

She reserved some studio time for a demo and asked a friend to do the sound engineering. She did everything else (the piano and vocals) herself, and three days later she had a tape. But when she brought it home to duplicate, she realized it was too "hot"—

the sound had been recorded at such a high volume that she couldn't duplicate it without distorting the music. On May 20 she called Fundis. She had finally finished the song, but she needed a few more days to get the tape copied.

"We're already done," Fundis told her. "Send it to me now. Overnight." She handwrote the lyrics on a sheet of legal paper and arrived at the Federal Express office just as it was closing. Then she sent her only copy of "Hearts in Armor" off to Nashville.

CHAPTER 15

P ASCHALL DIDN'T GET THE PACKAGE WITH JOHNSTONE'S TAPE until late the next afternoon. He opened it, then called Fundis, who was over at the studio working on Collin Raye's next album. The song is great, Paschall told him. But the producer was caught up in meetings all day and wouldn't have a chance to get to his office until the next morning.

The next day, Fundis had an early unpleasant meeting with an aspiring songwriter. He finally listened to the song in midmorning, and though he liked it, he thought they had enough ballads. At eleven that night, still at the office, he decided to put on "Hearts in Armor" again. This time he was smitten, and he knew Yearwood would feel the same way. He called Johnstone and left a message on her answering machine. "I really like the new song," he told her. "I'm not sure we can use it on this album, but we'll definitely use it next time."

On his way home, he drove by Yearwood's house and left "Hearts in Armor" in her mailbox, along with another tape by Jamie O'Hara and a note: "Check out the Jude ballad. O'Hara is for your listening pleasure."

Yearwood was heading home to Georgia for the weekend. It was the tenth anniversary of her high school graduation, and she had been invited back to Piedmont Academy to give the commencement address. She listened to the tapes as she drove to Atlanta. She tried to call as she drove through the Smokies, but her cellular phone didn't work. As soon as she hit Chattanooga, she tried again, and this time she reached him. "I love 'Hearts in Armor,' " she said. "We have to put it on this album." She also liked one of the songs on the O'Hara tape, "For Reasons." Maybe they could record both? Fundis agreed to put a session together for the next week.

Yearwood was nervous about that graduation address. She wanted to say something memorable; she simply had no idea what it might be.

She showed up on graduation day looking much as she had when she marched down the auditorium aisle to collect her own diploma a decade before. She wore a calf-length flowered dress, little makeup, glasses—much more college coed than country star. She had decided against notes.

"Ten years ago yesterday," she said after she took the podium, "when I was giving my salutation, it was pouring down rain, and no one could understand a word I said. I wish it was pouring rain right now. I talked with people from my class, and we couldn't remember who our speaker was, so I'm not going to assume that anything I say will be everlasting in your minds. . . .

"One thing, though, I did want to tell you how important it is to set a goal, even if it is something totally unattainable. I don't remember when I told my parents, 'I'm going to be a country music star.' . . . But if I didn't believe it could happen, it never would have happened. Whatever your goal is, no matter how farfetched it seems, don't be afraid. . . .

"A lot of people ask me, 'You finished your education, you graduated with honors, don't you think you wasted your time? No one asked to see your diploma when you got your record deal. Don't you think you should have moved to Nashville right after high school and made this happen?' I don't believe that. . . . I sing for a living, but I'm a corporation. I have twenty or thirty people that rely on me, and it's important for me to know how to run a business, and I learned that in school. . . .

"I felt that for what I wanted to learn there was no textbook. But I knew that it was a business, like everything else. And I had a plan: Move to Nashville, get to where the music was, get work, get my voice heard. It's never too soon to have a plan, because you never know when opportunity is going to come along. You can't necessarily create an opportunity, but you can be in a position to take advantage of it once it comes along. . . .

"Success for me is not selling a million records, it's doing what I'm happy doing. . . .

"I also want to thank the faculty at Piedmont for the quality of the education I got here. I didn't appreciate how important that was until I got to college and a lot of my friends couldn't cut it because they had such poor high school educations. . . .

"Thank you for asking me to come back and speak. I've never done anything like this before. My tendency would be to grab the microphone and take requests. I'm sure it was riveting and everyone is going to remember it forever."

The students and faculty stood and applauded, then the school principal took the podium and declared September 19, her birthday, Trisha Yearwood Day and gave Yearwood a parchment scroll honoring her "scholastic excellence, her perseverance of a dream, her commitment to family and roots."

There was, of course, a price for celebrity. Yearwood had precious little quiet time. Just about every hour of every day was accounted for. Between life on the road and life in the studio, solitude meant an occasional weekend with Reynolds. Fans expected autographs, radio programmers expected phone calls, reporters expected interviews. Country singers don't just smile and shake hands, they hug, they kiss, they run round-the-clock campaigns. The public face is constant cheer, effortlessly personable, easily accessible. They are the politicians of the entertainment industry, each a sort of chamber of commerce unto him- or herself.

Mostly, Yearwood looked past the flotsam, the foundered marriage, the friends who had unintentionally slipped by the wayside, songwriters and musicians who had been part of her life as a demo singer, who had tried to help when she was looking for a deal, who had never heard from her after her career turned asteroid. "I would have figured she would have kept in touch," said Kent Blazy, the writer she had met in college, who had introduced her to Garth Brooks. "The last time I ran into her, she said, 'I'll call and give you my new number.' I tried to get a couple messages to her, but I never heard back. Maybe I just overestimated our friendship."

It wasn't that Yearwood wanted to erase the past, she simply felt that she didn't have time for it. "I haven't talked to Kent in about a year, but I do talk about him," she said, as if invoking his name was penance for moving on. As she had told that crowd of reporters in Los Angeles, the only ones she kept close were her family—father, mother, sister—her fulcrum as she tried to balance her public and private lives.

By the midpoint of 1992, Yearwood was fast becoming an icon: the daughter every parent wanted, the young woman every small-town southern girl wanted to become. "I think I stand for taking charge of your life," was how she put it. "I feel like I'm trying to do that. . . . Some days are better than others.

"If I look at what I'm trying to do, I'm not trying to make any major political statement. Music is about raw emotion to me. When I listen to music, it's because I want to think about something or I want to forget about something. If anyone can get something from me, it's what I stand for as a woman, what it takes to be independent, to take charge of your life and the courage to follow your heart and do what you think is right, even in the face of criticism. That part has been hard for me. I was the girl from a small-town Georgia family. You don't rock the boat. I was in every club. I got straight A's. I didn't date bad boys. I didn't drink, and I didn't smoke, and I didn't stay out past midnight. No one talked about me because there wasn't anything to say. I had respect for my parents, and I still do. I still feel a responsibility to them. I don't want to do something that would make them be disappointed in me. I'm sure I have and I'm sure I will again, but the bottom line is I have a real respect for family. I think people know that about me. . . . Other than that I'm just trying to make a lot of money." And then she laughed.

Yearwood got back to Nashville on Monday and called Paschall to find out when the session was scheduled. The plan was for Friday night, but Matt Rollings wasn't available. He was heading off for the weekend for his girlfriend's brother's wedding. The only day he was available was Thursday. "Well," Yearwood suggested, "why don't we just do it as a piano vocal? Just like on the demo." Paschall checked with Fundis, and they scheduled two separate sessions, one, with just Rollings, for "Hearts in Armor," and the other for "For Reasons."

Yearwood spent Monday night sorting through boxes in her new house. There was a smallish study just off the living room, with its own closet and a small bathroom, and she turned that space into her office, putting her stage clothes in the closet, her awards on the wall. She called it the "Trisha Room,"—"I'm going to keep all my business stuff in there," she resolved. "That way I can close the door—and have a real life."

As she was hanging an iced-glass lampshade in the bedroom, screwing the fixture into the ceiling, the phone started ringing. Her answering machine picked up. "Hey Trisha, this is Garth. I was wondering if you could come in and sing a few harmonies on my next album." She jumped off the chair, left the lamp hanging, got to the phone before he hung up. She would love to, she said, and she had a song she'd like him to sing on as well; she'd bring a tape to his studio within the hour.

Much has been made of the so-called family of country musicians. But the fact is, Minnie Pearl never did spend any time with Roy Acuff off the Opry stage, and not much has changed. There isn't much socializing among the stars, a function, as much as anything, of the fact that they are very rarely in Nashville at the same time. There are really only two places where they see one another: backstage at the myriad awards shows and in the studio, where they do the harmonies that call back the origins of country music. They are sort of like so many class reunions; no one is expected to keep in touch until the next time around.

When she got to Jack's Tracks, where Brooks was working, the singer asked her to do harmonies for a half dozen songs, four for *The Chase* and "Unto This Night" and "Silent Night" for his upcoming Christmas album. Afterward, she handed him the tape of "Nearest Distant Shore." "When do you need me?" he asked.

"When can you come?"

He promised to be there at seven-thirty the next evening.

Fundis and Yearwood spent the day at the Sound Emporium, finishing loose ends on "Nearest Distant Shore" and adding her own voice to the harmonies in "Wrong Side of Memphis." Rob Hajacos, a fiddle player who had worked with Yearwood at the Eleventh Frame before ascending to the ranks of regular session players, came in at three to put the fiddle track on the section of "Wrong Side of Memphis" that Fundis had mimed at the session with MCA, the soaring string solo midway through the song: "I've had this dream from a tender age/Calling my name from the Opry stage/I can hear it sing loud and clear/Two hundred miles and I'll be there."

Hajacos was still working when Brooks walked through the door just before seven-thirty. He was wearing his usual studio uniform: Oklahoma State sweatshirt, sweatpants, Ball sneakers muting his "weight-lifter-in-toe-shoes walk," as one journalist had described it. He did not wear a hat.

Brooks gave Yearwood a quick, generic hug before he headed into the studio. By 7:40 he was in the sound booth, working over the chorus on "Nearest Distant Shore." Three takes later, he was finished. "Just push it way back on the mix," he said laughing. "Way, way back."

As he headed out through the control room, brushing Yearwood's cheek with a kiss, she tried to hand him a green AFTRA card for his signature. He pushed it away. "You don't need to do that," he said. "We're friends."

It was a nice gesture, but ultimately more trouble than it was worth. Union rules dictate that a singer's performance must be documented. Paschall spent half the next day trying to track Brooks down so he could get the form signed.

Yearwood spent Wednesday in the studio, reworking "Memphis" and putting her own harmony vocal on "Say You Will." For the most part, the changes were just a matter of a couple of bars, and Fundis ended up using none of them. He was content with the work she had done with the band.

She got home to find a message from Don Henley, asking which song she wanted him to do harmonies on. She called back and told him she was hoping for "Down on My Knees."

"I didn't think that was appropriate for me to sing with her," was how he put it later. He preferred "Walkaway Joe." He wasn't in love with the song, but he did believe it had commercial potential. Besides, Vince Melamed, one of the writers, was an old friend, a sideman on one of the Eagles' tours.

Yearwood was happy to accommodate him. The only question was when he could come to town. She wanted to be there when he put on his harmony. He suggested Saturday the thirtieth; he wasn't exactly sure when. He needed to go to Washington for some political business, and he could stop off on his way. She would, she said, be there.

* * *

She was due at the studio at two on Thursday to record "Hearts in Armor." Just before leaving home, she called Johnstone. "We're recording your song today," she said. "I think it would be an awfully nice album title."

The work went quickly, just Yearwood's voice and Rollins's piano in a spare sad duet. Two takes and they almost had it. Fundis called them back into the control room. "Let's listen to the demo one more time," he suggested. And they went back out and got the perfect take.

Yearwood and Fundis agreed that they wanted to keep the song simple. The only thing she wanted to add, she told Fundis, was a cello. Matraca Berg had put a cellist on the title cut of her first album, *Lying to the Moon*, and Yearwood thought that the instrument's melancholy resonance would work well on her own ballad.

"Should we put a harmony on this?" Yearwood wondered.

"I don't know," Fundis replied. "If it were the right person. It's such a solitary statement."

They listened and talked for another hour or so, then decided to call Johnstone and play her the song. Once again, they encountered the answering machine. "It's a quarter to two your time," said Fundis. "Trisha and I are sitting here, wanting to play you this thing we just cut, and I'm not going to put it on the damn Code-A-Phone."

Yearwood left just before midnight. Fundis stayed on, tinkering with "Say You Will" and "Wrong Side of Memphis." He had promised to have them ready for MCA at the beginning of the week, and it was already Wednesday. He left the studio at four, slept four and a half hours, and woke up in time to call Paschall. He had a nine o'clock meeting with Sony about Collin Raye, and there was no way he could make it.

Fundis arrived at the studio just after ten, called Paschall, and asked him to call the MCA contingent and invite them over to the Sound Emporium to decide on the first single. He was a bit worried about what they wanted, but at least Borchetta no longer seemed to be a concern.

The day after that first meeting, Hinton had called. He liked what he had heard, he told Fundis, and yes, he was going to talk to Borchetta about having a little tact. After that, Borchetta himself had called Yearwood to apologize. "I want you to say what you think," she told him. "It's okay." And she made sure to stop by the MCA offices to repeat it in person. Borchetta was, after all, a friend from her days at MTM, and as vice president for promotion, he was critical to her cause.

Yearwood and Fundis were at the Sound Emporium at five. The MCA contingent didn't arrive until nearly five-thirty, with several key players missing. Walt Wilson was stuck in a meeting, and Janet Rickman was laid up at home with bronchitis. With one exception, they assembled in roughly the same constellation as they had two weeks before. Borchetta took the seat to Hinton's right; it seemed protected.

Fundis played the two contenders in his order of preference, first "Memphis," then "Say You Will." When the music ended, the group sat silent until Bruce Hinton took the lead. "Let's hear them again," he instructed Fundis.

After the second "Memphis," Brown spoke. "That's a hit," he pronounced.

They listened once more to "Say You Will," but Brown had clearly spoken for the group.

"Play 'Memphis' again," said Shipley.

"That's it," said Brown when it had finished. And the group went rolling off into promotional possibilities. Once again, they talked about how good the video would be.

"We should play off ASCAP," said Shipley, referring to Yearwood's performance at the Country Radio Seminar months before. "We do something like . . . 'You heard it first at ASCAP.' "

Nobody ever came out and talked about problems with crossover, but the rationale for the decision seemed clear. This was still only Yearwood's second album, and she needed to be placed solidly in the country market. It was the sort of thing done far more easily with a song whose lyrics celebrated the Opry than an impudent love song that sounded as if it could be the latest single from Bonnie Raitt.

"Let me just play you one more thing," said Fundis. "We did this yesterday."

It was the first time he'd played "Hearts in Armor" since they'd recorded it. He was hoping it was as good as he had remembered.

It was.

"I don't know if it will work on radio," said Hinton, "but it's gorgeous."

Borchetta said not a word during the forty-minute meeting. He went in, as he put it, "with tape on my mouth" and kept it on throughout. The meeting, all agreed, went exactly as it should have the first time.

At a quarter past six, Brown peeled out of the lot in his silver Mercedes, and made a quick stop at home before cruising down to his condominium in Panama Beach, Florida, for a week. As his secretary put it, "He needs to rest before Fan Fair."

Garth Fundis didn't have the luxury of even a single day off. He had scheduled Yearwood's last recording session for Friday night.

Of the original players, only Bayers, Walker, and Mason could make the date. Pomeroy was off on the road with Don Williams, and Rollings was at that wedding. Fundis got substitute piano and bass players and added a fiddler, Rob Hajacos, who had worked on "Memphis." Hajacos arrived drinking something that appeared to be beer. Fundis eyed the bottle warily. "It's nonalcoholic," Hajacos said when he saw Fundis's look. "Excalibur. It's Friday, I thought I've got to have a beer, but I can't because I'm working. This is the alternative."

Yearwood showed up at a quarter past six, carrying a stack of photos. Kragen had prepared a marketing brochure using six pictures from the St. Nicholas shoot (cleavage and all). Four were from the "come hither" series in front of the makeup room mirror; there was also one of Yearwood in a graveyard, her dress slipping off her arms, along with one of her smiling from the front seat of her Mustang convertible, leather motorcycle jacket pushed down her shoulders. The photos had not been submitted for MCA approval.

"If I were to hang these in the drum booth, do you think you'd play better?" she asked Bayers.

"Will you sign something really good?"

"Maybe I could put it on the ceiling."

"That would be even better," he said, and the room filled with lascivious laughter.

Fundis beckoned her off to a corner, where he had piled a group of tapes. "If we have time for a second, which do you want?"

Fundis had brought along "Blue Guitar," just in case she wanted to give it another try. She wasn't interested. Instead, she picked out another O'Hara song, then asked Fundis to play "Hearts in Armor" for the band.

"Now that's something you should have been singing at the Eleventh Frame," Hajacos said when it was over, adding, "Did you get the job at the Fifth Quarter?" a Nashville steak house that hired talent on the cheap.

"Yeah," Yearwood replied. "Starts tomorrow. Tonight actually. So could we hurry this up?"

Hajacos handed out the charts for "For Reasons."

"Oh, my goodness," Yearwood exclaimed in mock southern belle dismay. "It has *damn* in it. Maybe we should just say *darn* instead. Never know what radio might think."

It took nearly an hour of run-throughs before Fundis thought they were ready to tape. The problem was tempo: It started at ninety-three beats a minute, moved up to ninety-five, then, just past nine-thirty, back to ninety-four. "I'm sorry to be so indecisive," Fundis said after the final switch. Finally, at half past ten, after five takes, Fundis was satisfied. There was no time for another song.

The band, though, wasn't ready to leave. "What's the first single?" asked Bayers.

"I guess they've decided on 'Memphis,' " Fundis replied.

"I want to hear it again. And 'Walkaway Joe'."

" 'Say You Will,' too," Mason chimed in.

Mason, Bayers, Hajacos, and Walker line-danced to "Memphis." They quieted down during "Walkaway Joe," then, during "Say You Will," Mason reprised his fandango.

When it was over, just past eleven, the band packed up to go. "You're gonna be a star," said Mason as he walked out the door. "I can feel it. You're gonna sell a million records."

The record, though, was still a long way from over. The next day, Don Henley was coming to town.

In terms of preparations, Henley's appearance might have been a lunar landing. It wasn't that his needs were so complicated— a chauffeured car, a hotel room—it was just that he couldn't seem to decide when he was showing up. At first it was Saturday afternoon, then Saturday evening. Finally he called and said he'd get there late Sunday.

Yearwood had originally planned to pick him up at the airport, but she was jittery when she woke up Sunday morning. The studio was her comfort zone, and as she put it, "I thought I would be better off if he just showed up and I was working."

Paschall was waiting for Henley at the gate when his flight got in at 6:35. The face was a little more lined than Paschall had expected, the square edges of the jaw a little softer, but the singer still looked good. His outfit hewed to the Texas-L.A. axis—black jeans, black T-shirt, faded jean jacket, slightly scuffed oxblood cowboy boots, and sunglasses, worn indoors.

Paschall introduced himself and asked Henley if he wanted to go to his hotel. Straight to the studio would be fine, he replied. They small-talked their way to the baggage claim, Paschall asking about Walden Woods, about Henley's last time in Nashville (a signing for a book promoting the Thoreau project), about when he had last been in the studio (quite awhile ago). Henley explained that he was going to Washington on yet another environmental mission. Developers were trying to expand the airport in Aspen, where he had a ranch, to accommodate 747s, and he wanted to put a stop to it. They ran into Dan Dugmore, a steel player who had worked with Linda Ronstadt, recently moved to Nashville from Los Angeles. Then a stranger walked up, asked if Henley was who he thought he was. Henley reluctantly acknowledged him.

"I love your stuff," the man said, and stuck his hand out to shake Henley's. Henley briefly took it, then turned to Paschall, instant bodyguard. "Let's get out of here," Henley said. In an instant, this forty-five-year-old man had turned into the rock star, the celebrity hounded by screaming crowds. His eyes locked into a twenty-mile stare, he hunched his shoulders against a pressing crowd of one, and they headed out to the car.

Henley got in, asked for the phone, and spent the rest of the fifteen-minute ride making calls. When they arrived at 7:20, Yearwood was in her booth, working on "For Reasons."

Fundis pushed the talk-back. "Hey, you got company," he said, and Yearwood headed into the control room. Yearwood introduced Henley and Fundis, and they talked about the flight and, once again, Henley's last time in Nashville. By seven-thirty, Laney was playing "Walkaway Joe," and Henley was listening and pacing. After it finished, he asked if he could hear it again. He heard it five times before he felt ready to go in and work on his vocals. Fundis had set up a microphone smack center studio. Henley put on his sunglasses and his headphones and took his seat in front of the control-room window.

Yearwood and Fundis sat together in front of the console. The producer was the one with a bad case of nerves. "I don't want to tell Don Henley he's flat," he said after one clunker, and handed the talk-back over to Yearwood. ("I have never seen him like that," Yearwood said afterward. "It was almost like he was a little kid—I ended up producing a lot of the 'Walkaway Joe' vocal.")

As Henley worked, Yearwood listened, not quite believing that this voice she had grown up listening to was now trying to work with her licks. "Trisha," he said, after one of the last lines of the chorus, "Sing me this lick, because I'm trying to sing it like you are."

She started laughing. "That's a Don Henley lick," she said. "I learned that little trill from you."

Henley finished just before nine. He hadn't had dinner; neither had Yearwood. They sent the driver to pick up sandwiches. After he left, Henley realized he was running out of cigarettes. Paschall was dispatched, and though Henley had asked for Marlboro Lights or Salems, he came back with both.

"We have another song we'd like you to hear," Yearwood said as they finished eating. "It's by Jude Johnstone, the woman who wrote 'The Woman Before Me.' "

That, said Henley, was one of his favorite songs from the first album. Laney put on "Hearts in Armor." Yearwood still wasn't sure if she wanted a harmony on the song, but if he heard a place where he could come in, maybe, just maybe, it would work.

"It's gorgeous," he said, but he did have one problem. The last line in the second verse was sung almost as if it was a question. It wouldn't have been spoken like that, he said, why sing it like that? "It's meant to stick out. It's fine the way it is," Fundis thought. But he didn't want to contradict Don Henley.

"What do you think?" Henley pressed. "Do you want to do a fix first?"

"I think we're going to leave it," Yearwood answered, without consulting Fundis.

"That's fine," Henley replied. "Let's get to work."

Henley looked at the lyric sheets, and for the next fifteen

minutes he ran through the song. Nothing quite worked, thought Fundis, who was wondering if he should simply leave Yearwood to sing alone. Still, he held his tongue. Then, a half hour into it, Henley found a harmony that worked. He sang his lines and looked up at the control booth.

"You know," he said, "I take it back about what I said about that lyric line. It's fine like it is."

With that, Fundis reclaimed his talk-back, and became the producer once more.

By ten, Fundis and Yearwood were happy with what he had worked out, but Henley wanted to press on. He worked another hour and then two, circling back over the same spots five or six times. Then, just before midnight, they got to the end, trying to figure out where he should be. "I think she needs to be on the last line by herself," said Fundis. "It's such a solitary statement. But it would be great if you could get on the line right before it." Yearwood had ended the song by repeating the last two lines ("I would finish what you started/If I had that chance again"). Henley sang with her through the first round and then left her to sing alone. He listened again to the two last lines and asked if he could try once more. He stayed silent through the first line, then joined her for those last six words. Fundis listened. "It makes it sound like there's hope there," he said. "I love it." And with that, they knew they were done.

Fundis sent the driver out to get some beers and wine coolers. They sat back, listened (Henley kept his sunglasses on), and had a couple of drinks, the first time there had been alcohol in the studio since Yearwood had started recording.

"I'm dying for a cigarette," said Henley. "Do you mind if I smoke?" Nobody, of course, did. Yearwood even asked for one of her own. She had smoked maybe two dozen cigarettes in her entire life, and the inexperience showed. She had all the right moves, and they all seemed a little posed. She looked like a teenager practicing to be an adult, rehearsing the part in the mirror.

"Could I have a tape?" Henley asked, yawning. "I promise not to play it for anyone." Laney recorded a cassette.

Henley thanked Laney, who thanked him in return. Then it was Fundis's turn, then Yearwood's. "You don't know how special this is to me," she told him.

"I really enjoyed it. It's been my pleasure. The singer before me must have been hard on you," he said, a play off the first line of "The Woman Before Me." "We'll be talking."

Yearwood walked him out to his car and repeated her promise to take him out for Nashville barbecue. He had an early afternoon plane, he told her, breakfast would have to do. He would call in the morning.

As she walked back into the control room, the star-struck young star opened the pack of Marlboro Lights that Henley had left behind. "I think I need another cigarette," she said.

For awhile then, Yearwood and Fundis just sat there and played the song over and over. Just after one, Yearwood picked up the phone and dialed California. Johnstone's answering machine picked up. "Hi Jude. This is Trisha Yearwood. We recorded a harmony with this new guy, Don Henley. I just wanted you to know."

She and Fundis listened to "Hearts in Armor" four times more. Just before two they decided it was time to head home.

Don Henley called Yearwood just after eleven. She was still in bed. It was too late for breakfast, and with Henley catching an early-afternoon plane, there wasn't time for lunch. He wanted to listen to the cuts again, he told her. He promised to check in from Washington. He called that evening. "There are a couple things in 'Hearts in Armor' I'm not happy with," he told her. "I'd like to come back and work on them."

The question was when. Yearwood was leaving in two days for another tour through Texas (Dallas, Longview, Houston), and she couldn't be back before Sunday. That was fine, Henley replied. He would meet her at the studio Sunday afternoon.

They met at the studio and worked until just after five. The changes, to both Yearwood and Fundis, were minor—he added a short, sweet lick at the end of the second chorus of "Hearts in Armor"; on "Walkaway Joe," he took two words to himself, echoing "Walkaway Joe" after the song's penultimate line. Henley was a perfectionist, going over his part a dozen times or more to get the right notes, the right inflection. "I wanted it right for her sake—and mine," he said afterward. "You know, vinyl is final." Reminded that records were no longer being made, he amended his aphorism. "Plastic," he said, "is drastic."

His plane wasn't leaving until nine, so Yearwood had time to make good on her promise of barbecue. They ended up at the Country Cabin, a middling diner near the Vanderbilt campus. It wasn't her first choice, but on Sunday night in Nashville, you take what you can get.

They spent much of the meal talking about the difference between rock and country stardom. Henley never let himself be photographed with fans, he told her. That's the way the tabloids get their pictures. And he refused to sign autographs. They, too, ended up being sold. It was a strategy meant to keep fans at bay, lessons no country star could afford to learn—especially now. In less than forty-eight hours, Trisha Yearwood was due at the Tennessee State Fairgrounds. Fan Fair, Nashville's five-day country-music petting zoo, was about to begin.

Part IV
THE FANS

From Fan Fair to Branson

> I been hungry too many times
> and I remember the times.
> These people have fed me. I
> won't ever forget it.
>
> —Loretta Lynn

CHAPTER 16

"*F*AN FAIR," EXPLAINED LOUDILLA JOHNSON, WHO, WITH HER sisters Kay and Loretta, is copresident of the International Fan Club Organization, as well as the Loretta Lynn Fan Club, "is simply the greatest thing that happens." Nashville's homespun hajj was first called in 1972, when the Country Music Association and the Grand Ole Opry joined to bring a little extra business to town. A hundred-odd stars signed up for that first fair at the Municipal Auditorium. Five thousand fans were expected, considerably fewer turned up. Irving Waugh, then head of WSM, shipped in recruits from a local army base to fill out the crowd.

The twenty-four thousand tickets to Fan Fair 1992 sold out three months in advance. For the better part of a week each June, singers come in off the road and spend their hours, unpaid, on the Tennessee State Fairgrounds. Their ten-by-ten-foot booths are crammed side by side in barns labeled for livestock: mule, swine, poultry, rabbits, and sheep. Two hundred-odd country stars, everyone from Garth Brooks to Tammy Wynette to George Jones to Kitty Wells, hold audiences with supplicants, who spend three, four, five, and six hours waiting in line to offer up gifts and receive the sacramental autograph in return.

"The country music fan isn't like any other," explained Evelyn Shriver, a publicist who has represented everyone from Larry Hagman (in his J. R. Ewing days) to Diana Ross. "They bring homemade gifts, they bring food—it's sort of an extension of family."

You can go to the back room at the Randy Travis museum cum store off Music Row in Nashville and see the offerings: quilts, carved likenesses, hand-painted statuettes of Jesus and the Virgin Mary. Before his first child was born, Garth Brooks says, he found out the baby's sex in order to accommodate fans. "We felt if the people knew what sex they were dealing with, then their gifts could be used instead of being stored away."

Woe unto the country star who isn't grateful for the attention. When Ricky Van Shelton refused to sign an autograph for Joan Hollis, a Connecticut secretary, after one recent concert, she vowed revenge. "I'm not going to see him anymore," she huffed. "And I'm not buying his records again, either."

"The thing that goes over here is abject humility," said Ken Kragen. "If you don't have it, they will come after you."

Country music's fans have turned history on its head. Just as they have torn down the pedestals beneath their stars, bringing their celebrities down to civilian level, so, too, have they collapsed the distance between past and present, kitsch and art, putting it all on an equal plane.

That old-is-good, new-is-better philosophy has made possible one of Nashville's more peculiar landmarks. This city, which bills itself as "the Athens of the South" because of its score of colleges and universities, also has its own version of the Parthenon, billed as "the world's only full-sized replica of the Athens original." It was first built of wood for the Nashville centennial in 1887; by the twenties the beams were rotting, and the whole structure was replicated in concrete. The Athenian Parthenon may be missing its Athena; not so its Nashville counterpart. In 1990, Alan LeQuire built what is described as "the largest indoor statue in the Western World," a forty-one-foot rendition of the Greek goddess (imagine the Midas Muffler Man in drag) complete with owl and shield, cast in blended fiberglass.

Along Music Row, history can be conferred almost instantaneously. The Hank Williams Museum displays Hank junior's steer-head-and-spur-festooned bathing trunks, as well as a special-edition liquor decanter with, as the display notes, a music box that plays "Family Tradition." Down the road, at the Nashville car museum, Alan Jackson's 1990 Mustang has been christened a relic. There's a certain antiseptic quality to it all, which helps to explain why, when the Opry show moved out to the spangling new theater at Opryland, National Life had, until the preservationists intervened, figured on tearing down the old Ryman Auditorium.

In this topsy-turvy world, Fan Fair is not just for those who want to see stars. It is a place where dreams can be bought for forty-five dollars a booth. Hank Sasaki, born in Fukuoka, Japan, had moved to Nashville three and a half years earlier, after fifteen years selling encyclopedias in his homeland. His booth, decorated with a kimono and cowboy boots, offered T-shirts illustrated with Japanese and American flags and emblazoned "Country to Country," along with his latest single, "I Want to Be a Japanese Cowboy." Dawne Anita Diffie, the aunt of the singer Joe Diffie and herself an aspiring singer, made the seven-hundred-mile trip from Broken Bow, Oklahoma, on her quarter horse, Doc. "All my life I worked as a secretary to support my music habit," she told *The New York Times*, which acknowledged the newest country boom by sending a reporter to chronicle Fan Fair. "Now it's time for my music to support me. I feel that my time is here."

Then there were those whose time had come and gone. Donna Douglas, Elly May Clampitt on *The Beverly Hillbillies*, was in town promoting her arts and crafts festival in Eureka Springs, Arkansas. She looked like a waxwork—cheeks rouged too pink, hair still in pigtail. Three years after his death, there was even a booth where, for ten dollars, Keith Whitley's faithful could join his fan club and receive a membership card, a biography, an eight-by-ten photo, and a subscription to the triannual Whitley newsletter which, among other things, provided an ongoing roster of Keith Whitley namesakes.

The booths at Fan Fair are generally homely affairs, arts-and-crafts projects constructed by loyal fan-club members. Doug Stone's was a minicave of fake boulders. Johnny Cash's had a Christmas motif, its tree festooned with June-and-Johnny-emblazoned ornaments. Lorrie Morgan held court from behind a faux adobe facade. Yearwood's pavilion, a Ken Kragen production, was an entirely different order of business.

"You're trying to get attention," Kragen explained. "You want everyone in the industry, as well as the fans, to be talking about it. The ballots for the CMA Awards went out last week. This is a time where visibility counts."

Toward that end, Yearwood bought space on ten Nashville billboards emblazoned with her likeness and the legend "PLATINUM BLONDE." She paid over twenty thousand dollars to have professional set designers build her an ersatz sound studio, complete with a full-fledged sound system and double-paned glass doors designed to eliminate all outside noise as effectively as any professional setup. The plan was to have fans march through, sing along with two choruses of "She's in Love with the Boy," and leave with their efforts immortalized on cassette.

The booth might well have been the most elaborate on the fairgrounds, but as Kragen discovered when he stopped by just before noon on Monday, it was also in violation of fair rules. Not only was it a good two feet higher than regulations allowed, but since it was airtight, it required its own air-conditioning system.

"It's going to have to come down," a thickset official told Kragen. "Didn't you see the regulations?"

"Is there any way we can make this work?" Kragen replied.

For ten minutes they dickered, the official demanding that he eliminate the air conditioner, Kragen insisting that it was impossible. Finally they cut a compromise: Kragen could have his two extra feet and his air conditioning as long as the booth was moved to another corner of the building, where it would be less obtrusive. It had taken forty-eight hours to put up the booth. There were less than twenty-four hours to take it down and rebuild it before the gates officially opened.

Kragen was unfazed. "It will get done," he said. "It has to."

Ten miles across town, at Opryland, his prize pupil was in the midst of dress rehearsals for the Music City News Awards. There are more awards in country music than at your average 4-H show. And the Music City News Awards, voted on by the magazine's subscribers, and aired on cable rather than network television, were not among the brightest lights. Yearwood had been nominated for something called the "Star of Tomorrow." For the singer, the main event of the evening was her date. Robert Reynolds was escorting her to the show, and it would be their first appearance as a couple at an industry event.

Yearwood had a short solo on the show, a chorus and a verse from "Wrong Side of Memphis." Kragen watched as she took the stage during dress rehearsal; she walked stiffly across the stage as she sang. It should have been an easy show, but Kragen was concerned. "I don't think she should be moving like that," he said. "She hasn't been rehearsed." He walked to the stage and grabbed her arm, imploring her to stay center stage.

Yearwood spent another hour getting ready for the show—having her hair done, her makeup put on, stepping into a custom-made off-the-shoulder, turquoise velvet gown. The back was cut low, the sleeves, at Kragen's behest, tailored full and long. She took the stage just after eight-thirty, about halfway through the program.

She started out strong, her voice mellifluous, her moves certain. Then, as she sang, the neckline slipped off her left shoulder. Then her right. Gravity took over. By the last line the neckline was down to her biceps, her strapless black bra was in clear view of the camera. There was no going back; the show was being broadcast live.

"I can't believe that happened," said Nancy Russell, who was hovering just offstage. The dress was but one of Russell's worries. After Yearwood's performance came the award for Star of Tomorrow, and both of her clients, Yearwood and Travis Tritt, had been nominated. "This is bad," said Russell, "having both of them. New artist? He's sold four million albums. She'd get it in a heartbeat if it weren't for him." Russell took a deep breath as George Jones walked out to announce the award.

"The winner," he said, "is Travis Tritt." The young leather-clad singer took center stage. He thanked Jones for his rendition of his own hit song, "Here's a Quarter, Call Someone Who Cares," then Warner Brothers, then Ken Kragen, then "especially my publicist, Nancy Russell."

"It is going to be a good week," Russell said.

Ten minutes later, the show was over, and Yearwood returned to her dressing room.

"I felt the dress go down, but I figured I would be better off to just keep going," she said as she walked in. "What am I going to do? Stop in the middle of the song and tug? If I'd won, I was going to thank those last-minute voters who called in when my dress fell off. I have to talk to Dolly about how she holds her dresses up."

As soon as she changed clothes, the dressing room became public turf. Ken Kragen arrived with George Christy, the Hollywood gossip columnist.

"What are you calling your new album?" Christy asked.

"We're thinking about *Hearts in Armor.*"

"I'm not so sure," Kragen said. "Doesn't it sound a little negative?"

"If you have any other ideas . . ." she said.

"What's the album cover?"

"We want to use one of the shots you see on the billboard," said Kragen.

"I don't think she should have her eyes closed," Christy advised. "You want to be accessible."

"I think you're right," Yearwood replied. "Aren't we supposed to have lunch tomorrow? Maybe we'll come up with something by then."

Yearwood was sufficiently chatty and charming, but every minute or so she glanced over at the door. Reynolds was hovering outside, not necessarily interrupting, but making his presence known. A friend of his was playing at a local club, and Yearwood had promised to go with him. Christy and Kragen stayed for twenty minutes of small talk; Yearwood and Reynolds got to the club at half past eleven. It was nearly two before she got home.

The next morning, the singer woke up with a blinding headache and a bad cold and missed a nine o'clock photo shoot for Dean Markley, a guitar-string manufacturer. She was scheduled to be at her Fan Fair booth an hour later. It was the last place she wanted to be.

While Yearwood was shaking off the effects of the night before, Kragen and Fundis were out at the fairgrounds surveying the reconstruction. The producer had worked until four in the morning setting up the sound system and had come back in hopes of seeing the operation in action.

At 10:05, Kragen's cellular phone rang. "She's not coming for another half hour," Kragen announced.

"I can't wait," said Fundis. "Hey, buddy, can I borrow your phone?" He dialed up his office; Paschall was already there. "How are you doing? I'm at the fairgrounds. No, she's not here. Listen, I've got Buddy Emmons coming in to play steel on 'For Reasons.' Just have him listen to the demo and do that in the right key. I'll get there as soon as I can."

Ten thousand fans were temporarily corralled in the fairgrounds' parking lot. The stampede to the stars was getting ready to begin.

* * *

On Monday, Laurie Lumbrezer and Linda Calvin, both in their twenties, had driven down eight hours from Fayette, Ohio. They had checked into their motel and set their alarms for three-thirty so they could get to the gates promptly at four.

"I was just too excited to sleep," said Lumbrezer. "I just had to see Garth." The young women had the line to themselves for the first hour or so. By ten the crowd numbered in the thousands. When the gates finally opened, the scene looked like the Pamplona bull run, ten thousand people who should have known better running as though their lives depended on it.

By 11:15 the lines snaked around the buildings. Security guards figured Garth Brooks's line to be eight hundred strong, and he wasn't scheduled to arrive until noon. There was a half-hour wait to get on a sleek black bus emblazoned "Clint Black," even though, as its driver, Mike "Jolly" Cole, conceded, "Clint doesn't use this bus—never did. It's just for PR." It would take two hours or more—in a separate line—to see the singer himself.

"I don't know who I'm in line for," said Helen Luck of Damascus, Maryland, "but it was a long line, so I figured it had to be good."

At 10:30, the Yearwood contingent (the singer, Arnold, and Gary Falcon, who was working security) had appeared at the Fan Fair gate. Two more security guards arrived to escort her to her booth. She walked through the double-paned glass doors at 10:45. Two hundred people were waiting.

For the next fifteen minutes, Kragen, Falcon, and Arnold worked out logistics—how many people could be taped at one time, who would handle the front door, who the rear. At eleven, Sound Studio Yearwood was up and running.

"Keep your hands in the ride," said Falcon, who was guarding the front door, as they ushered in the first round of fans: a ten-year-old girl from Murfreesboro, Tennessee, two brothers from Roland, Oklahoma, and a middle-aged woman from Wichita in a Garth Brooks T-shirt.

"This is my first year having a booth, so you'll have to bear with me," Yearwood whispered as "She's in Love with the Boy" came on. "My throat is a little weird, so you guys will have to do most of the singing. Don't be shy."

The effect was country karaoke. At first, the brothers and the

Kansan simply mouthed the words, but when Yearwood herself joined in, full throttle, the entire contingent began singing.

"We should ask if they're families," said Kragen as the first group filed out. "Then we can fit more people in."

Another group, six this time, filed in. Arnold offered a bit of backhanded encouragement: "The last group couldn't sing. You have nothing to worry about. Who knows, maybe we'll find a star." Dead silence through the first verse. Then Yearwood started coaxing them along. "You know you sing it in your car. You might as well sing it here." And prompted by a star, they managed a weak chorus.

And so it went: Move 'em in, sing a verse, a chorus, a half dozen snapshots, a tape, move 'em out. At about noon, there was a knock at the backdoor of the booth. An overweight woman, a half dozen "I'm A Regular Joe Diffie Fan" buttons pinned across her chest, tried to push through to take a picture. Nancy Russell, who had taken over guard duty from Kragen, shook her head no, but the woman pressed on.

"Won't you please just take a picture of her for me?" she pleaded, and for a moment the camera changed hands. "I can't," Russell replied. "If I do it for you, I have to do it for everyone."

"How dare you," the woman said. "How could you get my hopes up like that and then disappoint me."

And then she stomped off into the crowd.

Yearwood left her booth just after one for her lunch date with George Christy.

"I can't do this," she said as Arnold drove her to the restaurant. "I feel terrible. I'm just going to go in, say hello, apologize, and go home and take a nap."

As she headed into the restaurant to beg off, Arnold—her hired mother hen—worried. "She shouldn't have gone partying. I don't care what he says today. I don't care how much fun they were having. He kept her up too late. Today she's paying for it. She's a bright girl, but she has to learn her limits."

Kragen, though, wasn't particularly perturbed. She had had a few moments to talk to Christy the night before, so that job was done. As for Robert Reynolds, Kragen by and large approved. He wanted only two things from his clients' romantic attachments: "They should be supportive and not interfering." To his mind, Reynolds was covered on both counts.

Yearwood made good on her pledge to Arnold. She skipped an MCA party in favor of a few extra hours' sleep. At 7:30, she had to be back at Fan Fair. The record label was sponsoring a concert, and she was due on stage at 8:20. Two hours later, Reynolds and the Mavericks were going to be performing at the Ace of Clubs, and Yearwood was determined to be there.

Her dress for the MCA show was a scarlet twin of the dress she had worn the night before. This time a support strap had been added across her bare back. Her performance lasted just twenty minutes, long enough for the obligatory obeisance to Garth Brooks and her current single, "The Woman Before Me," which, as she told the audience, had just gone number one. And at the end, as she did at nearly every concert, she left them with "the one that did it": "She's in Love with the Boy."

She was back on the bus by 8:45, but the evening's obligations were not over. This was the first day of a relentless week; she had signed and performed, and still there was more. A reporter and cameraman from the E! channel, a twenty-four-hour entertainment network owned by Time Warner, came through, followed by Lee Adams, midday operations manager for WHYL in Carlisle, Pennsylvania. "I'm just so proud of you, you've come so far since I talked to you last year," Adams said, and handed Yearwood a plaque with gilded letters: "WHYL New Female Entertainer of the Year."

There was the obligatory hug. Then, as Adams walked out, Yearwood turned to Arnold, "Will you tell anyone that asks I feel sick? I don't want them to think I'm being a star." And she went to the stateroom to lie down.

Fundis, then Kragen, appeared on the bus, and Arnold turned to manager and producer for support: "Do you think she should go to the Ace of Clubs tonight?"

"No way," Fundis said. Kragen said nothing.

"I was hoping one of you big guys would tell her no," said Arnold. But when Yearwood emerged from her stateroom moments later, neither said a thing.

"There's news on Revlon," Kragen announced. "Garth wouldn't okay 'Shameless,' so they want to call it 'Revlon Country' instead." He brought out a trial version of the counter display, a gauzy portrait of a young woman in a wheat field, the copy set in the midst of the golden sheaves: "Revlon Country, filled with all the heart and soul of the music that inspires her."

" 'Revlon Country.' Well, it is neutral," said Yearwood. "It's not like calling it 'Nashville'. . . . I can't think about this now. I'm exhausted."

Five minutes later, Nancy Russell appeared at the bus door, and the singer headed for home.

Yearwood stopped at home, but she did not stay there. Her boyfriend's band was performing, and she was not about to miss it.

She got to the club at eleven and joined Russell in a small private balcony above the stage. Raul Malo was the main event, his sweet tenor filling the room with Hank Williams and Patsy Cline and a song dedicated to an aunt who had survived thirty years' detainment in Cuba before the government allowed her to emigrate to America. The crowd loved him, loved them.

Yearwood focused on Reynolds. He was an effective counterpoint to the Latino lead singer, equally good-looking, but more accessible—less drama, more easy charm. "I don't know," she said to Russell. "Maybe this relationship is a bad idea. He's too good-looking. He's probably only hanging out with me because he thinks it's good for his career. There are all those skinny girls out there. He could have any of them. . . ."

"Those girls have nothing on you," said Russell. "Nothing."

Yearwood sat silent. She knew Reynolds wanted her on stage for an encore duet with Malo on "Your Cheatin' Heart," but her voice was almost gone. Not only did she have three days left in her Fan Fair booth, she still had work to do on the album that would make or break her career. She had shown up for their performance, and that would have to suffice.

CHAPTER 17

*T*HE STREET ACROSS FROM THE COUNTRY MUSIC HALL OF Fame, the southern boundary of Music Row, is chockablock with establishments that do their best to blur the line between souvenir shop and museum: The George Jones Museum (best exhibit: the guitar case cum liquor cabinet); Jimmy Velvet's Elvis Presley Museum (best exhibit: olive green crushed-velvet bedroom set from Presley's Beverly Hills mansion); and the Hank Williams Museum (best exhibit: the powder-blue Cadillac he died in). Outside each stood a singer with a guitar, a set of small speakers, and a small container marked "Contributions"—a cacophony of unrealized ambition.

Marilyn Jeffries, a fortyish bottle blonde in spike heels, sailor shirt, and hot pants, was belting out "Sweet Dreams" in the parking lot between the Shoney's restaurant and motel and the Barbara Mandrell Christmas Shop. A handout described her as a one time contestant on *The Price Is Right* ("She won some great prizes on that show but the 'Showcase Prize' is yet to come!") as well as a former "Miss Truck Stop, USA." A banner across a folding table billed the show as "MARILYN JEFFRIES ON TOUR." Her itinerary, she said, included South Carolina and Virginia, with a daylong stop in Washington. "And on July thirtieth, we're playing for the president. You know, there's the White House and the Oval Office? We're playing at the Oval Office." (The White House has no record of her appearance.)

Across the street, in front of the Elvis Museum, Ringo Garza and his three sons had finally found their first gig. They could barely be heard over the rush of traffic and Jeffries's booming speakers, but they still managed a fairly rousing rendition of "Johnny Be Good."

Joy and Larry Dickie, who drove in from Newark, California, videotaped the Garzas, and placed two dollar bills in the open guitar case in front of the band. "We'll be at Fan Fair next year," Ringo senior said. "Getting started has taken a little longer than I planned, but we're finally on our way."

In the next doorway, a clown was making balloon animals.

• • •

Up at Fan Fair, the young new breed of country fan was on parade. "I'm into Confederate Railroad," said Kim Price, a blond waitress in a denim bustier from Spartanburg, South Carolina. She held out her fingernails, each painted in a Stars and Bars motif.

To stand by Travis Tritt's booth—an oversize Gibson guitar with the star inside the center hole—was to experience the full chasm of the generation gap. Just across from Tritt, behind a long table festooned with red, white, and blue crepe paper, sat Kitty Wells, one of most eminent of country music eminences. Tritt had a three-hour line; fifteen minutes would get you to the first woman to go number one on the country charts. Just after eleven, two teenage girls in halter tops headed into the building, looking for the end of Tritt's line. They looked over at Wells, mystified. "Who is that?" said one. "Who cares?" the other replied.

A moment later, a sixtyish man and woman passed by Tritt's booth after buying a couple of cassettes from Wells. "Oh, my goodness," said the man, his voice laced with sarcasm. "Should we wait for two hours to see if Travis Tritt will touch us?"

The biggest story of Fan Fair XXI was the ascension of a thickly bicepped ponytailed singer from Flatwoods, Kentucky. Billy Ray Cyrus generally appeared on stage wearing two or three layers of T-shirts, neck and sleeves scissored out to reveal a relief map of the male musculature. As his show went on, he would remove one, then the next, ending with the remnants of a faded Fruit of the Loom undershirt stretching across his brawn. The rumor, denied by Cyrus and repeated regardless, was that he had learned his moves as a male stripper at Chippendale's.

On June 4, Cyrus had made history. Thanks to "Achy Breaky

Heart," a thuddingly monotonous single written by a onetime wallpaper hanger, Cyrus's debut album, *Some Gave All*, had gone to the top of *Billboard* magazine's pop and country charts. Cyrus was the first Nashville act to have his first album grab both spots.

Cyrus's record label, Mercury, had done a savvy selling job, turning "Achy Breaky" into a dance and distributing his video, complete with dance steps, to thirty western clubs across the country in February, three months before the album was released. In the video, he was already a star, leaving his limousine to the shrieks of scores of fans.

Cyrus, a onetime cigarette-warehouse worker, was no earnest cowboy. Not only did his songs lack the finely crafted lyrics that Nashville songsmiths prided themselves on, his big hit owed its melody to "Tulsa Time," a ten-year-old Don Williams recording. What Cyrus was selling was sex, and sex made Music Row very nervous. The last time they had seen such crossover success was with John Travolta and *Urban Cowboy*. They worried that Cyrus might turn the new Nashville into a fad, as perishable as one of his torn-up T-shirts.

It was the sort of thing that was mostly whispered about over the watercooler, chatted about over cocktails. Then, on the afternoon of June 10, Wednesday of Fan Fair, a reporter for the Associated Press asked Travis Tritt what he thought of country's newest star.

"I don't think 'Achy Breaky Heart' makes much of a statement," Tritt said. "I just don't much care for the song." He allowed that he wasn't particularly thrilled with the video either. "He's stepping out of a limousine and being mobbed as he goes into a concert. This is a guy that's not even been recognized yet. This is his first single."

Even though he was saying what everyone else was thinking, it wasn't the sort of thing that was done in Nashville. Public criticism wasn't permitted in the country music family, and when Tritt spoke out, the news was as much his candor as his criticism. Which is why, even though the interview was supposed to have been embargoed for a month, it was reported on the radio that afternoon.

Yearwood learned of the fracas while she was waiting in her car in the parking lot outside the Sound Emporium. Tritt was being interviewed on a call-in show on WSIX, one of Nashville's four country music stations. "I think it degrades country tremendously," Tritt said of "Achy Breaky." "It comes out and it says that everybody in country music—instead of us producing songs that really get to the heart of the matter and really talk to the public—it says instead of that, what we're going to have to do to be popular in country music is get into an ass-wiggling contest."

Fundis pulled into the parking lot, and Yearwood gestured him over. "Can you believe this?" she said, as Marty Stuart called in to sympathize with Tritt. "Man," said Stuart, "You couldn't have opened a bigger can of worms if you said Roy Acuff was gay."

"Guess Ken's got his hands full," said Fundis. And they headed into the studio.

The plan had been for manager, producer, singer, and publicist to spend a couple of quiet hours together, but what with the Cyrus-Tritt snit, Yearwood and Fundis figured Russell and Kragen would be running late.

"Feeling better?" Fundis asked after they had taken their seats in front of the control-room console.

"Some," she replied. "Okay. Let's come up with a title for this album."

"Down on My Knees?" asked Fundis.

"I have a great album cover concept for that. . . . Okay, maybe I've had a little too much Robitussin," Yearwood replied. "I don't think 'Hearts in Armor' is negative."

"*Armor* is the problem."

"I don't think it's such a hard thing. I think it indicates strength. It doesn't have to be a happy title. What are our options? I could do a Garth thing. 'Fence This.' 'Rope These.' " She glanced down at her bosom. 'Wrong Side of Memphis'?"

"You don't want to put *wrong* in the title."

"Why don't we just call it 'Blue Guitar' and let them figure out why."

" 'Woman Walk the Line'?"

"I want a lyric. There's not another title for this album," Yearwood said. "It's got to be 'Hearts in Armor.' The only problem is the picture Ken wants doesn't fit. None of the pictures fit."

While MCA legally had control over her album cover, Yearwood was permitted to choose the art, subject to the label's approval. That was one of the ways she had justified the money spent on the St. Nicholas shoot back in March. Now, though, Hinton's objections weren't the problem; the pictures were. Their glamor didn't match what she wanted to convey. "I don't want to pick a title around a picture."

"Do you have any other ideas? Unless we come up with something that has nothing to do with the songs . . . which we could do."

"Let me call my sister."

She dialed Beth's number. "Hi. We're figuring out the album title. Is armor o-r or o-u-r? First spelling is o-r. What's the definition? Protective coating. Thanks. I'll call you back later."

"Okay," she turned to Fundis. "That's what I want to do. It's cool to me."

"I like it," said Fundis. "A lot of songs on the record are about leaving or loss or tough times. 'Move That Mountain' could be a possibility, but if we put that as the title, it's going to look like a gospel record."

"Okay," said Yearwood. "It's 'Hearts in Armor.' "

"Done," said Fundis.

And they shook hands.

"Now I get to think about liner notes. Can't I just say, 'Thank you—and Garth will tell you the rest'?"

"I want you to hear something," Fundis said. A few days before, Fundis had brought in Mac McAnally, the guitarist who had worked on her first album, to put a track on "Hearts in Armor." This was Yearwood's first opportunity to hear it.

"If Don Henley were here, this is how he'd listen," she said, putting on her sunglasses and slouching back in her chair.

"Now, just get your mind right," said Fundis.

She sat quietly as the song played through.

"Okay," said Fundis, before Yearwood said a word. "So it doesn't work."

"I just think it takes away. It makes it too ordinary, not so lonely, too warm. I still want to try the cello. I don't not like this, I just think anything else is too much. I'm scared to put strings in. Mac is simple and very tasteful. If anyone could have done it . . ."

There was a knock on the outside door. Fundis went to open it. "Did you hear Travis?" Kragen asked as he and Russell walked in. Yearwood nodded.

"Do not take this as an example," Kragen said. "For Travis that is what he is. . . . Your edge needs to be musical." He walked over and put his hand on Yearwood's knee. "Enough of Mr. Tritt. Let's hear your music."

Kragen had heard early versions of the songs, but he hadn't heard anything since Don Henley and Garth Brooks had put on their harmonies. As a rule, he kept his distance from the making of the music. His strength was selling the singer, not shaping her songs. This was his first trip to the Sound Emporium since he and Yearwood had started working together.

"Walkaway Joe" came on first.

"Boy, that's good," said Kragen.

"Can we make a pact that it's going to be a single?" Yearwood said. "I honestly think I can get Henley to work for us. I don't know in what capacity; maybe he'd do a performance video."

Next came "Hearts in Armor." It was the first time Kragen had heard the song.

"I don't know if that's a single," he said, "but it's mind-bogglingly good. Maybe that should open the album."

"We'll discuss it," said Yearwood.

"There's only one song that can follow it," said Fundis. " 'Move That Mountain.' "

"We'll discuss it," Yearwood repeated, her way of saying no. "Think we've brought in enough guest stars?"

"We're not finished," said Fundis. "I've got calls in to Emmylou and Vince."

Then they played "Nearest Distant Shore." "It's a beautiful song," Kragen said, "but it does feel anticlimactic. . . . The thing that's formulating in my mind is the quality of the record, the cleanness . . . I want to send it early to critics, to other artists. We want to create talk. . . . 'Hey, come on over. You gotta hear what I got.' I want a campaign going that's very high road."

The next order of business was the music video for "Memphis." Just as MTV had revived rock and roll in the eighties, Country Music Television (CMT), complete with its own bold-colored block-lettered logo, has been a major force behind the Nashville boom. CMT was created in 1983, and at first it was a fairly low-end operation. It changed hands twice in the eighties, with no significant improvement, before being purchased in 1991 by the owners of the Nashville Network—Group W and Gaylord Entertainment Company, the Oklahoma-based outfit that now owns

WSM and Opryland. By 1992 CMT had become the nation's fifth most popular network among twelve- to thirty-four-year-olds, the suburban cowboy's answer to MTV.

There were three videos released for Yearwood's first album. MCA paid for half of each film outright; the rest was recouped from her royalties. The financing was much the same for the first video for her second album—a fifty-thousand-dollar-budget split evenly between the singer and the label.

At MCA, Janet Rickman had solicited a half dozen "concepts" for the "Memphis" video. It was up to Yearwood to choose among them. Now, she pulled the first one from her handbag and started reading.

" 'A video for the nineties, reminiscent of the spirit of a woman determined to go by her gut instincts. A woman accessible, sensual, real and loaded with straightforward humor. . . . A visual treat loaded with unresistable [sic] personality of Trisha.'

"Do they think they're going to get this just by flattering me?" she interjected, then read on.

" 'The Action: Reflections of the approaching car. We crane down, snorkeling past the roof's textures. . . . The man slowly walks over to the soda machine and, as casually as possible, lounges against it. Boy meets girl, girl meets boy. Not that simple!'

"Oh, please.

"Next. 'It is hot. Really hot—even the shade of a tree brings no relief. We see a female counting twenty-dollar bills and laying them, one by one, into the palm of a sweaty old man. . . . She is paying the man for the car he is selling from his front lawn, a sixty-nine Tempest. . . . It is night. Parked at a roadside truck stop, the girl stretches out in her back seat. She reads a *Stars of Opryland* fan magazine. As the sun rises, she is back on the road. She travels along a rugged and dusty backroads highway. Her wheels screech to a stop, and she turns to look over her shoulder to spy a handsome young hitchhiker. She motions him in. They become fast friends. . . . The young man even takes the wheel and drives while the girl sits in the passenger seat, playing some tunes on her guitar. There are some flirtatious glances between the two travelers. The car is stopped by a wooded roadside area. Through the backseat window, we see the girl walking off into the distance. We see the arm of the hitchhiker reaching into the backseat. Is he going to steal something? He grabs the picnic blanket from the floor, pulls it out the window, and as he follows the girl into the woods we realize his intentions are romantic.'

"Not. I don't want to have a relationship in here. The song has nothing to do with that. This song is about independence. It's about leaving everything you feel comfortable about and going and doing what your wildest dream is. If anything, she's probably leaving somebody behind."

She picked up the next in the pile.

" 'She's driving a battered sixty-nine Tempest down the road, Mike the dog in the back of it. . . . She's wearing her big hair, complemented by a black leather motorcycle jacket and a short skirt. As she zooms by a sign for Nashville, she pulls into a worn and dilapidated service station somewhere on the outskirts of Memphis. As she pulls up to the gas pump, she obviously looks very inviting to the very young station attendant who's slouched in a lounge chair outside the station. . . . Trisha sits in the driver's seat, puts lipstick on, looking in her rearview mirror as the station attendant fills the tank, examining her every move. As he cleans her windshield, his eye catches her skirt, riding up her leg. . . . She slowly looks up at him. Embarrassed, he quickly looks away as she hands him the money, and she peels out into the road. She enters Nashville city limits as her Tempest races by the Nashville sign. She drives through the streets of Music City, passing museums, gift shops, and Music Row. . . . At a low angle, a shot of the Ryman Auditorium, the wheels of the sixty-nine Tempest enter the frame. The car door swings open, and Trisha's cowboy boot hits the pavement.'

"That's a cool idea right there."

"Did you see *My Cousin Vinnie*?" Kragen interjected. "That's the way Joe Pesci comes in."

" 'Trisha enters the hallowed space of the Grand Ole Opry,' " Yearwood continued. " 'Sunlight floods in the back . . . revealing Trisha in a warm silhouette. The dog appears by her side and follows her in. Trisha wanders around and finally takes a seat in the last row. The dog jumps up and takes the seat next to her. The lights in the auditorium go down, and the spotlight goes up onto the stage. Trisha is revealed on the stage in slow dreamlight motion. Suddenly we are transported back to the stage of a small club in Memphis. Trisha is onstage, smiling. The place is almost empty now with a few die-hards and hangers-on.' "

"Where's Mike the dog?" said Kragen.

"Let's lose the dog," said Trisha. "I love the idea of using the Ryman. I like it that it's Bobby Ewing—only a dream."

"Whose is that?" Kragen asked.

"Planet." The company, headed by a Yale-educated filmmaker named Gerry Wenner, had done the third video from her first album, for "That's What I Like About You."

"I should stop reading," Yearwood said, as she picked out the next one. "The doctor said reading out loud is the worst thing I can do to my voice." She pushed the pile over to Kragen.

" 'Sleazy nowhere bar. Deadsville. Local losers gathered around an impromptu stage. . . . No one really cares, not even a shaggy dog covering its ears in a corner.' This is just terrible. 'Slamcut to her closet being raped.' "

"I think we've heard enough," said Yearwood.

Kragen picked up the last in the pile. " 'It's obvious Trisha is taking it to the edge with "The Wrong Side of Memphis". . . . She's got lots on her mind and she's on the road with nothin' but attitude. . . . We'll have Trisha riding and playing and singing in a 'driverless' convertible. . . . Trisha will be all over the car doing different things. Sometimes singing, sometimes not. Always cool. Sitting on the back . . . sitting in the passenger seat, maybe even standing in the back seat.' "

Kragen stopped. "Planet is the best treatment, far and away," he said.

"I loved working with Gerry," Yearwood said. "I love the Ryman, the dog has to go. If we don't want to be literal, I can use my own car in this. Or," she said hopefully, "we could get a Harley."

"If the song is about a sixty-nine Tempest, let's try to use one," said Kragen. "Why give people a chance to criticize?"

As the conversation drifted, Kragen looked at his watch. "I've got time to watch the second half of the Lakers game," he announced, and moved toward the door.

Russell, still fretting about the Billy Ray Cyrus brouhaha, joined him. "I've got to deal with Travis," she explained.

(During Fan Fair, Cyrus met Tritt's criticism with silence. Seven months later, though, after accepting his trophy at the American Music Awards, a pageant sponsored by record sellers, Cyrus pulled a coin from his pocket. "For my critics," he said, "here's a quarter, call someone who cares," a gibe at the Georgia singer and his hit single.)

"So I guess 'Hearts in Armor' is it," Yearwood said when they were alone.

"What about the album cover?"

"I want to get the proofs of all of the shoot from Ken. I'm not sure what I want."

They circled back to the music. Yearwood was still intent to try a cello on "Hearts in Armor."

"Who was on Matraca's album?" she asked.

"There was a cellist and an arranger."

"If you had a fiddle player come in, they would just come in and do what they do. Why can't a cello player do that? I don't have a problem leaving it like it is, but I would like to know that the cello didn't work—like you needed to know about the guitar."

They sat still for a moment, then turned to the lineup for the album. They had already decided not to press the issue of "Devil in Disguise," but even without it they had twelve songs, and they could only use ten. "I'm still not thrilled with 'You Were Right from Your Side,'" said Yearwood. "Even with the new lyrics."

"That brings us down to eleven songs. 'Now She Knows'?"

"I like it, but lyrically and melodically it's a lot like 'Nearest Distant Shore.'"

"Same writer."

"Let's hold it."

Fundis started ticking off the remaining songs, sounding like an assembly-line foreman taking an inventory of work done and work still to do.

" 'Nearest Distant Shore.' Done. 'Walkaway Joe.' Done."

"We could try cello on that, too."

Fundis shook his head no. " 'Oh Lonesome You.' I talked to Vince. He said his voice is shot, I should call next week. 'For Reasons.'"

"I want to try Raul.'"

"When?"

"Next week."

" 'Down on My Knees.'"

"I think that harmony would be good for me or Vince."

" 'Woman Walk the Line.' I'm still trying to get in touch with Emmy. 'Move That Mountain.' My thought was not to use harmonies, just get a bunch of people—Vince, Emmy, Marty [Stuart], maybe Garth again, to sing a line or two."

"It feels like it's turning into a collaboration."

"We need something to make that song go. Let's listen to it."

As the tape finished, Fundis and Yearwood turned to each other and said, simultaneously, "Vince and Emmylou." They laughed and traded high-fives.

"After I get past this new artist stuff maybe I can use my own band," she said. Fundis ignored the comment.

"Well . . . let's see if I can get some work done. What needs fixing?"

"Want to try 'Woman Walk the Line'?"

She went into the studio and started singing the first three lines of the song. Fundis listened, pushed the talk-back. "You're still sounding off," he said. "Why don't you go home and get some rest, get rid of that cold?"

She was home before midnight, the earliest she had got to bed all week.

Thursday, day three of Fan Fair, was more of the same: four radio interviews, three hours at the booth, a half hour break for lunch, five more radio interviews, a break for dinner, then, at eight o'clock, what is called an "in-store," a half-hour acoustic set and autograph signing at a local record store, in this case, Tower Records.

Yearwood was performing with two other MCA acts: McBride and the Ride and Mark Chesnutt. Backstage, essentially a storeroom, was crammed with a full complement of agents, managers, road managers, and publicists. "Hi," Kragen said as he bounded in the door. "I'm here representing the Achy Breaky anti-defamation league."

Russell, in two layers of black T-shirts and a short black skirt, glanced over at Kragen. "He hates what I'm wearing," she said. "I know it. It's too rock."

Kragen walked over to Yearwood and launched into a discussion of her album cover. "I talked to Jim Kemp about using the photos on the billboards. Those are fine with him."

"I don't know if I like them," said Yearwood. "I think the photo should have something to do with the title."

"The photo is the highlight of the cover. The question isn't what goes with the title, it's which will sell the most albums."

"If I'm going to use that photo I'll have to change the album's title. Look, I don't want to talk about this now, I have a performance to do."

She finished her three songs just after ten, but that was just the beginning of her evening. By the time she had scrawled her last "Love, Trisha Yearwood" at a long table set up among the CD racks, it was twelve-thirty and her manager was long gone.

By Friday morning the end was finally in sight. There was a morning interview with KMPS radio out of Seattle, twenty minutes with an Irish TV show, half an hour with a reporter for a Canadian newspaper syndicate. At noon Yearwood had promised to sign autographs at the CMT booth.

Yearwood arrived on time for the signing, but she was escorted off before the end of her allotted hour. Billy Ray Cyrus was next on the schedule, and his fans were getting restless. Moments later the crowd parted as Cyrus, together with his bodyguard ("He used to do security for Michael Jackson," Cyrus's publicist breathlessly confided to a reporter) made a wedge through the throng. A small green step stool was brought out so the star could pose above his minions. He stayed up there a full three minutes, giving the crowd a succession of clenched fists and peace signs, their precise significance entirely unclear.

Cyrus signed for just over three hours. Outside, James Wordon, a long-haul truck driver from White House Station, New Jersey, had just finished calling his boss. He thought he might be in a little late on Monday.

"I slept outside twice," he said. "I wanted to see Garth. I ran, but I was too late. They let people in through another gate first. By the time I got there, the line had already been cut off. You have got to be extremely fast at this."

While he didn't get Brooks's autograph, he did get good seats for his concert.

"To be able to get to see the people that help you through life with their music," he said, made it all worth it. "Most of the songs Garth Brooks sings just fit me to a tee. Friends of mine hear the songs Garth Brooks sings, and they say, 'Oh, that's just like James.'

"I've already reserved my room for next year. It's not like I'm sleeping there, but you gotta take a shower every so often. I'm sort of looking forward to going back to work. I need to recuperate."

So did Yearwood, but she was due on her bus at eight o'clock Saturday morning for a ride to Fort Payne, Alabama, site of the annual June Jam, the biggest annual outdoor country concert in America.

CHAPTER 18

ALABAMA HAD NEVER BEEN MUCH OF A CRITICAL SUCCESS, BUT then again, critical success goes only so far. Alabama has sold more records, fifty million worldwide, than any group in the history of country music. When they put on the first June Jam in 1982, as a benefit for their hometown, 30,000 people came. In 1992 more than 62,000 people had paid $25 apiece to see a score of country acts do 20-minute turns on the stage. For the singers, it was an annual rite; a coda to the five-day Fan Fair blitz.

When Nancy Russell arrived at Yearwood's bus for the four-hour trip to Fort Payne, she was tired and tense. The Jam was the first time Cyrus and Tritt would be appearing at the same event since the sniping had started, and Kragen had asked her to run interference.

Yearwood turned up at 8:25 wearing an oversize Garth Brooks T-shirt. "Hi, I'm a germ," she said as she climbed onto the bus. "Germ" (pronounced with a hard *g*) is Nashville's answer to the groupie. Nobody professes certainty of the precise etymology of the term. "It's someone who gets in a star's face backstage and wants something from them," explained Bill Ivey, who heads the Country Music Foundation, "sort of a variation on the words germ and worm." Which, given the looks of many of them, makes a certain uncharitable sense. In the rock world, the ones who make it through the various levels of security seem to be shapely blondes. In country, where access is accorded to almost everyone, the hangers-on often look more like the outcasts in tenth-grade phys. ed., the last ones picked for the team.

The bus was off to Alabama by a quarter to nine, through the rain, down the highway, past the sign for the "ACUFF CUNTRY [sic] INN," past the billboard for "ROCK CITY. SEE SEVEN STATES." Yearwood played the most recent versions of the songs from her new album. "Praise God," said Ric McClure, the drummer, after "Hearts in Armor" came on. "Put a little more emotion in your singing, babe."

By ten all except Yearwood and Russell had retired to their bunks. The publicist pulled out the contact sheets from the St. Nicholas shoot so Yearwood could see her options for the album cover.

Yearwood picked out the graveyard shot. Her skirt was up, her eyes averted from the camera.

"We could put this on the cover," she said. "Let's create a little controversy."

"Ken doesn't think that will sell records."

They considered another shot—Yearwood sitting on some dilapidated stone stairs, her hair up, wrapped in a scarf.

"This one has a boob problem," said Yearwood. "Oh my God, there's cleavage."

After an hour, Yearwood had found nothing she both liked and thought would satisfy MCA.

"I just won't have a cool cover, that's okay. . . . You know how labels are, they don't want anything out of the ordinary. If I were pop, they'd let me do this."

The bus pulled into the Fort Payne Quality Inn just after noon. With thirty-odd singers' buses, the parking lot looked like a country music convention: Marty Stuart's *Texas Troubadour*, Earl Scruggs's old bus, was there, along with Joe Diffie's and an orange coach with the Hebrew word for blessing, "Mitzphah," inexplicably scrolled—and misspelled—across the back, Billy Ray Cyrus's temporary transportation until his own custom coach was finished.

Moments after Yearwood's bus had parked, there was a knock at the door, and Diffie, who had known Yearwood since her days as a demo singer, climbed on.

"How are you holding up through this?" he asked her. "I had two days up twenty-three hours straight. It's zombie city out here." Outside, a gaggle of overweight blondes were circling the vehicles. "They've got *germ* written all over their foreheads."

"I guess I should go in," Yearwood said. "I've got a one P.M. phoner to do."

With that, Russell and Yearwood left the bus, the publicist navigating the singer to her room. As they passed through the motel courtyard, Russell spotted Billy Ray Cyrus holding court for a reporter.

"Should I go see him?" Russell asked Yearwood.

"Your call."

Minutes later, the issue was decided for her. A helicopter, Cyrus's transportation to the concert site, landed in a field just behind the motel, and the heartthrob and his bodyguard ducked their heads and ran for the cabin. It looked like a scene from *China Beach.*

Yearwood headed back to her room for her phone interview with the *Springfield* (Mo.) *News Leader*, preparation for her appearance the next week in Branson, Missouri, the Ozarks town that had become an upstart showplace for live country music.

"Hi, it's Trisha Yearwood," she said to the interviewer as she lay back on her bed. "Yeah, I have a new album. Ten new songs. No, it's not a wild departure. I've had a year's worth of growth, and the album reflects that. I think my voice has gotten better, and I think some of it comes through on tape. Hopefully it gets better as you go. I don't know where it peaks out and gets worse, but we're on a roll so far. . . . No, I don't think Nashville has a patent on being the only place to play. . . . It's my first time to Branson; I want to see what everyone is talking about. . . . Yeah, my life has changed. I sort of think of it like starting up a business—for the first couple years I don't have much time for myself, I don't take vacations, all my profits get invested back into the business. You make the sacrifices, and then, in a few years, you have the rewards, and hopefully it's been worth it. . . . I'm looking forward to meeting you, too."

Russell went searching for Tritt as soon as the bus arrived at the concert site. She quickly discovered that he had yet to arrive. As for Cyrus, he had already helicoptered off. The only crisis of the afternoon had been entirely Cyrus's own making. After his encore—a second round of "Achy Breaky Heart"—the singer had decided to do a dive into the crowd, à la Axl Rose.

Unfortunately the stage was not set up to accommodate such antics. The crowd was fenced off about ten feet back, and Cyrus fell far short of their outstretched hands, straight into a mudhole.

A brace of security guards intervened as the fans made a rush for him. The fence held, no one was hurt. The fiasco did, however, leave performances running nearly three quarters of an hour behind schedule.

"What's he going to do if the next record bombs?" Yearwood wondered.

"Call Travis and ask him to slam it so he can get some publicity," replied Russell.

Yearwood spent the next three hours with her parents, who had shown up at the motel earlier in the afternoon. They generally came to every concert within a day's drive of Monticello. Just before she made her entrance, Jack Yearwood put his hands on her shoulders. "I just want you to know how much I love you, how proud I am," he said. Then, with his wife, he stood off in the wings as his daughter took center stage.

She was offstage and back on the bus by seven. Arnold brought her dinner from the steam tables. Gwen and Jack Yearwood came back with their own a few minutes later.

"Let's hold hands and say the blessing," said Gwen.

"I can't," said Trisha. "I already ate."

But Jack went ahead anyway, a breakneck-speed invocation ("Lordmakeustrulygratefulfortheseallthyotherblessingsamen") unintelligible to the uninitiated. "Until I was twelve, I thought he was speaking in tongues," said his younger daughter.

Afterward, she retreated to the back of the bus, alone. At about seven-thirty, her mother went back to talk to her. "Are you all right, dear?"

"No. I'm sick. I've got two days in Nashville, then I go on the road for a week. I have no idea how I'm going to get my album done."

"I'm sure you'll be fine, dear," Gwen replied, and hugged her. For a moment, at least, she seemed to relax.

Yearwood spent just about all of Sunday in bed. After a day at home with his family, Garth Fundis arrived at the Sound Emporium at seven-thirty, reveling in the prospect of a few hours alone at the studio. He wanted to start thinking about the order of the songs on the album. Usually, sequencing was the last thing he worked on, but this time, everything was running so late he didn't have that luxury.

He wrote out the name of each song on a small slip of yellow paper, and started shuffling them around. The idea, as he put it, was to "put on a show, keep the listener entertained. You don't want two songs in the same key. You want to break up the ballads with something upbeat."

He also had to take into account the songs' length. It didn't really matter for the compact disc, since CDs have only one side. On the cassette, though, he wanted to make sure that the first side was at least as long as the second.

"You don't want blank tape on the A side," he said.

"People get annoyed, they think the music has stopped."

He fussed with his yellow slips until just before four in the morning, coming up with a preliminary sequence. The record would start with "Wrong Side of Memphis," then go into "Nearest Distant Shore." "Hearts in Armor" would be the penultimate song. He considered "Move That Mountain" the encore.

There wouldn't be much time for sleep. He had to be back in the studio by noon on Monday; Raul Malo was coming back to town to do harmonies for "For Reasons."

Yearwood worried about her relationship with the Mavericks. It wasn't that she was nervous about tainting her image as the girl next door (the Randee St. Nicholas photos were evidence of just how ambivalent she was about all that). She was just concerned that her support of Raul Malo would look like a campaign to jumpstart her boyfriend's band. There is a long and unhappy history of successful female country singers and the men who scurried along after them—construction workers turned managers, sidemen turned producers, stories that played out like Norma Desmond with a drawl. Now that she and Reynolds had gone public, Yearwood took pains to explain that her respect for Malo was genuine, separate from her relationship with his bass player. She didn't want anyone to start whispering about coattails. After all, she had never even considered putting Reynolds on her record.

The executives at MCA were quite pleased with this new alliance. "Other female artists might have been worried about their image," said Tony Brown. "It wasn't what I would have pictured. The Mavericks are playing the same role for her that Rodney and Rosanne did with me. . . . She's hanging around with some strong personalities, which will do nothing except raise her awareness level." And it certainly didn't hurt that the band recorded on MCA.

Malo got into Nashville just before noon on Monday. Yearwood picked him up and drove him straight to his hotel before heading into the studio to work on her vocals on "For Reasons." Her voice was still in bad shape, but she had to come up with something for Malo to work with. After two hours, she ended up with a rough version of what she wanted—close enough that his version would match her finished vocals.

Malo slept through the afternoon. The Mavericks' tour was considerably less plush—and more grueling–than Yearwood's. With their idiosyncratic mix of rock and country camp—they were almost a postmodern country band, not unlike Lyle Lovett or k. d. lang. They were having roughly the same experience as those singers: great reviews, minimal radio play, which translated to a hard time getting dates at most of the bigger clubs and fairs. Walt Wilson at MCA had come up with a provisional solution, what he called "the lounge-around tour," a circuit of hotel bars. For a Holiday Inn or a Sheraton, an evening with a semi-known group represented little risk. The fees, though, were low, and there wasn't enough coming in to pay for a bus. They traveled by van, their instruments packed into a truck. Comfort—and sleep—were scarce. Malo's six hours' sleep at the Hampton Inn were the best rest he'd had in weeks.

It was just before seven when Yearwood delivered him to the studio. Fundis played him "For Reasons," and he worked for two hours before he felt ready to go into the control room and listen to his handiwork.

"It works," said Fundis.

"Thank you," said Malo. "I guess I'll be heading back to my hotel."

"We have something else we want you to listen to," said Fundis.

"I'll be back in town next week," Malo replied, not quite realizing what the producer meant.

"You're not going anywhere," Yearwood said. They put "Say You Will" on and sent Malo back into the studio to work up another harmony. By ten, he had finished with his second set of vocals.

"Guess I'll be going," he said once more, and once more, Yearwood and Fundis told him they had something else they wanted him to hear.

Fundis had already sent a first version of "Wrong Side of Memphis" to MCA, but when he heard Malo with Yearwood, he wanted to put him on the song. It was the hardest song for Malo to do. "She variates different notes so precisely," he said, "I can't do that except by mistake." It took him an hour, but finally he came up with a part Fundis was happy with.

Yearwood and Malo left just before midnight. She was due back in the studio ten hours later. Fundis had found a cellist to play on "Hearts in Armor."

Carl Marsh, the arranger, and John Catchings, the cellist, did not belong to the Nashville session scene. Though they had done other country records—they had worked on the Matraca Berg album Yearwood so admired—they mostly did pop and rock acts, among them ZZ Top and Amy Grant. This was the first time they had worked with Fundis.

Unlike the session players, they used scored music, a sixty-eight-bar melody composed by Marsh and played by Catchings. Essentially, Marsh and Catchings were to the regular session players what a cook who measures with teaspoons is to one who simply pinches out the proper ingredients.

Fundis generally addressed the Nashville players in broad strokes. With the cellist and arranger, each bar was dissected, each note minutely examined. Fundis and Marsh sat in the control room, while Catchings worked in the studio. Protocol dictated that the producer direct his comments to the arranger, who, in turn, told the instrumentalist what was required. "On bar thirty-eight we don't need that much separation between the notes," said Fundis, after Catchings played a two-beat E, followed by a D. "Thirty-nine needs to be smoother."

"I think if he plays again, he'll be fine," said Marsh, who then pushed the talk-back. "John, could you play bars thirty-eight and thirty-nine again?"

"On the third beat of bar twenty-nine, instead of the A quarter note, I'm wondering if we should just extend the B-natural," said Fundis.

"I'd rather he not use the passing note," said Yearwood.

Again, Marsh pushed the talk-back, directing Catchings to play the bar with two notes instead of three.

"That works," said Yearwood. It was a painstaking processs, and midway through, Yearwood's concentration flagged. Scott

Paschall came in with a draft of the liner notes for her album, and she turned her attention to checking the typed pages for errors. "Last time I just thanked MCA Nashville," she said. "I want it to be MCA Records this time—that'll include Al Teller."

Her dedications and thank yous were quiet testimony to the changes of the last year. There were no friends listed on this album; virtually all the names on this year's roster were part of the extended operation of Trisha Yearwood, Inc.: Sheri McCoy, along with Russell and another publicist from Evelyn Shriver's operation, Joe Harris, Malcolm Mimms, Fundis, Paschall, and the company that manufactured her T-shirts. She gave her love to her family, her thanks to her "family on the road."

She did include one nonbusiness notation. The line after her acknowledgements read "Proverbs 4:23" [Protect your heart, for it is the wellspring of life], courtesy of her sister, who was far more conversant with such things.

"It all looks okay," she said, finally, then read the last line out loud. " 'Thank you for a wonderful year!' Let's leave that out. I think I've thanked everyone enough."

Yearwood listened as the cellist went over his part one last time. "They'll never put this on radio," she said, and then she went to drive Malo to the airport.

After Yearwood left, Fundis listened to the cello track again. It was pretty, he thought, but there was a problem. The instrument shared the same register as Don Henley. When the two were on together, the effect was a sweet low blur.

While Fundis worried over "Hearts in Armor," Yearwood was still trying to figure out what to do about her album cover. She was due at MCA Records at four, and she had to choose a cover photograph. She still had no idea what she wanted.

Kragen had called the day before to suggest that she stop off and see a set of photos that Jim McGuire—the photographer who had done her first album cover—had taken two weeks before for *Harper's Bazaar*. There were a few black-and-white shots with Yearwood's own motorcycle jacket, another with a different black jacket wrapped stolelike around her shoulders, cleavage obscured. McGuire had sent Polaroids of the session to Kragen, and the manager thought one of them might just work for the album cover. The pictures were sultry, though not as prettified as the St. Nicholas portraits. The black-and-white composition lent them a somberness that, in Yearwood's estimation, fit the title "Hearts in Armor."

McGuire gave her copies to take to the meeting at MCA. Jim Kemp, it turned out, liked them as much as she did; he promised to have a couple of sample covers worked up by the time she was back in town the next week.

Yearwood left MCA for home, to pack for a week on the road. She also had to get hold of her ex-husband, who was still baby-sitting her dog, Roseanne, when she was out of town.

While Yearwood tended to domestic affairs, Fundis was due at the studio to do a final mix on "Memphis." Mixing a record is the aural equivalent of watching paint dry. It is long, repetitive, and painfully laborious (with Fundis, each song could take days), the individual adjustments virtually indistinguishable to the un-trained ear. Over the next weeks, as he mixed the album, Fundis would determine the precise sound of Yearwood's vocals, how much echo would be in her voice, whether the fiddle would be obscured by the acoustic guitar, how loud the harmony singers would be. The mix is a sort of chiaroscuro, the variation of light and shadow that allows the images to emerge.

Gary Laney spent two hours working on a preliminary mix for "Memphis." Fundis was supposed to be there at eight, but as the minutes turned into hours, the engineer started fussing with the furniture in the studio. He set up two speakers, three rugs, and an arm chair. "Sometimes you just have to hear something somewhere else," he said.

Which is what Fundis did when he came in, two and a half hours late. His daughter's Little League team had made the play-offs, and he had promised to watch her pitch. He sat back in the armchair, listened to "Memphis" three times over, and decided on a few minor changes. He turned down the vocals, making them less "bright" by turning down the treble in Yearwood's voice. He spent forty minutes adjusting the fiddle, turning down the other instruments to make it stand alone. At a quarter to twelve, he packed up a finished copy of the tape to bring to Yearwood. He wanted her to hear "Memphis" and the cello on "Hearts in Armor" before she got back from Branson, and her bus was pulling out at midnight.

CHAPTER 19

IMAGINE LAS VEGAS CONCEIVED BY ANDY GRIFFITH. WELL, maybe Andy Griffith with a little help from Liberace. Lots of lamé, lots of sequins—no liquor, no gambling, no girls. That's Branson, Missouri—population 3,706, and a theater for every 132 residents, 28 in all.

Branson is set smack in the middle of the Ozarks, the beautiful but impoverished mountains that straddle the Missouri-Arkansas line. This is Pat Robertson country, the place where George Bush, worried about losing the right, kicked off his ill-fated 1992 presidential campaign. At the Branson theaters, just about every show culminates with an ode to God or America or both. At Loretta Lynn's show in the Lowe Theater, a stage-sized flag unfurls as she sings "God Bless America." Boxcar Willie, who has owned a theater and museum (featuring his whiskey-decanter collection) in Branson since 1987, does "Jesus I Need to Talk to You" (also available on his album: "Jesus Makes Housecalls"). Shoji Tabuchi, a classically trained Osaka-born violinist with a Beatle haircut and a taste for sequined dinner jackets, finishes each night with an extravaganza of red, white, and blue: fireworks, lights, an American flag. He started playing country when he was sixteen, inspired after hearing a fiddler named Howard "Howdy" Forrester at a Roy Acuff concert. He went backstage that night and introduced himself, and some years later he reintroduced himself to Acuff in Kansas City, where he was working nights playing country music. Acuff invited him to appear at the Opry, and Tabuchi showed up the next Friday night. It took another decade and change for Tabuchi to discover Branson. He did his first show there in 1981; he now claims to have the town's biggest draw. Mel Tillis is one of the rare Bransonites with a secular finale. He sings "They Call the Wind Mariah," complete with the "Curtain of Rain," a technothunderstorm pumped from a trough below the stage to an overhead sprinkler.

Over five million tourists trekked to Branson last year, 99 percent in a caravan of tour buses, Winnebagos, campers, and cars. The interstate runs clear through to Springfield, then it's a straight shot down the three-lane Highway 65 to the outskirts of town. Traffic gets bad on the three-lane road, but the true horror begins inside city limits. Driving the five miles of County Highway 76, lined with twenty of Branson's theaters, can take an hour or more, depending on how close it is to showtime, which, as in Las Vegas, comes twice a day.

The building of Branson is an epic—dirt-poor hilltown turned Ozark Shangri-la. Until the coming of tourism, the hard Ozark land had never been good for anything except the occasional tomato patch. The area's only distinguishing characteristic was a large cavern just outside town, Marble Cave, named optimistically for the stone the cavern's explorers never did find. The cave was purchased in 1889 by an amateur archeologist named William Henry Lynch; his two spinster daughters ended up running it as a tourist attraction. In 1949, they granted a $5,000-a-year, 99-year lease on the property to Hugo and Mary Herschend, an Electrolux salesman and his wife. By the midsixties, under the direction of the Herschends' sons, the plot on top of the cavern had been turned into a fantasy mountain village, complete with grist mill, steam train, and blacksmith. They called it Silver Dollar City and gave out the coins as change.

In 1959, as the Herschends were starting up Silver Dollar City, four sons of a Baptist preacher named Donald Mabe started performing as "the Baldknobbers," named after a group of local vigilantes. The brothers set up chairs in the local police station, and their wives stood on street corners trying to lure patrons. Eventually the Mabes, along with another local family, the Presleys (no relation to Elvis), built the first Branson theaters along Highway 76. Their routines were not unlike the Opry: a little fiddling, a little singing, a lot of corny comedy. ("He's not too bright," says the Presleys' emcee, introducing one of the hillbilly clowns. "When I asked him what he thought about red China, he said, 'Looks good on a blue tablecloth.' ")

By the early seventies, the Ozark town had manufactured a reputation as one of the cradles of country music. In 1974, when Thomas Hart Benton was looking for the faces to fill his great mural in the Country Music Hall of Fame, he went to Branson. He found Raymond Buffett, a fiddler who lived in a shack surrounded by junked cars, and Chick Allen, whose instrument was the jawbone of an ass.

The first big name in town was Roy Clark. The *Hee Haw* fiddler and owner of the Sound Emporium built his own theater in 1983. The tourists were already there, coming half a million strong to see Silver Dollar City, accustomed to staying the night to catch the Mabes and the Baldknobbers. Clark invited his friends to perform for a week or two at a pass; Mel Tillis and Boxcar Willie liked it so much they decided to stay.

There has been talk that Branson could spell the end of Nashville, that the Ozark town is about to become the next big thing. That threat has been rather overplayed. The fact is, Nashville has never been much of a place to see performers—sure, there's Opryland, but that's only three theaters; the city has only four other concert venues that seat more than a couple of hundred. And in Branson, most of the performers are country music's elder statesmen and -women, who have outlived their record contracts and are looking to get off the road. The line on Music Row: "We breed 'em, they bury 'em."

That may be, but they are certainly going in style. Branson's biggest theater is the $13 million, 4,000-seat Grand Palace, opened in April 1992. Built by the same folks who own Silver Dollar City, it looks, in the words of Ray Stevens, like "Tara meets an atomic reactor." The facade is antebellum mansion, its pillars gleaming white against the Ozarks, the rear a vast pile of granite and steel cubes. That unlikely edifice was Yearwood's destination on the night of June 15. The next day she was scheduled to open two shows for Glen Campbell.

Yearwood's bus pulled out on time, just after midnight. The plan was to arrive in Branson just before noon, three hours before showtime.

The first couple of hours were quiet; Yearwood played her tapes; Haege put on an *Andy Griffith* rerun. Everyone was in his or her bunk by one. At two, Steve Hoker, the driver, saw his oil-pressure gauge starting to fall. He stopped, added a quart of oil, drove on. When the gauge dropped for the second time, he decided he had better stop.

He pulled off at the exit, went to wake Arnold, who woke up Yearwood. They wanted to use her cellular phone to call Nashville, but they couldn't turn it on. The batteries were dead.

Hoker went back to the front of the bus and switched on his citizen's band radio. "Stagecoach in trouble," he broadcast. "Stagecoach in trouble." In recent years violence on the highways has fractured the brotherhood of the road. But *stagecoach* is CB argot for a star's bus, and it's clear that the vehicle is benign. Hoker had picked his CB handle, "Coachmaster," to insure that truckers would be aware of his precious cargo.

Fifteen minutes later, his call was answered. The trucker estimated he was probably fifteen minutes away. He would pull off when he got there and give Hoker a lift to the nearest phone. Hoker called Trent Hemphill back in Nashville and told him that his bus had broken down. Hemphill promised to have another there as soon as he could, though it probably wouldn't be before daybreak.

Back at the bus, Arnold smelled smoke. He woke Garcia and the two went to investigate. A small fire was smoldering in the engine. They got the extinguisher from inside the bus, put out the fire, and waited. They were a hundred miles east of St. Louis. So long as the new bus arrived by five that morning, they would have no trouble making the matinee show.

Finding a bus in June, though, would not be easy. It was fair season, and anything that wasn't broken was out on the road. Yearwood got the only vehicle Hemphill had, an '82 coach nicknamed *Blue Thunder*, which had come back that night from a tour of duty for Dolly Parton's crew. It had been the first bus acquired for the Hemphill fleet, and it looked it. There was no water in the bathroom sink, and the toilet didn't quite work, either.

Blue Thunder arrived just after seven o'clock. It would be close, but they still ought to be there for the early show. "I just love country music," said Tammy Rogers as she carted her fiddle case across the shoulder of the road.

Hemphill had promised to send the bus clean, but the bunks had the feel of the beds in a motel with hourly rates. Ric McClure turned up a half dozen toothpicks in his quarters; Lisa McLaughlin found a wad of hair and cracker crumbs in hers.

Unlike their regular bus, where the windows pushed out for emergencies, this one had top-hatches for emergency exits. Twenty miles down the road, the back hatch blew off, turning the stateroom into a convertible with its top down. They lost forty minutes as Hoker circled back to look for the thousand-dollar part, to no avail.

The bus made its first stop just after nine. They were about twenty miles east of St. Louis, five hours from Branson. They might make the three o'clock show if everything went right. By now, no one expected it would.

Everyone shuffled off at the truck stop, whose only distinguishing characteristic was a bank of thirteen phones, each occupied by a sweaty driver. Arnold tried to call the Grand Palace; no one was answering the phones. As the bus pulled out, Yearwood got nervous: "Would someone check if Jay's in his bunk? We've left him before." The bass player was discovered in the stateroom, working on his tan.

"We still need to call Branson," said Yearwood. Just after eleven, Hoker pulled off at another gas station. "This time, only Leonard gets off," Yearwood ordered.

Arnold was back in less than a minute. "Phone's dead," he announced.

Hoker made a choppy U-turn to another gas station across the highway. "One more of these, and I'll be throwing up," said Rogers.

"Maybe this means we're not supposed to go to Branson," said Yearwood.

"Maybe there *is* a bright side to all this," said Rogers.

Arnold finally got through to Branson; he told the theater's manager that Yearwood wasn't likely to make the first show. "This is a first for me," he said when he got back on the bus. "Thirty years on the road and I haven't missed one yet. . . ."

As the morning wore on, the bus turned into an inferno. It was 95 degrees out, and the air-conditioning unit wasn't up to the weather. It didn't help that the plastic window and door seals were leaking a steady stream of hot, humid air. For the rest of the way, everyone tried to stay as unsweaty as possible. Yearwood changed into an oversized T-shirt. Lauer stripped down to his boxer shorts. Arnold even took off his hat.

"I'm going to head back to my bunk," Yearwood said just before noon. "I might as well sweat laying down." Within a half hour, everyone followed.

By two, the band members were in the front of the bus, debating the chances of making the three o'clock show. "Remember this episode on *The Partridge Family*?" said Hager. "You know, the one where the bus breaks down and they go on stage wearing their regular clothes and David Cassidy says, 'We'll be right back after we change'? The audience applauds and they just go ahead and play anyway?"

"Gee, Jay," said Rogers. "That's kind of like us."

"This isn't *The Partridge Family*," said McClure. "If we go on, we need to get dressed."

"That's a Trail Boss decision," said Rogers.

"You wake him," said Garcia.

"Ric brought it up," she said.

So the drummer headed back and woke up Arnold, who, in turn, roused Yearwood, who was in foul humor. The bus passed the signs for Elvis-A-Rama, the Baldknobbers, and Shoji Tabuchi.

"What should we do?" asked Rogers.

"Whatever you want me to do," Yearwood said to Arnold.

"We are going to prepare, regardless," Arnold announced.

Yearwood didn't move.

"Am I still awake?" asked Hoker, who had been going for fifteen hours. Suddenly, an RV, driven by a blue-haired lady, veered in front of him. "I've never been a drinker," he said. "But I might start tonight."

"Sounds like a country song," said Arnold. And for the first time in hours, everyone laughed.

It was nearly three o'clock when the bus finally pulled into the parking lot behind the theater. No one had bothered to put on stage clothes. As it turned out, it didn't much matter. As soon as he got backstage, Arnold found out that Debbie Campbell, Glen's daughter, had taken the stage in Yearwood's place. Until six weeks before, she had been a stewardess for Southwest Airlines. Now, she was on a six-month leave, trying to establish a singing career. She had just started as an opening act at the Roy Clark Theater.

The phone was ringing when Yearwood walked into the motel

room a half hour later. It was Kragen, wanting to discuss her album cover.

"Ken," she said wearily, "this is not a good time."

Yearwood was an unusual act for Branson—a lot younger and a lot less traditional. But the Grand Palace was experimenting with newer talent, with mixed success.

That night, Yearwood finished, as she usually did, with "She's in Love with the Boy." As she sang the chorus, she looked out into the audience. "All of a sudden they looked at me like, 'Oh, that's who she is.'" She was prepared to do an encore, but there wasn't enough applause to justify going back on stage. "The audience just sat on its hands," she complained.

Glen Campbell, who had been hired by the Grand Palace for a six-week engagement, stopped by her dressing room just before his show.

"I haven't traveled by bus since Tanya and I were together," he said after hearing about the singer's transportation troubles. He liked Branson, he said, because there were no bars. "I stopped drinking," he explained. Even better, a stint in Branson meant six weeks off the road. "You get tired of waking up in motel rooms and looking for something with the area code printed on it so you can figure out where you are."

Campbell's show was an exercise in nostalgia. He wore a lime-green embroidered suit and hit all the favorites—"Gentle on My Mind," "Rhinestone Cowboy," "By the Time I Get to Phoenix." For his finale, "Amazing Grace," he not only sang, he played the bagpipes as well.

Yearwood signed autographs for two hours and headed back to her motel just before midnight. She still had no idea how she was going to get out of town. She had declared *Blue Thunder* an unacceptable means of transportation, but it wasn't clear if there was an alternative. Hemphill called soon after. He had fixed the oil line, he told Arnold; they could have their bus back by noon.

The only problem was lodging. Since the band hadn't expected to stay overnight, Arnold had rented only three rooms. He called around, trying to find extra space, but this was Branson: "No vacancy" all around. The women slept two to a bed; most of the male members of Yearwood's crew ended up sleeping on the bus.

The bus arrived on time the next day, and they pulled into the

Best Western in Marinette, Wisconsin, just after eight. Yearwood got a full night's sleep, but she was still tired. It was also unseasonably cold. They would be playing outdoors, and it hadn't occurred to anyone to bring along any winter clothes. Yearwood was not in good humor, and a badly prepared reporter from the local paper didn't help matters. He met her on the bus, where her new publicity pictures were piled on the table. He took a look at them, looked at her.

"Is that you?" he asked.

"Yes," Yearwood nodded.

"Boy, it doesn't look like you."

It wasn't the sort of thing that made for an easy rapport.

"So what do you think about Billy Ray Cyrus?" he asked next.

"I have my opinions, but I don't see any reason why I should share them with the press. I wish Billy Ray Cyrus the best."

Arnold watched as she talked, and he worried. She had been the easiest performer he had ever worked with, and he was starting to see a change. It was a bad run, he reassured himself. She would be all right.

And by the time they finished the next show, the next day, on Obitibway Island, north of Saginaw, Michigan, she was. They had been on the bus for ten and a half hours, and she had been expecting the worst. It was a free show, sponsored by WKQQ, the local country station. It was still cold; she was still testy. Then she went on stage. She opened with "Say You Will," and the crowd was on its feet. By the time she hit the songs they knew, they were screaming. She did three encores.

"I've seen them do that for Garth," she said afterward, "but they've never done it for me."

She invited the band out to dinner. They found a restaurant on the water, and went through a copious amount of wine.

They cruised into Nashville at six in the morning, nine hours before they had to set up for their next show in front of the hometown crowd at Opryland. She had five days straight in Nashville, five days to finish her album.

CHAPTER 20

FUNDIS WAS AT THE STUDIO AT NINE-THIRTY ON MONDAY MORNing. Yearwood was supposed to be there at ten. Emmylou Harris was due in at noon, and Yearwood had to finish her vocals for "Woman Walk the Line" so Harris would have something to work with.

The appointed hour rolled by, then 10:15, then 10:30, with no sign of Yearwood. "I want to get this album done," Fundis said, pacing the floor. "She said she had to drop Robert off somewhere before she came in. I'll rent that boy a car myself if that's what it takes." Then he stopped himself. "I have to let that part go. It's only going to create problems with our relationship if I don't."

At 10:45, Yearwood ran into the control room, went straight for Fundis, and hugged him. "I'm sorry," she said, "I'm sorry," and repeated it once more for good measure.

Fundis shook his head. "It's okay. How was Branson?"

"Not a good time. I missed a show. Glen Campbell's daughter subbed for me."

"I want you to hear 'Memphis.' I did some more work. I ended up leaving your vocals out of the harmony."

Yearwood smiled as the fiddle solo came on. "That, I really like."

"You wanted the fiddle up, you got the fiddle up."

"I like it. I want copies for the band before the video because it's so different. I've been listening to 'Hearts in Armor.' I can't decide about the cello."

"I know," replied Fundis.

"It's fighting against the vocals. The simplicity is lost."

"It knocked me out before we put it on," said Fundis.

"You know how we debated on the harmony? The coolness and the emotion are lost with the cello. It's competing with it. When I listened I just kept thinking, 'Oh, man, how am I going to tell Garth I don't like it.' "

"I felt that way the day we did it. Maybe the cello was too low. Maybe a viola is the answer."

"We could try it. At this point it might make sense just to leave it alone."

"Let me work with it. Okay, it's time to go in there and cry your heart out." For the next ninety minutes, she worked on "Woman Walk the Line." She was still working when Emmylou Harris walked in at noon. Harris—a slight woman of forty-five, face scrubbed except for the kohl liner surrounding her eyes—carried a worn carpetbag and wore an oversize paisley T-shirt, a tiny denim skirt, and a jean jacket. Her legs were bare, and she had on a pair of tasseled loafers. Except for her hair, a tangle of gray curls, and her Cartier tank watch, she could have passed for a college student.

Fundis greeted Harris with a hug. The two had known each other since the early seventies when Harris had come to town, sick as a dog, to sing on an ill-fated album being recorded by Don Williams's guitar player.

Harris was already seated by the time Yearwood came into the control room. Yearwood greeted her with uncertain familiarity, half-handshake, half-hug. "I've been hearing such great things about you," said Harris.

"Thanks," Yearwood replied, then sank back into unaccustomed silence, shyly watching as Harris fiddled with her glasses, then looked over the lyric sheet.

Fundis played the tape twice, and on the second play, Harris sang harmony against the recording. When it stopped, she turned to Yearwood.

"Wow. You sound great. You know, this is a pretty good song. I forgot about it. To go on top of you is going to be hard. Will you sing the melody?"

For a minute or two, their sopranos joined.

"Shall we do it?" asked Harris.

Fundis nodded, and she went out into the studio.

Yearwood let out a deep breath. "I'm trying to remain calm. I'm going to remain calm. Emmylou Harris was singing with me, and she's going to be on my album, and it's going to be cool."

Harris stood in front of the control-room window and put on her earphones, placing one hand over each. She looked like a child holding on to her earmuffs in a high wind.

Fundis played the song once more. Harris waited through the first verse, then sang the first line of the chorus. "Tonight I want to do some drinkin'," she sang, stopping just short of where the recording ended. "I have to hold it up the long way," she said.

"The Emmylou way," Fundis added.

It was a phrase-by-phrase, line-by-line process, each sung over and over until both singer and producer were happy. By 12:30 they were still only on the third line. "Yes I'm as good as what you're thinkin'," she sang, "thinkin' " coming out sounding almost like "thankin'."

"This is not easy," she said.

"It's a tough part, but you're going to get it," said Fundis.

"Thinkin' thinking thinkin'," said Harris, trying to mimic Yearwood's pronunciation.

"You don't need to match her exactly," said Fundis.

For the next hour she worked through the second chorus. "Two more lines, then one more song," said Fundis, pushing the talk-back.

"I think she should sing the last line by herself," said Harris, referring to "Don't bother sitting at my table," the line that had been repeated at Matt Rollings's suggestion back when the song was first recorded.

"Just try it once," said Fundis.

" 'Don't bother sitting at my table,' " she sang, way high above Yearwood's vocal. "I think you're right," he said. "It's basically, 'Leave me alone, buster.' "

"More like, 'Get the hell out of here,' " said Harris.

"I think we're there," said Fundis. "Of course, I want you to be happy with it . . . up to a point. Just kidding."

"Can I hear the whole thing one more time?" Harris asked.

She sat on a stool in the studio, put on her glasses, and listened.

"It sounds good to me," said Yearwood.

"Then what are you biting your nails about?" Fundis asked.

"I've bitten them for twenty years. I bit them long before I met you, and I'll bite them long after you're gone."

"Emmy, we've got one more for you. Want to come in and listen?"

And he put on "You Don't Have to Move That Mountain." The chorus started the song:

> *You don't have to move that mountain*
> *Just help me Lord to climb it*
> *You don't have to move that stumblin' block*
> *Just show me the way around it.*

"You sing too high, girl," she said to Yearwood after those first four lines. "Nanci Griffith and I want to get T-shirts that say, 'We don't sing as high as we sound.' I can get breathy—but Vince is the one who can really sing high."

Harris went back out into the studio just after two and started singing the second line. "Just help me lord to climb it," she sang, over and over. "I'm still not getting 'just help me,'" she said, and tried twice more.

"What about 'stumblin' block'?" asked Fundis.

"This *is* the stumbling block," Harris replied.

"Try this," said Fundis, and sang it himself.

"She goes a half step down midway through," said Yearwood. "I'm not sure. . . ."

Fundis pushed the talk-back. "Trisha has a suggestion. Why don't you stay on the same note."

She tried it again. "What do you think of it?"

"I'm wrestling with 'block,'" he said into the talk-back. Then he switched it off. "This is not killing me," he said to Yearwood. "I love her voice, but . . ."

"Let's just let it go. We could be here hours."

With that, Fundis walked out into the studio.

"Are you coming out here to fire me?" Harris asked.

"We could work this out," he started.

Harris took off her headphones and got up. "You know things aren't going well as soon as the producer leaves the control room," she said.

"Want to stay for lunch?" Fundis asked. He got out a menu

from the local Middle Eastern restaurant. Harris and Yearwood both decided to try falafel. Neither had ever had it before.

"My Daddy would love this," said Yearwood after she tasted one of the crunchy brown patties. "It's fried."

The subject turned to health and the rigors of the road. Not long before, Harris had had a bout of pneumonia. More recently she had been hit with the same cold Yearwood had had.

"You have to be careful," she said. "Especially in dressing rooms. Free tip from someone who's been doing this awhile: When we go in, we tape up the vents."

They finished lunch, and Fundis started packing up his gear. "Vince is coming at six," he said. "I may be late—I've got a meeting. Please be on time."

Vince Gill doesn't just have a reputation as one of the best golfers on Music Row—he averages par golf, with a three handicap. He is also one of Nashville's better musicians. Gill, thirty-five, born in Oklahoma, had started his career in Los Angeles playing bluegrass. He switched to country because, as he put it, he wanted to be able to afford the down payment on a house. He was originally signed on at RCA by Tony Brown. But Brown left two months later, and Gill languished for three years with little success. His fortunes finally turned in 1989, when he joined Brown at MCA. In all, he had sold over five million records since switching companies, nearly two million on the last record alone.

His only liability, as far as MCA was concerned, was that he was too nice a guy. Executives worried that he didn't act like enough of a star to be received as one. His entrance into Yearwood's studio was in keeping with that reputation. He showed up twenty minutes early, wearing a polo shirt, battered khaki shorts, and a white painter's cap. No one was there, not even Laney. Gill sat down in the anteroom, switched on the television, and watched the news.

Laney arrived just before six. Yearwood showed up five minutes late. "We had Emmylou over here," she said after they exchanged the standard hug, Nashville's answer to the Hollywood air kiss. "We put her on one thing, then tried another, and fired her. We said we were going to use you instead." Gill winced.

They waited until 6:15, but there was still no sign of Fundis. "Well," said Yearwood, "we might as well get started."

Laney put on "Oh Lonesome You." Gill listened, and after one round he went out into the studio and sang the first chorus.

"Is that part too high?" he asked.

"Just do whatever you're comfortable with," Yearwood said into the talk-back. Then, with it switched off, she added: "Dang Garth for not being here. I hate this part. I hate telling him what to do."

"Let me try it a little lower," Gill asked. "Once more, please."

Laney put on the tape.

"That felt good."

"It sounded good," said Yearwood. "Want to listen?"

Then, to Laney: "We're going to have to give him something else to do. He's getting this too quickly."

By 6:30, Gill had finished all but the last line.

"This seems way too easy," said Laney. "It seems like we should be spending a couple hours on this."

"Don't think about it," said Yearwood.

"You might get another golf game in before dark," Yearwood said through the talk-back.

"Great," said Gill. "Do y'all get a producer's fee on this?"

"This is the new Nashville," said Yearwood. "Let the artist do the overdubs."

"It's the Bowen way," said Gill. "I've worked on eight zillion of his records and never saw him."

"Maybe it's better that way."

By 6:40, Gill was back in the control room, finished. Fundis was still missing. Gill wandered around, lay on the sofa, and leafed through a copy of *The New York Times.*

"We might as well listen to the next one," Yearwood said finally.

"Another high one," said Gill, after he had heard "Move That Mountain." He folded the paper in his lap and sang a harmony a good half-octave higher than the part Harris had tried earlier in the day.

"I haven't taken on a high one like that in a long time."

"It'll be good for you," said Yearwood.

"I don't know about that. It ain't real manly."

As Gill headed out into the studio, Fundis intercepted him in the hallway.

"Hello, baby," he said to Gill.

"Dahling, dahling, so wonderful to see you. I do love this song," Gill said.

"He's going to do both harmonies," Yearwood explained.

"I didn't like doing this at all," she said to Fundis when they were alone in the control room. "I guess if you were going to leave me alone with anyone, though, Vince was the best."

"I knew you'd be okay," he said.

And with that, she passed the talk-back over to her producer.

June 25 was supposed to be Yearwood's final day in the studio. She was scheduled to start at eleven, but Reynolds was in town, and, as usual, she was running late. This time Fundis didn't take any chances. He picked her up and brought her to the studio himself. Even so, they showed up at one.

When she walked in, she took a sheet of yellow paper out of her purse. On it were written three items:

> *D on Walkaway Joe*
>
> *CK last line of Down on My Knees*
>
> *Oh Lonesome You*

They started with "Walkaway Joe"; Yearwood had dropped a *d* from "revealed" in the song's last verse. She headed into the studio and spent twenty minutes working on the line, perfecting that single word. Next, they listened to "Down on My Knees." Yearwood was concerned that the last line was slightly flat. They listened. It wasn't quite dead-on. "I hear bunches of things that aren't perfect, pitchwise," she said, "but I'm willing to let them go because of the performance."

They moved on to "Oh Lonesome You," trying to figure out if Yearwood should add a harmony to the one Gill had done the week before. She went out into the studio and sang a few lines, then headed back into the control room. "It's kind of harsh," she said after she had listened to it. "Maybe I should do something different." He put on the recording, and she sang against it. "I don't know if I like that either," she said. "Let's try it with one harmony."

"Vince's?" asked Fundis.

"Not mine. Do you really think it needs more?" she asked, after listening to the one-harmony version.

"Not really. With two, you miss the lead vocal."

"Vince gets lost, too."

"Details, details," said Fundis, and he put his arm around her.

"I'm so glad you think like me," she said.

"Walt Wilson on line one," came a voice over the intercom, and Fundis picked up the phone. The marketing director wanted to alert Fundis to a meeting the next day. MCA's department heads were expecting to hear a current version of the album, and he wanted to know the status of "Devil in Disguise."

"It's a nonissue," Fundis told him. "It's on the soundtrack, and that's it."

"You know, you still have a problem with Scott," Wilson said.

"Paschall? What's he done?"

"Borchetta," said Wilson.

As Wilson explained it, though Yearwood and Borchetta had made reparations, the chief lieutenant of promotion had continued to voice reservations about the album.

"I appreciate his opinion," said Fundis, "but I go with my gut, and we make the best record we can. It just so happens that everyone else is flipping out except him. The thing is, he hasn't said anything to me, so as far as I'm concerned it's a spineless way to bitch. This really pisses me off. It's been weeks, and I haven't heard a word about it until now."

"What should we do?" Yearwood asked as Fundis got off the phone.

"If it matters that Scott doesn't like it, then we need to address it," he said. "Maybe I sounded a little shitty there."

"Not to me," said Yearwood. "I saw him at the Ace of Clubs. He came up to me happy as could be. We didn't do anything wrong. If several department heads were saying that, I would worry. But it does bother me that he's going to be on the phones selling this thing. . . . If he doesn't believe what he's selling, maybe I should call Shelia."

"I'll call Tony," said Fundis.

She held up her yellow sheet; each item had a check mark next to it. "Does this mean I'm done?"

"I guess so," said Fundis. It should have been cause for celebration, but after hearing about Borchetta, neither Fundis nor Yearwood was feeling particularly festive.

The timing could have been better, but that night there was a party for Jude Johnstone, whose song, "The Woman Before Me," had made number one in *Radio & Records*. Number One parties in Nashville are not formal affairs. This one was held in the front office of Johnstone's publisher, Bug Music, another of those parceled-up Victorians along Music Row. The hors d'oeuvres were modest and Mexican—a few taquitos, a half dozen bowls of tortilla chips, and some mild salsa. There were a few liters of Italian wine and a cooler full of beer.

Johnstone arrived just before six, her husband and two-year-old daughter in tow. It was her first time in Nashville, the first time she had met the singer responsible for her greatest success. "Thanks for my house," Johnstone said after they were introduced. She and her husband had just bought a home in Cambria, on the California coast, with the proceeds from her song. They talked for a couple of minutes, then Scott Borchetta walked in, wearing a Mavericks T-shirt.

"Well, it's nice to see there's something he believes in," said Yearwood.

Borchetta went over to greet her. Yearwood managed a tight smile, then turned away. It wasn't a big party, maybe twenty-five people, but Yearwood circled the room for a good half hour without ever saying a word to Borchetta. At about six-thirty she headed out to her car and brought back a mock-up of her album cover, with one of the McGuire photographs, to show to Johnstone. Midway down, in clean script, were the words "Hearts in Armor." Johnstone smiled. "Geez, I just love seeing my song there. I'll be right back. I want to show it to my husband." She left Yearwood standing in the doorway, an easy target for Borchetta.

"I'm getting claustrophobic," she said to Reynolds, "Let's get out of here." Then she headed out to her car.

Fundis had finally talked to Tony Brown several hours after Yearwood left the studio. Brown apparently wasn't even aware that Borchetta was still talking down the album. "I'll deal with it," he told Fundis.

The producer was somewhat calmed, but he decided to deliver the new tape of the album himself. Yearwood was heading out on the road for a two-week swing (Detroit/Kansas City/Texas), and he wanted to be at the meeting if anything went wrong.

The meeting turned out to be a nonevent. The talk was mostly about Revlon. The MCA executives wanted to know when the perfume was coming out, to make sure it wouldn't deflect attention from the album. As for the record itself, the reception was warm. Scott Borchetta had not been invited.

• • •

When you're in a road band, there is no such thing as a paid vacation; there are no sick days; getting time off requires arranging for a replacement. Which is how Leonard Arnold ended up playing music in front of a crowd for the first time in thirteen years.

Johnny Garcia's girlfriend was expecting a baby in August. He figured he would have to miss a show or two, so with Yearwood's blessing, he was teaching Arnold to take his part. They had worked on two songs, "She's in Love with the Boy," and "That's What I Like About You," saving most of the work for the end of July so the lessons would be fresh.

On July 3, Yearwood again played Billy Bob's in Fort Worth, drawing a considerably larger crowd than she had three months before. It was a late night; Garcia and Alan Haege, the sound man, had closed down the bar at the Stockyards Hotel next door and then, rather than keep their respective roommates awake, moved their party onto the bus. At about three, Garcia's girlfriend tried him in his room. When he didn't answer, she called Arnold instead. Her water had broken, she told him. If Garcia was going to come home, now was the time. Arnold told her he thought Garcia was on the bus, which was parked in front of the hotel. She called the front desk, and the clerk went and roused him. He got home the next morning, an hour after Matteo Leonel Garcia was born.

"From then on," said Arnold, "It was just, 'Do the gig.' "

They got to their hotel in Houston just after two and went over to the site early, so Arnold would have some time to work before sound check. He sat on the bus with Lauer for an hour, working over each piece, chord by chord. "Write the list out bold," Arnold told him. "With keys next to each. If I can't do something, we'll figure out a new way."

By the time they went on stage for sound check, it was 99 degrees out, and the humidity made it as thick and sticky as a good South Texas barbecue sauce. The stage had no overhang, and the sun was still high in the sky. They worked for twenty minutes. Arnold was bleeding sweat. A half hour later everyone was back on the bus. It was the only air-conditioned spot on the fairgrounds. Arnold stayed back in the stateroom, working on his parts.

Two hours later it was showtime. Arnold wore blue jeans, a calico cowboy shirt his wife had made for him, and blue suede boots. The sun set just before they went onstage, but the heat was still brutal. Someone on the fair committee brought him a towel with ice cubes inside; he wrapped it around his neck.

They started with "Say You Will," the hardest piece in the set, since the guitar player was responsible for the introduction. Arnold did it just fine. He smiled, he laughed, he hooted, he was thrilled to be back on stage, performing, where he would have been if he hadn't had a wife and two children to provide for. "I want you to give this guy a special hand," said Yearwood, when it came time to introduce the band. "It's his first gig with us."

And then it was over. Everyone left the stage except Arnold. He just sat behind his amplifier, towel wrapped around his neck, looking up every so often as the Fourth of July fireworks flamed through the sky.

Part V

THE CAMPAIGN

The Nashville Sell

> You can't be fish *and* fowl; up in New York they say country music's on the pop charts now, but you can't be country and be on the pop charts at the same time.
>
> —Wesley Rose

CHAPTER 21

"MOST MUSIC VIDEOS ARE PUT TOGETHER AT THE LAST minute," said Tom Calabrese, the balding, ponytailed Los Angeles producer who was hired to work on Yearwood's video. "Wrong Side of Memphis" was true to form. The week before the shoot, the director, Gerry Wenner, was in Barcelona filming the pop singer Tevin Campbell for a special Olympics presentation, Yearwood was off in Kansas City visiting with Reynolds's grandmother, and no one was sure if they would even be allowed to use the old Ryman Auditorium, the setting for the film's climactic scene.

Two weeks before the three-day shoot, Calabrese put in a half dozen phone calls to Robert Kimbro, the manager of the Ryman, which had become a standard stop on the Nashville bus-tour circuit since the Opry left in 1974. Each time, he left a message. He never heard back. Finally, Kimbro picked up the phone himself. His response was immediate and frosty: "We have contracts with tour buses, they're coming in until five P.M."

"Bring them in," said Calabrese. "Let them watch. We'll do whatever it takes. Pay whatever it costs."

"I'm just not interested," Kimbro said, explaining that others who had filmed there had left the place a shambles. It wasn't the money, it wasn't the time. He just didn't want the Ryman involved.

Calabrese figured himself to be part of the problem. He was from out of town, and there was no reason for Kimbro to feel he should go out of his way. The producer tried not to panic, but he knew that if they didn't get the Ryman they would have to rethink the entire concept of the film. He made two calls, one to Janet Rickman at MCA, the other to Ken Kragen in Los Angeles. Both agreed to see what they could do, and both did the same thing. First Rickman, then Kragen, put in calls to Hal Durham, general manager of the Grand Ole Opry.

Durham was equivocal with Rickman. While he would talk to Kimbro, he told her, he couldn't promise anything.

Kragen waited until the next day to call. "I don't like to overrule my managers," Durham told him. "We don't normally allow people in there—we've turned a lot of people down." But Kragen was a past chairman of the Country Music Association, and he still carried considerable Nashville clout. "I'll see what I can do," Durham promised.

The next day, Kimbro called Calabrese. "I have been instructed by my superiors to allow you to film," he told the producer.

"I hope I'm not putting you out too much," Calabrese replied.

Kimbro said nothing.

Yearwood hadn't had to deal with much action in her first video. "She's in Love with the Boy" had models acting out the song's lyrics while Yearwood sat on a straight-backed chair, the wind tousling her hair as she sang. She spent most of her second, for "Like We Never Had a Broken Heart," sitting on a big brass bed—a performance that was unfortunately similar to her static stage show. She played it sassy in "That's What I Like About You": The hammock-dumping scene was the first time she had done more than simply sing. This video would be the first time she played it sexy: hair slightly beehived, off-the-shoulder shirt, cats-eye white sunglasses—a blond Nefertiti, circa 1969.

Filming was supposed to start at 10:30 on Monday, July 6, in the offices of Planet Pictures on Music Row. Yearwood was in good humor when she showed up to get primped two hours early. Reynolds was in town for the week, and it was, she said, "almost like a real relationship." He had been with her in Texas (she finally switched to the stateroom), and he had even promised to go along to Memphis for the final day of shooting. She was, so far, juggling the impossible: life on the road and a life of her own.

She had her full entourage in attendance: Felts was doing

makeup, Smoot was doing hair, and McCoy was along to make sure her outfits were in order. Janet Rickman, MCA's publicity chief, was there to make sure everything went well.

As Yearwood was turned into a beauty, she and Rickman compared notes on growing up southern and smart.

"If you can skate by on your looks, maybe you don't have to develop brains," said Rickman. "I never had that problem."

"I have a college degree because I never won any beauty contests," Yearwood said. Things had changed a bit, she allowed, in the last year. "Everybody describes my skin as porcelain now. Before, they just called it pale." Conversation ceased as Felts lined Yearwood's lips.

Gerry Wenner had been directing music videos for six years. His first country music job was with Carlene Carter, who hired him to do the video for "I Fell in Love" after seeing some dance videos he had done for an R&B singer named James Ingram. Since then, he had worked with Randy Travis, Travis Tritt, and Dolly Parton. Like most everyone who worked in Nashville, he was grateful that the country musicians were so easy to work with. His only complaint was the budget, which averaged half what he would have for L.A. films—for roughly the same amount of work.

Filming a music video is considerably less complicated than making a full-fledged movie. Not only is it shorter, it's impossible to flub a line since there is no audio being recorded. The only sound is a recording of the song itself. For Gerry Wenner, the key to making money was getting it done fast. They had three days for the four-minute film, and the first day they shot three scenes before noon.

In the first scene, Yearwood stormed out of the house (ostensibly on the wrong side of Memphis, actually the Planet office). In another, she packed up her suitcase. Just before midday, Yearwood, Wenner, and their seven-member entourage were filming across from the Ryman. The scene was Yearwood's arrival in Nashville. She watched as a generic country star (a model hired for the occasion) was mobbed by fans. The "fans" were passers-by recruited at the last minute, among them a fiftyish woman and a cowboy-hatted man who looked to be no more than thirty. "This is my husband," she said to Wenner after he had finished shooting, as though there might be some question about the relationship. "He's a songwriter. Could you take some tapes for Trisha?"

"I'm sorry, I can't," he said, and an assistant pulled him away.

On the edge of the crowd was a young man wearing a black Guns N' Roses T-shirt. "Who's that?" asked a woman standing next to him, pointing over to Yearwood. "She's supposed to be Garth Brook's girlfriend," he replied.

This was the week that everything was supposed to come together. The record was supposed to be finished; the video was to be filmed; and Revlon was coming to town to discuss the last details for the perfume. But while the video was going just fine, the perfume was a question mark, and the record that was supposed to secure Yearwood's star in the firmament was still being tinkered with.

Garth Fundis was spending virtually every hour in the studio working on the record. His wife and children were off with relatives in Florida. At best, he was home six hours a day. On Friday, three days before, Yearwood had had Sheri McCoy take some Chinese carryout, with flowers, to Fundis at the studio for sustenance. He had eaten it for three days straight. On Monday, the lilies were wilting petals all over the control-room desk.

At about two that afternoon, Kragen walked into the Sound Emporium with two representatives from Revlon in tow—Cecil Kanale, one of the women Yearwood had met in Tampa, and Allyn Seidman, the executive in charge of public relations. After Kragen made his introductions, he took a close look at Fundis's pallid complexion.

"How long have you been here?" he asked.

"Since April," Fundis replied. Then he asked if they wanted to hear the album.

As "Woman Walk the Line" came on, Fundis turned to Kragen. "That's Emmylou," he said.

"Emmylou Harris?" asked Seidman, in that tone of voice reserved for running into a friend in an unlikely neighborhood.

"Yeah," Fundis replied, "she came in to do a harmony."

At the end, after "Hearts in Armor," Seidman and Kanale applauded.

"Nice little country record, isn't it?" said Fundis.

Kragen and the Revlon people were gone by four. They had a

meeting at MCA, and they were planning to stop by to watch the last scene of the day, the filming at the Ryman Auditorium.

• • •

The old Ryman is a glorious wreck. While the preservationists kept the building from being razed, there has been little effort to restore it. The auditorium has become a monument to neglect, especially the second-floor balcony, a jumble of upended pews and rusted Coca-Cola signs from deserted snack stands.

Downstairs, there is a motley gift shop (Minnie Pearl hat earrings, complete with price tag, go for $4.95) next to a museum of sorts in a half dozen glass cases—the Roy Acuff collection, memorabilia donated after the singer moved to Opryland. Some highlights: a Leaning Tower of Pisa lamp, a ceramic figurine of five dogs playing poker, a pair of black oxfords labeled "Elephant Hide shoes made on Mekon [sic] River in Thailand." In all, a sort of glass-encased tag sale.

Kitsch and all, Yearwood was thrilled to be on the stage where Hank Williams and Patsy Cline had sung their hearts out every Saturday night. Her only complaint was the heat. It was 92 degrees outside at 5:30 and no cooler inside the auditorium. Not only was there no air conditioning, the fans had been turned off. The humidity was running to 90 percent. It felt like the inside of a Dutch oven.

Yearwood waited for her call outside the Ryman in an air-conditioned mobile home, rented for the occasion, talking promotion possibilities with the two Revlon representatives. The main subject of the conversation was the name of the perfume. Revlon had been testing names all summer and had finally come up with "Wild Heart." It was the first title she actually liked.

"We want to launch it the day after the CMAs," said Seidman.

"Make it late," said Yearwood. "If I win, I'm going to be out celebrating."

Kragen reiterated his suggestion for a Reba/Wynonna/Trisha concert, perhaps to benefit Revlon's chosen charitable cause, breast cancer. He repeated his title for the show, "Righteous Women Together." The Revlon contingent looked underwhelmed.

"We could reverse the initials," said Seidman. "RTW. Ready to Wear."

They moved on to the album cover. It turned out that *Harper's*

Bazaar had a three-month hold on McGuire's photo shoot. In order to use the portrait she wanted they would have to receive a release from the magazine. McGuire had made the request; he had yet to receive a reply.

"What are our alternatives?" asked Kragen.

"None," Yearwood replied.

Calabrese knocked at the door. It was time to head into the Ryman. The producer had been vaguely flirtatious all day, arm on her shoulder, hand around her waist. Now, walking into the auditorium, he asked her out to dinner. "My boyfriend is in town," she replied, and Calabrese backed off.

Yearwood worked three quarters of an hour on two scenes—one simply walking in the auditorium door, the second sitting in one of the pews, head tilted back, eyes closed as though in a dream.

She moved onto the stage just past six. She twirled her skirt and sang, matching the recording, which was playing in the background, word for word. Though the recorded version would be used on the video, she couldn't simply lip-synch the words. The match never worked out quite right.

"She's much easier to work with than she was last time," Wenner said as he filmed her dancing. "She looks better than I expected—and she's really moving. She seems much more seasoned."

As filming passed an hour, then ninety minutes, the Revlon executives started to get a little fidgety; Kragen took them to dinner. By the time they got back, just before seven-thirty, Yearwood and crew had gone.

The ride to Memphis was scheduled for Tuesday afternoon. They would be filming driving scenes, road signs, and a sequence at a dilapidated gas station. What Wenner wanted was backwoods. He found it in Fly, Tennessee.

Fly is about fifty miles west of Nashville. It isn't much to speak of. "I'm not sure how many people live here," said Billy Joe Sewell, owner of the garage, which seemed to be the only commercial establishment in town. "I really don't know where Fly starts and where it stops."

The video filming was the biggest thing that had happened in Fly in a couple of years. Bruce Weber had shot some sequences for *Vanity Fair* on a horse farm just outside town, but he hadn't used local models and hadn't let anyone watch. Wenner and Calabrese hadn't counted on observers either, but by the time they got to Fly, sixty or seventy people were gathered at the gas station. Sewell had invited his family—wife, children, brother, cousins—who had in turn invited their friends.

Yearwood had no interest in venturing out into the crowd. "I don't want to create a commotion," she said, when someone asked if she would sign autographs. "I just want to get this done."

Mary Beth Felts surveyed the motley assembly, then started telling hillbilly jokes: "What did the hillbilly say when she lost her virginity? Get off me, Pa, you're crushing my cigarette. . . . Heard about the hillbilly who went to a family reunion? He was hoping to get lucky."

The only one who seemed to be enjoying the locals was the driver of the trailer, who wandered out into the crowd and started doing magic tricks, cutting a small section of string, then, with a few incantations and a flourish of a handkerchief, joining the pieces back together. Midway through the filming, a little girl passed out from the heat. Yearwood insisted that she be brought into the bus, where she gave her a cold compress and an autographed picture. They filmed for an hour, and by three o'clock they were on the road to Memphis.

Back in Nashville, Fundis spent his first morning in a month away from the Sound Emporium, closing the purchase of the studio at his lawyer's office. By three, though, he was back in the control room to finish up the viola section on "Hearts in Armor."

The week before, Fundis had done a single session with Kristin Wilkinson, a viola player who had also worked on the Collin Raye album. He had been sufficiently satisfied to consider adding two or three more sections, which was why this session had been scheduled.

Wilkinson arrived at four, and they got to work almost immediately, adding a new viola section midway through the song. Fundis recorded her second effort. "Something's wrong," he said.

"I know what it is," she said. "I'm using a new bow. I've got the other one with me—I wasn't thinking."

She played again.

"It ain't knocking me out," said Fundis. "And if it ain't knocking me out, Trisha's going to hate it."

"You afraid of her?" asked Laney.

"No," he said. "I know her."

"Could you play even softer?" Fundis asked after Wilkinson had tried it again. Then he switched off the talk-back and added, "And a little more in tune?"

They worked for ninety minutes, and still it wasn't knocking him out.

"Didn't we have the mike placed differently last time?" Fundis asked Laney. "It didn't sound quite as warm."

Laney went out into the studio. He pulled the mike down, closer to the viola.

"That's still not it," Fundis said after they had listened to the result.

Wilkinson tapped her foot on the floor, the sound muffled by one of the frayed oriental rugs. "I don't remember this being here last time," she said.

Laney pulled the carpet away, and this time Fundis was satisfied.

Wilkinson finished just before six. Fundis had just two more things to worry about. The next day he would begin to have the tape mastered, the last step in the recording process, and he had to messenger the current version to Yearwood to make sure she approved of the new viola section.

• • •

On July 8, the MCA marketing department met for the first time to discuss plans for *Hearts in Armor*. Marketing in Nashville is still fairly bare-bones: no television blitzes, few print ads, no billboards—at least not on MCA's dime. Walt Wilson, the head of marketing, had two goals for the meeting: They had to prepare a presentation to the independent rack-jobbers, the middlemen who decide which records are sold by the large discount department stores like Wal-Mart and Kmart. And then he had to devise a marketing plan for Uni Distribution, the division of MCA that dealt directly with record stores.

MCA had rented a conference room in the Vanderbilt Hotel, which had just been purchased by Loews. The property wasn't up to the chain's usual standards, and Loews was working hard to improve it. You could hear jackhammers pounding away as the eight marketing people gathered to decide how to sell Trisha Yearwood's new album.

With *Hearts in Armor*, Yearwood had set out not to re-create her successes but to expand upon them, and the album was a considerable departure from her debut. From "Wrong Side of Memphis," all lighthearted rhythm and blues, to the bluegrassy "You Don't Have to Move That Mountain" to the shattering emotion in "Down on My Knees" to the reckless desire of "Walk-away Joe" to the elegant, elegiac "Hearts in Armor," Yearwood's album eclipsed everything she had done before. It was quite unlike anything else produced by the Music Row pack. Yearwood wasn't straight-ahead country. She wasn't bluesy like Wynonna Judd. She wasn't a songwriter, a folk balladeer, like Mary-Chapin Carpenter. She was trying to forge a role as a new breed of diva, bound neither by musical nor geographical conventions.

But for all of its achievements, the challenge for *Hearts in Armor* was clear. Even though Scott Borchetta had twice been rebuked for his criticisms of the album, his point was essentially correct: *Hearts in Armor* had no mass-appeal single like "She's in Love with the Boy." The album was a finely honed piece of art, all agreed, but it still needed a hook.

Ken Kragen showed up for that meeting with Garth Fundis, who brought the most recent version of the record. ("Most record companies wouldn't let me be here," he confided. "They're too paranoid to let a producer hear what goes on.")

Yearwood's manager began the session, bragging about a deal he had just made for Travis Tritt at Warner Brothers. "He's spending one million dollars to promote two albums," he said. "He told them that he would match them dollar for dollar."

"It certainly is aggressive," said Wilson, making it clear that MCA had no interest in trying to match that deal.

The next order of business was the Country Music Association Awards. Though the ceremony wasn't until the end of September, the preliminary nominations had just been made. Although she had a shot at best female vocalist, her best hope was the Horizon Award, given each year to the act that has "shown the most significant creative growth and development in overall chart and sales activity, live performance professionalism and critical media recognition." The CMA board nominates up to fifteen singers for the award. Those names are then presented to the CMA's seven thousand members, who then pick five finalists, then the winner. Yearwood was tied for first place on that initial slate with Collin Raye.

"The nominations will be announced August thirteenth," said Kragen. "I figure she'll be up against Brooks & Dunn and Marty Stuart. He's the one to worry about—he has lots of friends."

Next, Kragen brought out a mock-up of Yearwood's album cover. "I'm not crazy about it," said Steve McCord, one of the marketing people. "She looks hard."

"There is a tension there that wasn't in the Randee St. Nicholas shoot," said Fundis.

The more immediate problem, though, was whether *Harper's Bazaar* would give them authorization to use the shot.

"They can't stop us from using it," said Kragen. "I talked to Malcolm Mimms about it this morning. There was a Supreme Court decision that involved a similar issue. Unless McGuire signed a written contract, they have no case.

"Nobody can figure that *Harper's* would sue—or what they would sue for. The only damages are a broken contract, and the only person who would lose is the photographer, who they would never use again. If push comes to shove, let's roll the dice and use it. Besides, Revlon is a huge advertiser in *Harper's*, so we can put a little muscle on them from that end. We might as well roll ahead, because the downside is limited."

Fundis put his head in his hands. "Poor McGuire," he said, "poor McGuire."

Wilson pulled out a format for the marketing sheet for Uni. "Okay, guys, what can we say about Trisha that sets her apart?"

"Who's she touring with?" asked Michelle Myers, a member of marketing staff.

"She's in protected situations," said Kragen. "Large clubs, fairs, generally headlining. Her fee is up to fifteen—after the first she's going to twenty."

"Are you thinking about expanding the band?" asked Wilson.

"Now it costs her eight or nine thousand dollars to put on a show. After paying commissions she brings in ten. She's still only netting one a show."

"Merchandise?"

"On a good night, thirty-five hundred dollars. We're still at a point where expenses are wiping out profits. We're trying to expand, but we don't want to get crazy."

"Okay," said Wilson. "What are we saying about this album?

I don't think we're going to sell this on hit singles. I think you sell the whole package."

"I tell people I think she's singing better than the last album," said Kragen. "I also tell people the fact that those people are on it—that they would come in, that's about as heavy as you get in terms of credibility."

"Where would you position her? We can't say she is the best female in country—we have Reba and Wynonna."

"I'd say, 'Poised to become the Linda Ronstadt of the nineties.' "

"We've got to be sensitive to the country market."

"Ronstadt started in country. You have that letter from Don Henley."

"The problem is that Linda has become such a chameleon. Would kids today know her?" asked Dave Weigand, another marketing person. "The stuff they've heard has been Nelson Riddle and the Spanish stuff."

"But we're not talking about the current Ronstadt," said Fundis.

"How about, 'Quality without compromise?' " proposed Kragen.

"Would a twenty-year-old girl buy with that line?" asked Wilson.

"How about, 'From the person who brought you "She's in Love with the Boy"?' " interjected Steve McCord.

" 'The woman who brought you "She's in Love with the Boy" has taken it to another level,' " said Kragen.

"*Evolution* is the word I'd use," said Fundis. "Hopefully she hasn't peaked yet."

"I like tying it to 'She's in Love with the Boy,' " said Kragen. "That's what the consumer knows."

"I don't want to walk away from that younger crowd," added Wilson.

"It isn't a young record," said Fundis.

"We want those kids," said Kragen. "The acts that have sold over two million—Billy Ray, Garth Brooks—the difference is kids. If you saturate the country market, you get two million. Beyond that, you have to get kids."

"I would be happy with two million," said Wilson.

"That should be the target," said Kragen. "If we get three, there's a breakthrough we can't anticipate."

"Okay, how do we differentiate her from what's on the market?" asked Wilson, once again trying to get that copy line.

"She is the hot new female," said Kragen. "That is the key. She is the hottest-selling debut artist in history."

McCord went up to a chalkboard, pulled out a marker, and started writing lines. "Quality without compromise. Hottest-selling debut artist in history."

"Why don't we listen to the album?" suggested Fundis. Wilson turned down the lights.

After "Down on My Knees," Pam Russell, another marketing staff member, looked up. "That's crossover city," she said.

At the end, after "Hearts in Armor," Kragen turned to Fundis. "Good job, Garth. You let her voice be so clean and out there. If ever I've seen a song showcased. . . . I've got an idea. What about, 'A woman in perfect harmony'?"

There was a silence in the room. Wilson nodded. It was the first thing anyone had heard that worked. McCord wrote the line on the chalkboard. "How about 'Trisha Yearwood in perfect harmony with . . . ,' " he suggested, and wrote "Garth Brooks, Emmylou Harris, Vince Gill, and Don Henley, only on MCA."

"Don't forget Raul," said Fundis.

"Cross out *only*," said Wilson. "It sounds like they don't get along. The only problem we're going to have is getting clearance on Garth's name. You know how he feels about his name being used."

"Let's not go to Bob and Pam," said Kragen, mindful of Yearwood's troubled relationship with her former managers. "I'll go to Liberty—Jimmy and I go back to First Edition."

"He's not going to like his name being first," said Fundis.

"Let's get a new harmony singer with name A," said Wilson. "Okay, we've got it. Now what's the plan for dealing with the rack-jobbers?"

Once again, Kragen led the way. He wanted to present it to them as an event: Rent a limousine, take them to a studio, serve a champagne lunch, and play the album. The only trouble was finding the right situation for each location; there were seventeen in all.

"What are we going to do in Amarillo?" asked Russell. "Recording studio? Amarillo is the end of the world."

"Maybe you can just play it in the limousine," suggested Kragen.

"We need to get started," said Wilson. "We have to have orders in the first week in August—when's the earliest we can have tapes?"

"First of next week," Fundis replied.

Kragen told the group he wanted to take out an advertisement with a collection of quotes endorsing the album.

"Movies have the luxury of previews," Wilson reminded him. "We don't get print until thirty days after we launch."

"I recently read a book called *The Power of Optimism*," Kragen told the group. "One of the neat tips it had was ten things optimists do. Optimists share good news. When I have something, I'll tell anybody. It works. It opens the door. I want to do that with this album. I want to get quotes from people like Henley to use to promote the album."

After that bit of Panglossian wisdom, the group broke for lunch.

After lunch, the marketing department went to work on the wording of the proposal, Kragen left for California, and Fundis had the final mixes of the album messengered to Yearwood in Memphis.

She had spent the morning with her band, filming the club scene in the video. It gave them a small role in the album, and they had a good time, but it was still all too clear that it wasn't their music. "The hardest thing," said Tammy Rogers, "was figuring out the new fiddle part. I knew it wasn't me on the tape, but it had to look like me."

The tape with the final mixes arrived in Memphis just before they headed off on a three-day run to Vandalia, Missouri, Fort Loramie, Ohio, and Indianapolis. Everything was set except "Hearts In Armor." Fundis sent three versions of the ballad: one with the viola track from the first session, one with the part that had been added the day before, and a version with a few bars of the acoustic guitar they had tried weeks before.

The bus pulled out of Memphis just before midnight. About an hour down the road Yearwood went into the stateroom and put the tape on. By the second cut, the room filled, and everyone was listening in. For the most part, it sounded good. But she was worried about "Down on My Knees." Was there too much echo?

They pulled into the parking lot at the Twilight Motel in Vandalia at about six, and about four hours later she made it to her room. She reached Fundis at a quarter to eleven at George-town Masters, where he was putting the final touches on her album.

"The mix sounds good," she said, sounding altogether unen-thusiastic. "The new viola lick is cool—but I still don't like the acoustic guitar." Then she paused. "Don't you think there might be too much echo on 'Down on My Knees'?"

Fundis was silent. He'd had mixed feelings about the acoustic guitar himself; omitting that was no problem. But "Down on My Knees"? That, to his mind, was one of the best, most powerful cuts on the album. He couldn't understand what bothered her. She agreed to listen to it again and call back later.

Yearwood hung up the phone and sat still for a minute. She went back out to the bus to play the tape again. She pulled out her calendar, trying to figure out just when she'd be home. There, before her, were the next three months. The blocks of places and dates overwhelmed her. It would be October before she had any time to herself, autumn before she could expect to see Reynolds again. The video was over, and the album, the most important thing of all, was finally just about finished, and she wasn't even there to see that it came out right.

She really was a country star, really had her tour and her album, and it felt as if she had mortgaged her life for a dream. She sat there, on the velveteen sofa, in her stateroom in the back of her bus, and she cried.

CHAPTER 22

*F*UNDIS WAS AS UNHAPPY AS YEARWOOD. HE HAD LEFT HOME at nine-thirty that morning in the midst of a family crisis. It was his son's thirteenth birthday, and the boy had planned to spend the day at Opryland with his younger sister and a friend of his. But the friend had canceled, and he lost interest. His daughter felt slighted, and soon the entire household was in a funk. Fundis, though, had no time to help settle the situation. He was due at Georgetown Masters for the last step in the recording process. "I keep thinking my son is turning ten and we're going to go fishing, but it's not like that," he fretted as he drove to work. "I'm missing years off their lives."

There are two steps to mastering an album, editing the songs into proper sequence, separated by proper intervals, and then doing a last fine-tuning to make sure that the volume is the same on the ten songs. Both steps serve the same purpose, knitting what had previously been discrete parts into a whole.

As Fundis headed around the second-floor landing of the mastering studio, a three-story wedge in a strip mall a block off Music Row, he saw Mark Miller, Garth Brooks's sound engineer. He had started mastering Brooks's fourth album the week before, he said, but had been unhappy with the results. He ended up going back into the studio to remix four cuts.

"Lucky you had time," said Fundis.

"Lucky he was here to approve it."

"I hear his wife had a baby yesterday."

"Yeah. They were going to induce labor in two weeks because

he had two weeks off. The water broke last night. They were lucky he had a couple days off."

"Good timing. Are they still in the double-wide?"

"Yup. Until they finish the mansion."

As they talked, Carlos Grier, one of three engineers at Georgetown, joined them. "I guess we should get started," said Fundis, and they moved into a windowless room crammed with editing equipment, machinery that would set the time elapsed between songs. Unlike many producers, Garth Fundis did not leave that job up to his sound engineer. The pacing, he believed, was part of the show. "There are times when it's appropriate to let a listener rest between songs," he said. "There are times when it should butt right in, take the audience by surprise." It was a subtle part of the process, but Fundis had a hard time delegating any part of his productions, one reason why he handled only three or four acts at a time.

Grier put the tape on and, after each song, made a rough approximation of where he thought the next should begin. He then played it over for Fundis. They worked through the first four songs without Fundis changing much. Then, on the transition from "Walkaway Joe" to "Woman Walk the Line," Fundis asked him to repeat the sequence.

"Take out a half second," said Fundis. "They have to butt into each other, otherwise it's going to sound like dead space."

Grier rewound the tape, eyeing the digital counter, essentially a location device, stripped with a time code, not unlike the meter on a standard tape recorder, just calibrated much more finely. He changed it from 1:17:29:69 to 1:17:29:19, eliminating fifty hundredths of a second. They listened again, then moved on to "Oh Lonesome You." Grier played the O'Kane song twice.

"Did you use a different mike with her?" Grier asked. Fundis shook his head no. "She sounds a little more smooth than she did on the last album. Better actually." They listened to the song again. "Unless someone screws up, this will be platinum, easy," said Grier.

Then came "Down on My Knees." "I think this is the best mix on the record," said Fundis, mostly to himself. "If there's one song I don't want to redo, it's this. Well, she's out wrestling with it in her fog. I trust her. I think she'll be okay. Let's just hope it was because she had too late a night."

Then Grier put on "For Reasons."

"That's the wrong one," said Fundis after a few seconds. "It's supposed to be 'Move That Mountain.' Wait a second. It did feel good. Maybe that's the one that should be in there. Katie's going to kill me."

Fundis had given his final sequencing order to Katie Gillon, the executive in charge of keeping track of such things, five days before. It was already weeks late, and he had promised there would be no more changes.

"If you're going to switch," said Grier, "now's the time."

"Why do I create these problems for myself?" Fundis said. He listened to the transition again. "Give me a minute. Shit." And he walked out of the studio to call Gillon.

"Can I swap 'For Reasons' with 'Move That Mountain'?" he asked. "I'm sorry, Katie. It was just an accident—but it's better for Raul to not be followed by Don Henley. I'm sorry. But if we had gone with the fifth single, we wouldn't be having this problem."

He hung up the phone and walked back into the studio. "I hate this," he said. "My stomach is in knots." He took a deep breath, told Grier to keep "For Reasons" after "Down on My Knees," and they went on. As soon as they completed the transit from "Move That Mountain" to "Hearts in Armor," Fundis grabbed his bag and flew out the door. He had a twelve-thirty meeting with Dean Dillon, and he was already twenty minutes late.

When Fundis returned, just after three, the day had turned for the better. The meeting with Dillon had gone well, and he had finally talked to Yearwood. She had apologized for her funk, and they had worked out a way for her to hear the album before it was shipped to the manufacturing plant.

"How are you doing?" asked Denny Purcell, proprietor of Georgetown, when Fundis walked in.

"Better," he said. "I just don't handle stress well."

"I've never seen you like that," said Purcell.

Purcell described himself as a "sonic therapist." "I'm the last stop," he said. "By the time they get to me they have heard the thing thousands of times. The bass might be making them crazy, it might be the steel. They need someone they trust to listen and tell them it's okay."

Purcell had done his best to make his studio inviting. There were eight different juices in the refrigerator, an espresso maker, and on one wall the "Relief Center," a dispenser containing single doses of a half dozen assorted analgesics.

Purcell, who grew up in Indiana, got to Nashville in 1971 and worked briefly as a sound engineer. He left town for California for a couple of years, and when he came back the only job he could get was in a mastering studio. Eleven years later, he joined with Norbert Putnam, producer of Joan Baez, Dan Fogelberg and Buffy St. Marie, among others, and Ron Bledsoe, the one-time head of CBS Records' Nashville office, to build Georgetown. After five years, Putnam got divorced, and Purcell bought his stake in the studio. He wanted to buy out his third partner, but, as he put it, "Ron won't sell out to me at a reasonable price."

With good reason. As one of only three mastering studios in Nashville, Georgetown handled 50 percent of the *Billboard* country charts, 60 percent of the Christian music, and about 25 percent of the *Billboard* 200, roughly three to four hundred albums a year. At five thousand to seven thousand dollars per album, it is quite a lucrative business.

Purcell's second-story studio has full-length picture windows; acoustic tiles line the walls. Against one of them was balanced a giant stuffed Bugs Bunny holding a 1958 Harmony Stratotone, one of Purcell's collection of vintage guitars.

His equipment, which adjusts the apparent relative volume and timbre (not necessarily the actual sounds, but what the ear hears) of an album's songs, is custom. The shell of the console was made by Georg Neumann, a German company. The interior electronics were designed by the same engineer who created the computer system that keeps a tally of cars' laps at the Daytona Speedway. His two limiters, which literally level out the range on a recording, and their control box are vintage models from the fifties, made by a company called Fairchild. A hand-lettered label on top of the three said, "Fairchildren." Each had a separate tag: "Pepina," "Hassie," and "Little Luke," named for characters in *The Real McCoys*.

When he masters an album, Purcell first listens to the music alone, writing down his thoughts on ten by four-and-three-quarter-inch index cards. He then goes through them with the producer, playing any sections he thinks should be changed. The cards for "Wrong Side of Memphis" and "Nearest Distant Shore" were virtually blank. For "Say You Will" he wrote, "Come down on *make*." The idea was to match the apparent volume level in "Say You Will" to the song before. By changing it on the second word of the song, that is *make*, the listener would not perceive that a change was taking place.

At four, when Purcell started working with Fundis, he switched the *make* down a full decibel, then he and Fundis listened to the song. "I want *you* down and *say* up," said Fundis. The idea, again, was to make the volume level of the song uniform, so that listeners wouldn't have to adjust it themselves.

"Let's bring *say* up a full db," said Purcell. "If that's too much, we can go down. Besides, we are going to hotbox it anyway," he added, referring to a process, used on every album he masters, that increases the volume by three to five decibels. By the time they worked their way through the rest of the album, it was nearly seven, and Fundis called it a night. He had promised to be home to take his son out shopping for his birthday.

On Sunday afternoon he met Yearwood at the Sound Emporium with a mastered copy of her album. She sat quietly through the first six songs, waiting for "Down on My Knees." She listened once, then asked to hear it again.

"I guess it does sound cool," she said.

"I knew you'd come around," Fundis replied.

The only thing that didn't work was "Hearts in Armor," which sounded noticeably louder than the song before it. On Tuesday, he went back to Georgetown to adjust the volume. When he listened to it again, he realized the problem was in the mix. The vocals themselves were too loud. "It hurt to listen to them," he said. He went back to the Sound Emporium and reworked the song. On Wednesday he was back at Georgetown, doing the final mastering. He finished by early afternoon.

Federal Express picked up the tape at 9:30 that night, shipping it to manufacturing plants in California and Kentucky. *Hearts in Armor*, just under a month late and $4,721.74 over budget (mostly for extra studio time), was finally finished.

The music might have been completed, but the album cover was still a problem. McGuire had finally heard back from *Harper's Bazaar*. The business manager refused to release the photograph. If MCA used it, McGuire told Kragen, it would destroy his relationship with the magazine. He suggested an alternative: If

Yearwood could come to the studio for an hour, he would recreate the shot; the *Harper's* art director had told him that would be no problem.

Yearwood made a second visit to McGuire's studio with the same jacket, the same hair, and the same makeup. He put on the fan, blew her hair back, and started shooting. Forty minutes later he had duplicated the portrait.

He developed the film as soon as she left. When the images emerged, he knew he had what they wanted.

The record was ready. Now it was up to MCA to sell it.

• • •

The classic radio promoter is a fast-talking, slack-jawed salesman whose job it is to court the radio stations and wheedle them into putting his songs on their playlists. In the old days he would use a fistful of bills to make his case. That became officially illegal in 1960, when Congress passed a statute making payola a misdemeanor punishable by a maximum fine of ten thousand dollars and one year in prison. To date, no one has ever served any jail time on payola charges, and as Fredric Dannen documented it in *Hit Men*, the law hardly put a stop to the shenanigans. Through the sixties, seventies, and eighties, a network of independent operators took over the dirty work (so that record companies could claim ignorance), with hundreds of thousands of dollars changing hands. By the end of the eighties, though, even that game was getting somewhat perilous. A new set of indictments were handed up in 1989 and 1990, which, even though they mostly ended up with dismissals or acquittals, were a source of considerable concern in the pop and rock world.

The payola scandals never came to Music Row. It wasn't that the country music promoters were necessarily more upstanding than their counterparts in rock and pop, it was just that when it came to promotion—as with everything else in Nashville—there were simply less expensive, and equally effective, methods of persuasion. "Everything here operates on friendship and favors," says Lynn Shults, onetime vice president of A&R at Capitol Records and currently director of operations for country music at *Billboard*. "Anybody that ever paid cash is stupid."

What MCA Nashville did pay for was a junket or two a year, airfare and lodging for scores of radio programmers to places like New Orleans or Chicago, where they would be wined and dined and serenaded by the label's latest act. Yearwood wasn't on that circuit this year. "Memphis" had been debuted back at the radio seminar in February. The sole piece of promotion programmers received was a two-by-three-inch refrigerator magnet, shaped like a highway sign, that said, "Wrong Side Of Memphis."

As far as Shelia Shipley, head of MCA's promotion department, was concerned, there really wasn't any need for an expensive push for Yearwood's newest single.

"She's coming off a number one record," she explained. "Radio stations have been waiting for this."

As promotion people go, Shipley is cast against type, and that measured response was typical Shipley. She was the only woman heading up a promotion department on Music Row—a small woman, dressed schoolgirl proper: calf-length skirts, patent leather flats, ruffled blouses—and she had got there by dint of quiet efficiency. Shipley grew up in rural Kentucky, where her mother worked in a factory making overalls and her father was a logger. She was married before she was seventeen, had her son while she was still a teenager. At thirty-nine, she had already been a grandmother for two years.

Shipley got to Nashville when she was twenty-three, intent on getting a job in television, but no one would hire her without a college degree. She ended up as a receptionist at a record company, moved to the promotion department at RCA in 1979, and was hired by MCA in 1984. Six months after she got there, she was put in charge of the department. Her wall was cluttered with the obligatory gold and platinum records toted up in those years. Above her desk was a plaque inscribed with the philosophy that she believed had made them possible: "The world is not concerned about the storms at sea. The question is did you bring the ship into port."

On July 20, that ship was the first single from Trisha Yearwood's new album.

The week before, MCA had bought the bottom quarter of the page of *Radio & Records* "Hot Fax," which alerts the record and radio industries what the new singles will be. On July 13, they sent, by overnight mail, five hundred CD singles to radio stations across the country. Today they would call each of them, to tally up how many had put the song on their playlists. The first goal was to have more stations add "Wrong Side of Memphis" than any other song that week. The second was to have it go number one the week of the Country Music Awards.

* * *

There are two master chart-keepers, *Billboard* and *Radio & Records* (*R&R*) with *The Gavin Report* keeping tabs on the smaller markets. Each has its own group of "reporting" stations—*Billboard* has 110, *R&R*, 205—a selection made on the basis of the size of the market, that is, the population within reach of a given station's signal. Stations clamor to be listed as reporters. They are the elite group that get those trips to New Orleans, the ones supplied with the first copies of a single.

The criteria for playing a song on the radio vary from station to station. Some base their selection on listener call-in, but increasingly the selections have become more objective, with independent contractors hired to survey the radio audiences. They play a few lines from the song, then ask whether the listener likes it and whether he or she is familiar with it. Would they like to hear it more? Have they heard it enough? If the answer to the second question is yes, the record is considered to have run its course, or, as a promoter would put it, "burned."

It used to be that both publications relied on telephone surveys, in which radio stations would simply report what they were playing and how often they were playing it (light rotation meant two to three times a day; medium, three to four; and heavy, five to six). The publications would then multiply the frequency by the size of the marketplace (the larger the marketplace, the bigger the multiplier), add up the results, and post them. If a song was doing better than it had the week before, it got a bullet on the chart, a sign of upward momentum.

In 1989 *Billboard* changed the way it tracked what was being played. It installed a computerized system on 110 stations (82 in the top markets) that electronically monitored radio play. The need for polling was eliminated. *Billboard* simply reported what was actually being played.

"It met with tremendous resistance," said *Billboard*'s Shults. Record promoters argued that the *Billboard* sample was inadequate, that it didn't represent the smaller markets where country records could be broken. But that wasn't the only reason: A national promotion director measures his or her success in number one records, and *R&R* tended to change number one records far more often than *Billboard*. Quite simply, under the old system the promoters felt that they might have more influence over the results. Most turned their lobbying efforts to *R&R*.

By the end of 1992, though, promoters were starting to feel that *Billboard*'s computerized monitoring might, in fact, present a more accurate picture of the marketplace and that that information might well aid their marketing efforts. Still, change was coming slowly, and on July 20, when "Wrong Side of Memphis" was released, MCA was still focusing its efforts on *R&R*.

The promotion department spent that Monday working the phones to see if Yearwood's latest had, in fact, been added. Usually Shipley spent her time handling administrative matters, with Scott Borchetta heading up the phone squad. But today Borchetta was out of the office, and Shipley was handling the phone banks herself. Her first call went to WTNT in Tallahassee, Florida. Yes, Yearwood had been added. Then Orlando came in and then Panama City. By a quarter past ten, Yearwood's tally was up to seventy-two stations. Rosie Fitzpatrick, another member of the promotion staff, came in to report her tallies. The country station in Augusta, Georgia, hadn't put Yearwood on, but promised to next week. Who was added? Shipley asked. Collin Raye, she replied.

More and more stations have started using telephone recordings so they don't have to take the promoters' calls themselves. When Shipley called KPLX in Dallas, that recording told her precisely what she didn't want to hear: The only new add was Collin Raye. "Son of a bitch," she said after the recording clicked off. "I've got to hear what it is." She pulled out a copy of the CD and put on the song, "In This Life," a sweet ballad. "It's a hit," she announced after the first verse. She switched the player off. "That's going to sell him a lot of records." Shipley didn't know Raye shared his producer with Yearwood; it didn't much matter. It wouldn't pull her ship home.

In all, though, the day went well. By the end of the afternoon "Memphis" had 123 adds, topping anything Yearwood had done before. "We could have it," said Shipley, "if it weren't for Collin Raye."

At seven she drove over to the *Radio & Records* office to get the official results: Yearwood came in with 128 adds; Collin Raye had 129. Garth Fundis had produced the most added record for the week, but it wasn't Trisha Yearwood's.

CHAPTER 23

O<small>N</small> J<small>ULY</small> 17, <small>AS</small> "W<small>RONG</small> S<small>IDE OF</small> M<small>EMPHIS</small>" <small>WAS MAKING</small> its radio debut, Trisha Yearwood was in St. Clairsville, Ohio, for an hour-long turn at the Jamboree in the Hills, which bills itself as "the Super Bowl" of country music concerts. The Jamboree is four straight days of country music. Yearwood was scheduled to appear along with Lorrie Morgan, Diamond Rio, and the Oak Ridge Boys. There was a surprise guest that Friday: Sean Young, the actress who had made a small sensation in the backseat of a limousine with Kevin Costner in *No Way Out*, then again when she showed up on the Warner lot, unannounced, in a Catwoman outfit, determined to win the part that ultimately went to Michelle Pfeiffer, had apparently decided to diversify her career. She would be making her debut as a country singer at the Jamboree.

Yearwood got to the site, a cement stage set into the back of the Appalachian foothills, at four. There was a trailer set up for press interviews. As Yearwood talked, one of the promoters approached Arnold, asking him if the singer wanted to meet the actress. Arnold escorted Yearwood over to Young's trailer. After introductions, Young brought out a waist-length wig she had bought for the occasion. It looked not unlike the pelt of an underfed black bear. "What do you think?" she asked.

"I think you should do whatever makes you feel the most comfortable," Yearwood hedged.

Young removed the wig.

The actress went onstage later that afternoon. She did three songs, two up-tempo, one ballad. All were originals, none was on key. She pranced around the stage, dancing something that looked like a cross between the two-step and the Swim. Mercifully, that has been the last heard of Young's new career.

Yearwood and company left the motel about eleven. It was a long run; they were scheduled to be out on the road for nine more days. They hit the Du Page County Fair in Wheaton, Illinois, six days through. The performance went well enough. There was sufficient enthusiasm for an encore. After they had played the Presley song, Yearwood and Lauer headed onto the bus—the keyboard player to the bathroom, Yearwood to the stateroom. As she opened the door, smoke started billowing into the hallway. She walked toward her vanity, somehow reasoning that the problem was her electric curler. Seconds later, she was enveloped in smoke. She backed out, slammed the stateroom door, then ran to the bathroom. "Tim," she called out, "get out. The bus is on fire."

An off-duty fireman named Rick Kammes working security for the fair was the first to see Yearwood and Lauer run off the bus. He told a policeman to call the fire department, then climbed onto the coach to check on the flames. He made it through the front room and the hallway. By the time he got to the back of the bus, he was on his knees, crawling through the stateroom. The fire was coming from a back closet, but it was too smoky to put out on his own. He turned around and backed out, and by that time reinforcements had arrived: a squad car and two full-fledged fire engines. The firemen bashed out the bus windows and snaked hoses into the stateroom. A swollen river of water flushed through the bus, cresting just above the second tier of bunks. Outside, the singer and her band made a loose ring around their coach. Arnold went off looking for a phone. Hoker stood outside the cab, close to the driver's seat, watching in slack-jawed horror.

It took half an hour to extinguish the flames, two hours more to clean up the charred, waterlogged mess. In a pile of smoky, soggy fabric in the back closet, the firemen found the source of the flames. The electrical outlet for Yearwood's cellular phone had apparently shorted out, sending sparks flying off into her clothing.

Virtually everything on the bus had been burned, smoked, or

soaked. There were three days of the run left, and they had nothing to wear and no transportation. Hemphill was supposed to have a new bus in Wheaton by noon. The band spent the morning doing laundry, salvaging what they could of their clothes. Emergency items—underwear, toothbrushes—were procured in a mall just across the highway. They ended up wearing the same stage outfits for the next three performances.

The replacement bus pulled into Nashville just after dawn on Monday. For their next runs they were assigned a new bus with its own driver. The last anyone heard, Hoker was working with Guns N' Roses.

Yearwood would be in town fewer than twenty-four hours.

• • •

By August 1, Yearwood had had seventy-three performance dates, and she was looking at the prospect of forty-nine more before the end of October. According to her schedule, she would be in Nashville fewer than thirty days through the summer and early fall. In fact, she would be there less than half that time. Home, for Yearwood, was becoming an increasingly tenuous concept. Her house was more a layover than a home; the living room was virtually empty, and her dog seemed to favor her house sitter.

After that teary scene at the Twilight Motel, she resolved she would have a personal life. She wanted to be with Reynolds, and on her days off she was, wherever that might be. When she flew to meet him in Dallas that Tuesday, she had four days before there would be another flight to another city to catch up with her band and another three-day run of her own.

It was an exhausting regimen, but, as far as Yearwood was concerned, it was better than the alternative. Her handlers were less certain. When Yearwood was with the Mavericks, it was harder to find her, harder to keep her informed, harder for her to keep up with the radio and newspaper interviews that were the foundation of her career.

Yearwood spent her days in Dallas shopping; evenings she sat in the back as the band played in a seedy bar in a downtown hotel. On Friday they moved out to the Hilton, a smoked-glassed high rise across from the airport. MCA was bringing in its marketing department, as well as the local distributors, for the occasion. Yearwood wasn't pleased when the local papers reported that she was going to be part of the show. She didn't want to deflect attention from the Mavericks. It wouldn't be easy, though. MCA had stocked the hotel with two hundred copies of an issue of *Country America* magazine with Yearwood on the cover. Before the show, she was the one asked for autographs.

Malo, though, didn't seem put out by Yearwood's presence. This night there was a sellout crowd, their biggest of the week. "I feel real comfortable here," said Malo midway through. "It's hot, it's sunny, and people know how to say my name." The next song was "Deep in the Heart of Texas."

Two hours into the set, Malo summoned Yearwood from the audience. He kept center stage. She stood off to his right, singing harmony to his lead on "Your Cheatin' Heart." At the end, he invited another singer up from the audience, Tracy Byrd, a fresh-faced Texan who had just been signed by MCA. "We're going to do a song I always thought a country band should do," Malo announced, then swung into "Twist and Shout." Neither Byrd nor Yearwood had ever sung the Beatles tune, but the audience was enthusiastic and the singers were game. It was a bumpy, rambunctious performance. At the end of the last cooing harmony, Malo called out his thanks to the audience, then threw his hand out to the harmony singers: "Ladies and Gentlemen, Tracy Byrd, Trisha Yearwood. Forgive 'em." And the singers and the band filed from the stage.

As Reynolds walked toward the bar, a fine-boned blonde in tight jeans approached him. "Wow," she said. "Great show." Yearwood walked up from behind, took her boyfriend by the arm, nuzzled up to his cheek, and then kissed him full on the lips. The blonde surveyed the situation and walked away without another word.

The next morning Yearwood was on a plane to St. Louis. At three that afternoon she was due in Owensville, Missouri, where she was the headliner at the Gasconade County Fair.

Yearwood got to the motel just after two. An hour later she was on her bus, parked just behind the bandstand. You could hear them auctioning off country hams as the band set up on stage.

The Gasconade fair was a small festival in a county that, economically speaking, was about average for the state. In the vernacular of the country circuit, it was "a dust bowl." The venue was a scarred athletic field. The audience supplied its own chairs.

As the wind swirled through the park, everything got covered with a dingy veil of dry brown dirt.

One of the biggest booths belonged to the Missouri State Trappers Association. The hunters had hung a macabre gallery. One photo showed a coyote corpse, half its fur gone, starved to skin and bones. The second showed another dead coyote, considerably plumper, caught in a trap. "Nature's control method," read the caption under the first photo. "Man's control method," read the second. Two rifles were being raffled off to raise funds for the local chapter. Another kiosk sold pillows emblazoned with logos for Harley-Davidson and Metal Maniac, along with bath towels printed with the Stars and Bars and a bit of wisdom from Hank Williams, Jr.: "If the South would've won we would've had it made."

Over the past weeks, the band had made a few changes in its performance. Instead of simply waiting onstage as Yearwood walked on, the musicians entered playing, and, at the end, joined hands center stage, bowing to the audience. "Just like a pop act," said Lauer.

Yearwood opened in Owensville with "Say You Will," then, to tepid applause, moved into "Who Turned Out the Lights." The weather was bad, her speaking voice was slightly hoarse, and her singing robbed of its usual power. She made it through the show without incident or enthusiasm. At the end of the hour, McClure, Lauer, Rogers, and Hager headed to center stage, joined hands, then looked at one another in panic. Yearwood had already walked off, making their last flourish look faintly ridiculous.

"I have a sore throat," Yearwood told Jarrah Herter, her trainer, back in the stateroom. "Could you tell Leonard I don't feel like signing?"

Unbeknownst to the singer, though, the fair director had just cornered Arnold and asked if she was going to sign. Since he had heard nothing to the contrary, Arnold answered that she would. Moments later, Herter found him and gave him the message that Yearwood wasn't feeling well. Arnold headed back to the stateroom. "We told them we were going to sign," he told her.

She looked up in frustration. "I guess I'm not the boss anymore.

I guess no one listens to what I want to do." She stood up and strode past him, out to the T-shirt stand where she sat and signed autographs in the evening mist.

It took ninety minutes to sign her way through a hundred fans. She returned to the bus in silence, went back to her stateroom, and shut the door. Fifteen minutes later, Lisa McLaughlin headed in; she wanted to tell Yearwood how well they had done that evening. Yearwood was sitting by her vanity, in tears.

"Can I do anything?" McLaughlin asked.

"No," she said. "It's my job to be happy and smile all the time."

"Everybody deserves a chance to cry," said McLaughlin as she pulled Yearwood's door closed.

That was the last anyone saw of the singer until the bus pulled into the parking lot at the Holiday Inn in Cedar Rapids, Iowa, just after nine the next morning. Arnold was, as usual, the first one out. He returned with bad news. Their rooms weren't ready and probably wouldn't be for another hour or two.

Half an hour later, the band had moved into a grim ground-floor coffee shop. Yearwood shared a table with Rogers, Herter, and McLaughlin. Just before ten, Arnold walked in, and Yearwood beckoned him over.

"My throat is still sore from sitting out in that dew," she said, eating her pancakes.

"Maybe one day you'll be so famous you won't have to sign autographs anymore," he replied.

"Maybe one day I'll be in charge of my own show."

"Are you trying to tell me something?"

"I felt like you forced me to sign."

"We told them we would do it, and I hate to disappoint people once we've said we're going to do something."

"Well, sometimes people just have to get disappointed."

Once more, Arnold worried that the woman he so enjoyed working with was slipping away. He had seen it happen before, perfectly reasonable people turned impossible because of the demands of road life—the interviews, the constant meet and greet, the endless smiles.

"The only way they can have any kind of effect is to say no," he said afterward. "And the only way they can get anyone to listen is if they say it real loud. Eventually they turn them all into monsters."

Now, he tried to steer the conversation to another topic. "How was Robert?"

"Great. I just wish I could have him out here somehow. I hate leaving him."

"I'll be your love slave," Arnold said, laughing. "Let's do it this way. Let's always tell them you *may* sign, never commit. That way we can always get out of it."

"Makes sense," said Yearwood, and finally the mood broke. "I'm sorry. I hate this. Please be my friend again." She reached over and hugged him.

They had five hours before they were due at the Great Jones County Fair. Yearwood slept and exercised. By afternoon, she was in considerably better humor.

"I've got some required listening here," she said, and pulled out a tape sent to her by a disc jockey she had met at one of her shows. On the road, they are known as underground tapes, recordings that are copied and sent from radio stations to performers and back again, in a sort of music-industry chain letter. This batch included an infamous recording of Linda McCartney singing a horribly off-key version of "Hey Jude" that a sound engineer had recorded on the sly, along with such gems as "We're from West Virginia and We Wear Shoes" ("We've got modern expressways going every which way/If you come here for a laugh/you can kiss my country ass/This is West by God Virginia and we wear shoes"); "I've Finally Gotten to Where You Told Me to Go" (the chorus: "It's hell without you"); and "Where's Hank Williams When You Need Him?"

They headed to the fairgrounds just after lunch and parked behind the bandstand. Everything was running late. The seating for Yearwood's concert doubled as the track for the demolition derby, and the contest was well into overtime.

Yearwood wandered off the bus to watch the crashing Camaros. Among the backstage spectators was a teenager with a ripped-up football jersey that read "Monticello."

"I want his shirt," she told McLaughlin. "Can you get him back to the bus?"

McLaughlin did as ordered; five minutes later, the puzzled teen was standing in the front of Yearwood's bus.

"I'm from Monticello, Georgia," Yearwood explained. "I want your shirt. I'll trade you for one of mine."

"I've got a clean one at home," he offered.

"This one's fine."

And he stripped off his torn jersey, replacing it with a white Yearwood special. She put her palms on his back and signed, "Love, Trisha Yearwood."

This night in Iowa was a considerable improvement over the evening before. The audience stomped and clapped, and Yearwood returned the favor with an encore. "Do you want to sign?" Arnold asked as he escorted her from the stage. This time she said yes.

The musicians headed over to an area just above the bandstand, labeled "Beer Garden." Jay Hager, uncharacteristically, went along. He had broken up with his girlfriend several weeks before, and now, instead of being glued to the phone, he was starting to spend time with the band. Before the breakup he had sought the advice of his fellow travelers: Did it make sense to drop her? Was he doing the right thing? Everyone encouraged him to make the break, and, in all, he seemed relieved. The biggest loss, he laughed, was his free supply of plaque-fighting dental floss.

• • •

On the face of it, Yearwood was doing fine. She was happy with her album, the Revlon deal was signed and moving ahead. The perfume's debut had been postponed until February, which, as far as she was concerned, was just as well. With a five-month lapse between the album and the perfume, she wouldn't have to worry about sullying the critical response with commerce. And everyone said she was a shoo-in for the Horizon Award at the CMA Awards.

Still, there were more and more incidents like the contested signing session in Owensville. There was too much travel, too much baked chicken wolfed down at picnic tables, too many breakfasts in bad motels. For the first year, even the first few months of the second, it had been an adventure, but the rattlesnake round ups and the apple festivals were fast losing their allure.

Along the way, there had been a change in the relationship between the singer and her band. Her success, they were realizing, was not their own. It was something that happened with every new band, rediscovered as each new star made it big. They saw now that she was the star and they were her supporting cast, there for the ride, easily replaced.

The fire became the crucible for their dissatisfaction. The issue was insurance. They had all signed waivers releasing Yearwood from liability should any of their possessions be damaged while they were out on the road. It's a routine practice, the kind of thing that hardly ever means anything. In this case, though, a couple of the band members had lost hundreds of dollars worth of clothing, and now the waivers meant that they probably wouldn't be reimbursed.

Even though he had lost only about fifty dollars worth of clothing, Lauer was the only one who didn't quickly reconcile himself to the loss. "Good management wouldn't allow that to happen," he said. Good management, he believed, would cover the losses. Then there was the matter of salary. Yearwood might have a platinum record and a deal with Revlon, but he was still getting just $250 a show—$50 less, he found out, than the members of players in another band whose leader had yet to have Yearwood's success.

For Lauer, it was a slow burn. He kept to himself for a two-day run through the Midwest and another four-day haul up to Rhode Island and back. But after an afternoon show in Bethlehem, Pennsylvania, as the male members of the band gathered in their room at the Holiday Inn, Lauer started talking about how unhappy he was about the insurance. Johnny Garcia chimed in that he was upset by Yearwood's attitude. During the show that night he had missed a lick on one song. Afterward, Yearwood had walked over and whispered, "Real smooth move." It wasn't much, but it was the sort of sarcasm he wanted no part of.

An hour or so later they boarded the bus to head back to Nashville. Yearwood retreated to her stateroom; the band crowded up front. Lauer announced he was going to talk to her. As the bandleader, he felt it was his responsibility to tell her he thought the situation was not acceptable.

McClure, alone among the band members, pleaded with him to stay silent. "You don't understand. This is a good gig. Give her time, be patient. It will work out."

Lauer wrote off McClure as Yearwood's pawn. He went and knocked on the door, and told Yearwood about his concerns—the money and how her attitude hurt morale. Afterward, she went back to the band members herself. Each in turn told her that no, they knew she meant well, that she was under a lot of pressure. Which left only Lauer to be dealt with.

When she got back to Nashville, she called Malcolm Mimms. She wanted to know what the insurance situation was and if she was paying the band enough. On both accounts, her lawyer told her, she was treating her band fairly—given how new she was and how much she was making per show.

"The money is being invested in the future," she told Lauer later. "There will be rewards."

"It's your future, not mine," Lauer retorted. "I want to be paid now." They argued to a draw.

Yearwood was already spending very little time with the band. After that confrontation, she spent even less. She started skipping sound check, staying in her hotel room so she could work out and do interviews. Generally she appeared just before showtime, and, at the end of the run, flew off to wherever the Mavericks were performing. Her only confidante was Jarrah Herter. Her trainer became her liaison with her road manager, her messenger to the band. Yearwood abhorred confrontation, and by letting Herter communicate for her she was able to avoid it.

CHAPTER 24

BY MID-AUGUST, THE MCA MARKETING CAMPAIGN, SUCH AS it was, was going full throttle. More than 50 rack-jobbers had been wined and dined, 3,500 posters had been sent to record stores, 100 15-second spots ("flyswatters," in industry parlance) had been purchased for CMT. Two single full-page advertisements ("Don Henley/Garth Brooks/Vince Gill/Emmylou Harris/Raul Malo in Perfect Harmony With Trisha Yearwood") had been purchased, one in *Billboard*, the other in *Country Music*.

"Wrong Side of Memphis" was heading steadily up the charts, though it was not the fireball MCA had hoped for. By the week of August 29, it was ranked number twenty-seven in *Billboard*, while Collin Raye's "In This Life" was at number nineteen. Four hundred thousand copies of *Hearts in Armor*—fifty thousand more than the marketing department had projected—had been ordered by distributors and record stores nationwide. All that was hanging fire were the reviews.

Pop records often have elaborate launch parties, but as with everything else, Nashville has never spent a lot to court the press. There was talk of a listening party for *Hearts in Armor* in Memphis, but by mid-August, Yearwood was mostly on the road, Fundis was on a much needed two-week vacation with his family, and no one was pressing to entertain. As Susan Levy put it, "there simply wasn't time."

On July 22, Levy had sent out 250 cassettes to reviewers around the country. There was no promotional material, no photographs, just a tape and a copy of the liner notes.

The minimalism was not by design: If Levy had waited for the compact disk enclosure to come back from the printer, the tapes wouldn't have gone out until the second week of August, much too close to the album's September 1 "street date," the day the tapes and CDs were supposed to arrive in record stores. Yearwood's songs would have to sell themselves—which was precisely what Bruce Hinton had wanted back in March when he was so concerned about Yearwood's new portraits. (Hinton, not incidentally, ultimately got what he had wanted months before. Although four shots inside the CD booklet were from the controversial St. Nicholas session, the all-important cover portrait was not.)

Two things would propel sales: if "Memphis" became a runaway hit—and if the reviews were good. "Memphis" was dubious, but by the end of August, the signs on the media front were more than encouraging. Levy heard that a review had been assigned by *Rolling Stone*, which hadn't even looked at Yearwood's first album. ("Frankly," said Levy, "there was no reason for them to.") And on August 28, *Billboard* came out with a rave review ("As good as Yearwood's debut album was, it pales in comparison to this one . . ."), as well as a front-page story headlined, "IT'S TRISHA'S YEAR TO SHINE."

Billboard had been the first national publication to cover Yearwood. Timothy White, who had been named editor in December 1990, first heard her in early 1991, when he paid a call on Bruce Hinton. "He just handed me a tape and told me it was a new young female they had just signed," White recalled. "There was no hustle, no blowing smoke up my chimney." White liked her music ("She sounded woodsy," he said, "a girl walking nervously through life"), and two weeks after her first album was released he assigned a story on the singer. When he heard her second album, it only confirmed his belief.

White liked to regard his publication as something of a tip sheet, and he scheduled the second story—on the cover with photo—to come out before the record hit the stores. "I want us to have stuff early," he said, "and I want to do it well so other journalists will get in the habit of stealing from us." Whether White had successfully cast *Billboard* as the industry standard is unclear, but there was no question that the *Billboard* articles were a bellwether.

September 1 brought reviews in *USA Today* (three stars out of four) and *The Houston Post:* "Some have compared her to Linda

Ronstadt, but Yearwood's not that soulless a technician. . . .
There's . . . not a bad cut on 'Hearts in Armor.' If you do the
right thing and buy [it] don't expect to listen to anything else for
a while."

Levy was encouraged, but she figured it would take the rest
of the national press a few weeks more to acknowledge the album.
"Everyone lets the cassettes sit," she said, "then they read something in *The New York Times,* and go through the stuff on their
desks trying to figure out where it is."

On Sunday, September 6, the *Times* weighed in with a rave in
the Arts and Leisure section. *Newsweek* followed with a brief
mention in a pop music roundup: After going through a score of
new pop and rock records, John Leland closed with a paean to
the new country albums. Yearwood, he wrote, "leads the field
with . . . the strongest female vocal performance to come out
of Nashville in years." *The Los Angeles Times,* which had given
Yearwood's first album a middling review, gave her second four
stars.

Perhaps most satisfying to the people at MCA were the three
and a half stars from *Rolling Stone:* "The denim shirt has given
way to off-the-shoulder sweater. The cascade of light brunette
curls has been made long and straight. The country girl is now
a dazzling beauty. Happy to report, this make-over in pursuit of
mass appeal applies only to Trisha Yearwood's appearance. Not
only has her music retained its edge, but it has grown. . . . On
a disc that offers much to admire . . . Yearwood's singing is the
most compelling element. . . . The adventurousness of *Hearts in
Armor* serves notice that Trisha Yearwood has the potential for
a long, significant career."

As soon as he saw the *Rolling Stone* review, Bruce Hinton called
Ken Kragen.

"Remember those conversations about how we wanted to crop
her picture, not wanting a lot of cleavage, about how we didn't
want it to be a distraction, how I wanted the critics to go straight
to the music?" he said. "This review does exactly what I was
trying to accomplish. It says we got our cake and ate it, too. It
says this highly attractive person makes incredible music. I
couldn't have planned it better."

Yearwood made a quick trip to New York City midaccolade
to promote the album—a photo shoot for *Entertainment Weekly,*

an interview on *Today*, two meetings with Revlon. She traveled with an entourage of three: Nancy Russell, Sheri McCoy, and Maria Smoot, her hairstylist.

The *Today* spot was scheduled to be shot at 10:00 A.M., in a room at the Regency. By nine, Yearwood was in Smoot's room, getting her hair washed and styled. As Smoot rolled Yearwood's hair on giant curlers, Madonna's newest video played on MTV. "I just hate her," said Smoot. "The girls in my shop brought her record in, just to get at me. They love her, though. Paid to see her movie twice."

"I went to see her movie," Yearwood volunteered.

"Why?"

"It was an education to me as a businesswoman. Whatever you think of her, she knows what she's doing."

Twenty minutes later, they were down in the suite, talking to a *Today* producer named Joanne LaMarca. Though the piece was being taped on September 2, the plan was to hold it until September 30, the morning of the Country Music Association Awards. "You have two hit albums, you were named top new female vocalist by the Academy of Country Music, now you're up for female vocalist and Horizon awards at the CMAs. How does it feel?" LaMarca asked.

"It's been quite a year. I feel lucky. . . . I don't know if ten years ago I'd be selling as many records. It's kind of like you wake yourself up and pinch yourself. It's hard to believe it's really happening."

LaMarca asked about her music business degree and its role in her career.

"No one asked to see my diploma when I signed my deal, but I do think it helped. . . . It's like starting a business. The first two years you don't take vacations, all your profits go back in."

"Did you ever have a day when you thought, 'I can't do it, I'm getting out'?"

"I never had a day when I felt like I'm going to pack up and go home. I just felt if I kept at it, it would happen—and it did."

She talked about Revlon, about the image of country music. She answered all the same questions for the umpteenth time, but this time she would have an audience of four million.

"The image of country music isn't what it used to be. It is Dolly Parton, but it's also Lyle Lovett and Mary-Chapin Carpenter. I might wake up and want to put on a fringe jacket, but I'm a lot more likely to wear black leggings and a big shirt."

LaMarca asked about Yearwood's market ("twelve-year-old girls, which makes me feel a little responsible"), if Yearwood had ever got anyone's autograph when she was a kid ("Reba McEntire was at a mall when I was about fifteen. I still have it on my wall at my parents' house. . . . I'm not real pushy. I wouldn't ask Elvis even if he came in—which he might do at this very moment").

"What's it like to be nominated up there with Reba now?"

"I look at that as an honor. I feel too new. . . . I am amazed and honored to be included; it's like winning without winning."

"What next?"

"I don't want to be trying to do hit records in twenty years. I want to enjoy it for as long as it lasts, and I know it's not going to last forever."

The interview went on for forty minutes. Ultimately, Yearwood's answers would be edited down to a three-minute segment. There was little time for small talk at the end. Yearwood was already running late for her photo shoot.

"Want to see a picture of my boyfriend?" the producer asked, apropos of nothing, and produced a snapshot of a mustachioed man, shirtless on the sand. "We met in Cape May."

Nancy Russell maneuvered Yearwood out the door. "There must be some kind of natural disaster about to happen," said Russell, who had been dating a young rock-and-roll musician for about a month. "Everyone gets a boyfriend, then the world blows up."

The next stop was the *Entertainment Weekly* shoot at Industria, the fashion photo studio owned by Fabrizio Ferri. McCoy had brought two racks of clothing.

"You can have anything you want," she said.

"Good," Yearwood replied. "I hate to wear something that I love, then find out I can't have it. It pisses me off."

She put on a tailored black jacket with red cuffs and lapel. The photographer put her in a chair and shot for forty-five minutes, the camera full on her face. They broke for lunch, a spread of grilled chicken and vegetables, and started up again just after two. By three they were an hour behind schedule, and Russell had had enough.

"We've got to get moving."

"We'll be fine," said Yearwood. "We'll be fine."

"It doesn't help when she says that," groused Russell. "If she's late, it's my fault. Damned if you do, damned if you don't." She walked out, leaned against a car, smoked a cigarette. "I've never seen a photo shoot that didn't go overtime."

They were three quarters of an hour late for their next appointment, an interview at Unistar Radio Networks, which provides programming to some thirty-five hundred stations throughout the country. Russell left Yearwood in the studio and found a phone. The day was nearly over, but she had other fires to douse. Travis Tritt had, for reasons unknown, forgotten to do an interview with *The Detroit News*. She spent twenty minutes trying to track down the reporter, to apologize and to reschedule. "This is bad," she said. "He's performing there next week."

Yearwood, she added, was getting almost as difficult to pin down. Russell had been trying to schedule a couple of newspaper interviews, but Yearwood couldn't seem to find the time. "When she gets time with Robert, she doesn't want to do interviews," she said. "It's not easy."

Later, on the elevator down from the Unistar interview, she tried to get Yearwood to change her mind. "You can't do it all," the singer replied. "You just can't. There aren't enough hours in the day to do everything people want."

The next morning she caught a flight to Washington for a four-day run through Virginia, New York, Ohio, and Wisconsin. After her show at the Central Wisconsin State Fair, the bus dropped her off at O'Hare Airport in Chicago. The Mavericks had a three-day stint in San Francisco, and Yearwood intended to be there. She would return to Nashville on September 11. Originally she was booked on an early-morning flight, but she changed it to early afternoon. She would be cutting it very close for Tim Lauer's wedding.

It was a big Nashville wedding, five hundred guests, among them the members of Yearwood's band and crew. Tammy Rogers played a Bach cantata on her viola as guests filed into the Brentwood Baptist Church. Ric McClure was one of the six groomsmen. Jay Hager turned up with his dental hygienist, much to the dismay of the rest of the band. "He asked me what I thought of her, and I told him he was right to get rid of her," said Arnold. "Now they get back together. I feel like a jerk." He avoided their table at the reception.

The bride's father, Ben Peters, was a songwriter of considerable renown ("Kiss an Angel Good Morning," "When the Last Teardrop Falls"), and so there was also a contingent from Music Row, including Jim Fogelsong, the former head of both Capitol and MCA, the songwriter Curley Putman ("Green Green Grass of Home"), and Eddy Arnold. Loudilla Johnson, in turquoise chiffon, sat at a corner table with her two sisters.

The only person missing was Trisha Yearwood. The singer, who had known the groom longer than anyone else in her band, missed the ceremony as well as the reception.

She was, however, on time for her bus's departure; they were scheduled to perform at the National Association of Broadcasters the next day in New Orleans. The group had gathered by the time Yearwood arrived, with two additions to the usual entourage: An acoustic guitar player, Jim Hurst, had been added so the band could more precisely replicate songs from the new album, and there was a substitute keyboard player while Lauer was off on his honeymoon. Yearwood showed up dressed to travel: black sweatshirt, gray sweatpants, scrubbed face. "I can't believe I missed the wedding," she said as she got out of her car. "I just can't believe it." She looked around. "Where's the bus?"

"Not here yet," Arnold replied. Yearwood got out her cellular phone and handed it to Arnold, who walked away from the group to call the new driver, Terry Ford, who lived a couple of hours outside of Nashville. "He thought we were flying this date," the road manager said when he returned. He called Hemphill, and they promised a bus within the hour.

"We might as well go get something to drink," said Arnold. He suggested the Third Coast, one of the Music Row restaurants within walking distance.

"I can't," said Yearwood. "I look like shit."

Finally, though, she relented. "If anyone recognizes me, will you say I'm someone else?" she asked Arnold.

"Want to borrow my sunglasses?"

"Do I look that bad?"

She managed the three-block walk, through three clusters of Nashvillians, unnoticed. She sat with Arnold, Tammy Rogers, and Lisa McLaughlin and talked about wanting a vacation, one where only Arnold would get her phone number. "If I give it to Ken he'll call three times a day," she said.

"I got to tell you," said Arnold. "I wrote a song last night. 'Mr. Mom.' "

"Got to get it on tape," said Rogers.

A woman with long brown hair, in a black leotard and tight jeans, came up to the table. She looked like a young Joan Baez. "Matraca Berg," she said, offering her hand to Yearwood. The two had met once or twice, but Berg, the cowriter of Yearwood's current single, wasn't sure if the singer knew who she was. "I just wanted to come by and say hey."

"Have you written anything else lately?" Yearwood asked.

"I'm working on stuff for my new album."

"If you've got any rejects, please send them."

There was a pause in the conversation. "Well," Berg said finally, "thanks for the record."

"Thank you for the song."

Berg turned and headed away.

"She's a great songwriter," said Yearwood. Then, as Berg's thin frame receded into the distance: "Shit. I knew I'd run into somebody skinny with make-up on."

Yearwood had had a total of seven hours sleep in two days when she and Arnold arrived in Burlington, Vermont, at eleven on Saturday morning, after a quick trip to Georgia. The band would meet them at the fairgrounds. The fair director picked them up at the airport for the ride through the Green Mountains. It was a sharp blue New England day, trees splattered yellow and orange against the sky. Yearwood slept through the autumn glory in the back seat of the van.

They got to Tunbridge at noon. Yearwood went to the fair director's house for a shower; Arnold went straight to the fairgrounds. He had expected to find the bus parked behind the bandstand, but there were only a few horse and cattle trailers. "This is bad," he said. "What did I do to make them not be here?" He went looking for a phone and called the Holiday Inn where the band was supposed to have spent the night. It turned out that the bus had broken down in Knoxville, and they had got in eight hours late. They had just left for the fairgrounds.

The bus arrived about an hour later, its cab decorated with crepe paper and "Happy Birthday" spelled out in glittery letters.

This was the day Yearwood turned twenty-eight. The grounds of the grandiosely named Tunbridge World's Fair—just off the Yankee-perfect main street—were just about the prettiest they had seen all year, a line of white colonial buildings, set like a gem into the hillside. There was a barn set aside for antiques, and booths selling homemade maple sugar and cheddar cheese. This being health-conscious Vermont, they also had turkey burgers and ginseng tea.

From the moment she arrived at the fairgrounds, Yearwood left the bus only three times; twice to sing, once to sign autographs.

The bus pulled out of the fairgrounds at nine-thirty, and they were back at the Holiday Inn by ten-thirty. Yearwood was coaxed to the bar, where Herter had arranged for a birthday cake. Yearwood sat between Herter and McLaughlin. Lauer and his wife were at the far end of the table. It was the first time he had seen Yearwood offstage since the wedding. She did not mention her absence, and he certainly had no intention of asking.

The bar had a dance floor and a two-man band—a vocalist with a bad toupee and his sidekick on the synthesizer. Every manner of hit—country, pop, rock, and Motown—had been programmed into the machine. The singer bumped and ground his way through "Heard It Through the Grapevine" and "Sexual Healing." Except for a group of five middle-aged women, Yearwood and company had the place to themselves. The singer played mostly to his distaff quintet. "This is for Reenie," he said, and segued into "Everything I Do I Do for You," moving out onto the dance floor, circling one woman, then another—a poor man's Engelbert Humperdinck. As he sang "Achy Breaky Heart"—a recent addition to his repertoire—Yearwood blew out her candles.

Jim Hurst, the new acoustic player, ordered Yearwood one tequila after another, and she drank them with reckless abandon. She had never been a drinker, but she was determined to keep up. The bus pulled out well past midnight, the entire band somewhat the worse for wear.

"Everybody off," Arnold shouted as they pulled into Springfield, Massachusetts, at 5 the next morning. "I paid for these rooms, and we're going to use them." Yearwood walked off looking wan. The singer was suffering from her first serious hangover.

* * *

Between her trips to see Reynolds in San Francisco and Dallas, Yearwood had fallen weeks behind on her interviews. Russell had rescheduled with a vengeance—three interviews before Sunday noon (two newspapers, one magazine) and seven on Monday (two television stations, four radio stations, and one newspaper). Yearwood slept through the Sunday series. Russell was furious.

Yearwood did four shows in two days at the Big E!, a six-state fair in West Springfield. A long white limousine shuttled her from the hotel to the fairgrounds.

There would be two more stops in mid-September, then, at the end of the month, five straight days in Nashville, her longest stretch at home since June. They wouldn't exactly be days off, though. The last week of September was CMA week, the most sacred of Nashville's trinity of holy weeks.

Part VI
THE TROPHY

Country Music Association Awards Week

All I ever wanted to do was pick and sing. . . . All this other stuff drives you squirrelly.

—Bill Monroe

CHAPTER 25

Monday of CMA week was the day when, according to the MCA battle plan, "Wrong Side of Memphis" should have gone to the top of the charts. But it had become clear weeks before that it wasn't going to work out that way. The promoters at MCA were working four songs in the top seven that week, and Yearwood's was presenting the most problems. Stations were reluctant to move it from medium to heavy rotation, and even more ominously, the week before, two stations had dropped it altogether. According to Jay Phillips, the man responsible for programming one of those stations, KXXY in Oklahoma City, the song had no business on country radio. "Too blues," he said. "The thing that got us to this point is nouveau traditional. Take Alan Jackson. The thing he has going for him is you know what to expect. . . . As far as Trisha goes, well, us country folks have a saying: 'Dance with the one that brung ya.' "

Phillips had a strong opinion, but it was a minority opinion, and on September 28, Scott Borchetta was working hard to keep it that way. Losing KXXY would keep "Wrong Side of Memphis" from going number one, but he still had hopes of getting it into the top five.

By early afternoon, it was clear that it wasn't going to be easy. David Haley, who handled the Midwest, walked into Borchetta's office just after two. "We have a potential situation at KSUX," he said.

"What's the problem?"

"Babe is frying," Haley replied. And so it went for the afternoon. KILT in Houston refused to move it from light to medium. KYGO in Denver wouldn't move it from medium to heavy. Borchetta wasn't sure how many stations were playing her and how frequently (the service that tracked them was on the fritz), but he wasn't hopeful.

Bruce Hinton walked into Borchetta's office just after five to check on their songs' progress.

"Is Sheinberg still coming in for the CMAs?" Borchetta asked. It would be the first time MCA's president, Sidney Sheinberg, the man in charge of all of the company's operations (movies, books, records and theme parks), had been to Nashville since Hinton took over.

"Our billings just came in," said Hinton. "He ought to be here. Where's Trisha?"

"She'll probably come in at six," he said. "It wasn't that I didn't like the album. I wanted it to work. I just didn't hear that breakaway single. It's not like I wanted to be right."

As it turned out, "Memphis" did better in *Radio & Records* than Borchetta had expected. Collin Raye, who had been number one the week before, dropped to seven, leaving a little room at the top. Yearwood ended up at four. "Memphis" wouldn't drive droves of record buyers to their local Wal-Marts, but it wouldn't be an embarrassment either.

The next week, barring extraordinary circumstance, the song would start heading down the charts. There was one outside chance that could put it back in contention: the CMA Awards.

"It wouldn't be enough for her to win," said Borchetta. "If her performance goes well *and* she wins *and* she looks great, it could make a difference. With Trisha it can go either way. There are times when she has looked great and times where she has won and she hasn't looked so fabulous. I've heard about it afterward, and it hasn't helped."

Over the last months, Don Henley had told Yearwood that he would be happy to godfather her album, do whatever he could to put her in the limelight. Yearwood happily took him up on his offer, conscripting him for both the CMA show and the "Walkaway Joe" video. His only request was that no one know about his appearance at the CMA—no advance announcements, no hype. It was Yearwood's show, he told her, and he didn't want to deflect attention from her.

While Borchetta was working Yearwood's record, she was off with Henley, filming the performance sequence for "Walkaway Joe," scheduled to be released as a single on October 19. The director, again, was Gerry Wenner. This time Planet had been the only company consulted. Wenner planned a two-part film: The Yearwood-Henley duet, shot in color, would be intercut with a story sequence, done in appropriately downbeat black and white. He had hired actors for the love-gone-wrong story; those scenes would be shot later in the week in Texas. Henley and Yearwood were filmed in a barnlike set constructed especially for the video. They sang in front of an eight-paned window, storm clouds shifting by the glass. They worked until ten, and afterward she went home and ate takeout Chinese with Robert Reynolds, who had come into town to escort her to the awards show.

Nancy Russell picked her up at eight-thirty the next morning. Yearwood was scheduled to be at the Roy Acuff Theater out at Opryland, where ten radio stations had set up tables to interview the stars. The singers were escorted from table to table, cafeteria-style, five stopwatch-timed minutes at each.

Each deejay had pretty much the same patter, and Yearwood had pretty much the same answer: Your videos are so sassy. ("I look for songs with a little attitude. I think country music should be fun, and I try to portray a little fun.") You're up for Horizon award and female vocalist. How does it feel? ("I feel lucky to have a ticket to the show.")

As Yearwood walked from WYAI (Atlanta) to WUSN (Chicago), a pale young woman, a Dresden doll in a flowing flowered dress, walked by. "Martina McBride," noted Russell. "They're trying to set her up as the next Trisha." Then she moved on to fret over the awards. "She is going to win, isn't she? She has to. We've covered everything. Everybody has done everything that can be done."

The *Entertainment Weekly* piece—with an A-plus endorsement—had come in the week after the trip to New York ("Trisha Yearwood . . . with her second album, *Hearts in Armor*, announces herself as one of the finest intrepretive singers ever to grace the genre"), and that same week, *Newsweek* ran a full-page profile headlined "A New Country Star Is Born." There had been a single-sheet mailing to the entire CMA membership—a portrait of Yearwood with a quote from Robert Oermann of *The*

Tennessean ("Move Over Boys, Here Comes a Star"); a swatch of advertisements in *Billboard*, each one with a plaudit from a different publication; ten more billboards bought for a week in Nashville, giant blowups of the CMA mailing; and a fancy pop-out ad in the program for the awards show—all paid for out of the coffers of Trisha Yearwood, Inc.

While Russell angsted, Yearwood interviewed, answering yet again how she felt about everything that had happened this year ("honored and excited") and just how nervous she was about the awards ("very"). Just before eleven, as she headed to WUBE (Cincinnati), she turned to Russell. "I've got to get out of here," she said. "I was supposed to be at the dentist's fifteen minutes ago." She was scheduled to get her teeth cleaned before the show the next day. Three interviews later, she was finally on her way.

Yearwood arrived at Emerald Studios at one for another four-station relay, then headed over to Russell's office for the last fitting of the two outfits she would be wearing on the show. Getting the clothes made had not been easy. Yearwood had been in town so seldom that she hadn't had time to see the designs. McCoy wasn't sure what she would do if Yearwood didn't like the outfits: a black jacket with red cuffs—a customized version of the one from the *Entertainment Weekly* photo shoot—and a long black jacket, zipper in front, Western stitching in back. No Marilyn Monroe, no sequins, no fringe. McCoy spent a half hour pinning the outfits on. They were deemed acceptable, and the dressmaker had eight hours to put in the last seams.

Next stop: the Union Station Hotel for eight more stations. A balding man in a bowling shirt and a tag approached Yearwood, only to be ordered back by the only man in the room in a suit and tie. "Contest winners, stay with your station," he said, and the contest winner retreated back to a half-circle of folding chairs around WQYK, the country station in Tampa. "I won through a drawing," he explained. "I work at a nuclear plant. But I write songs on the side."

Russell maneuvered Yearwood around the nuclear-plant worker cum songwriter to a table belonging to a Sacramento country station. "I understand you had a little trouble with *The Tonight Show*," the disc jockey said, and Yearwood found herself explaining one of the odder media events of the year.

Yearwood had first appeared on *The Tonight Show* under the

Carson regime. Six months later, after Jay Leno took over the show, Kragen had arranged for a second appearance on October 16 to promote *Hearts in Armor*.

A month before her scheduled appearance, though, Kragen had a set-to with the show's producer, Helen Kushnick. A *Tonight* booker had called Kragen looking to put Travis Tritt on the show, but Kragen had already promised the singer to Arsenio Hall. He offered to have the singer appear a week afterward, but that wasn't good enough. Kushnick told him to cancel Tritt's appearance on *Arsenio;* when Kragen refused, she told him Tritt would be permanently banned from *Tonight*. The next day Kragen was informed that Yearwood was being canceled as well.

"That was her mistake," he said. "Once she threw Trisha off the show, I had nothing to lose." He took his complaints to the press, and they made headlines coast-to-coast.

Within two weeks, Kushnick had been fired, and Jay Leno's shaky hold on the *Tonight* job had been further shaken. (Eventually NBC chose to keep Leno rather than bring in David Letterman.) Kushnick's departure was mentioned in virtually every national publication, and in each of them, Yearwood and Tritt had walk-ons. Ken Kragen had managed to get his two clients more publicity for their nonappearances than anyone ever got for actually showing up.

"I feel like I got in the middle of someone else's traffic accident," Yearwood said of the situation, "but I'm proud of my manager for having the courage to speak out. I think this way things will get better for everyone."

Three stations later, Yearwood sidled up to Russell. "How many have we done?"

"I think five," Russell replied.

"I'm spent," said Yearwood.

"We've got to get through this," Russell said, and pointed her toward the next table. Every station in the room was included in *Radio & Records* weekly poll, and to leave without talking to each of them would be to violate one of the cardinal rules of country: Never alienate a reporting station.

They were out the door just after six. As they waited for the valet to bring their car, Suzy Bogguss and her publicist walked by. Though Bogguss had been in the business longer, she was still part of the sorority of sophomore acts; after three albums, one of her singles had only just recently broken into the top ten. She was up against Yearwood for the Horizon Award, but was considered enough of a longshot that their rivalry stayed friendly.

"How are you doing?" Yearwood asked.

"Totally fried," Bogguss replied as Russell's car pulled up.

Yearwood had a ninety-minute break before she was due out at the Opry to rehearse with Don Henley.

Nashville traffic runs like Nashville music: There's the occasional renegade who jams up the works, but the roads generally run smoothly. When there is a snarl, natives blame the tourists, drivers from New York and L.A. who assume it's somehow okay to cut across four lanes of traffic if they miss their exits on I-40. On the day before the Country Music Awards, traffic was a nightmare—bumper-to-bumper down the Briley Parkway, dead halt on Opryland Drive. The trouble was an out-of-towner named George Bush.

Fifteen hundred Republican stalwarts—Roy Acuff, Crystal Gayle, George Lindsey ("Goober" from *The Andy Griffith Show*), and Lee Greenwood among them—came out for a campaign rally at Opryland. Younger Nashville generally kept its distance. Garth Brooks was nowhere to be seen. Even Reba McEntire, who had paid several calls to the Bush White House, stayed away. But while the turnout may have been mediocre, the presidential entourage still managed to create chaos in its wake.

Just before eight o'clock Nancy Russell and Sheri McCoy, Ken Kragen and Trisha Yearwood were in three separate cars caravanning to the Opry hall; none was moving. Russell was the first to get out. She found an Opry security guard and demanded to know why they couldn't move. They were scheduled for rehearsal, she said, and they were already late. "Everyone's late," he told her. "The president is moving. Nobody moves when the president moves."

While she waited, Russell contemplated the dangers of public life. "Can you imagine being a political leader and not being sure if something you'd eaten had been poisoned? I'd be completely paranoid."

"I'm sure you would be," said McCoy.

It took nearly half an hour, but finally the president moved off the Opryland compound, and by a quarter to nine Yearwood was on the Opry stage rehearsing "Walkaway Joe." The performance had already been subject to some serious lobbying. The Country Music Association had originally wanted to limit Yearwood's performance to two and a half minutes, a restriction that would have meant eliminating one of the song's verses. If she couldn't sing all the lyrics, Yearwood told Fundis, she wouldn't sing it at all. Fundis then approached the CMA. The song's story made no sense without all the verses, he said. The organization relented. She would still have to eliminate a chorus, but she would be able to preserve the integrity of the song. She and Henley would be singing the song live; only the instrumentals would be recorded. There would be no second take.

Yearwood stood center stage front with Henley in the shadows, nothing more than a silhouette. Kragen watched from the front row as they walked through their paces. "I think they ought to come together," he said, and left his chair to advise them. If Don Henley was going to be there, he wanted to take full advantage. "At the end," he told Yearwood, "why don't you say, 'Ladies and Gentlemen, Don Henley'—just to make sure people know he's there." Next, Kragen went back to the control room to see how they looked on camera. The only problem was Yearwood's microphone. She kept pushing it up toward her mouth as if she was singing into an oversize lipstick container.

"We want to see that beautiful face of hers," said Walter Miller, the show's director. "Don holds his down, and we can hear him just fine."

Kragen ran out to the stage to relay Miller's instructions. They ran through the song a second time; this time the microphone stayed down. But when Henley walked over to Yearwood, he strayed a good foot-and-a-half away. "Together," Kragen implored, "together." Yearwood reached her hand out to Henley, hooked it through his elbow, and pulled him close.

"Want to try one more?" Kragen asked.

"Only if he wants to," Yearwood demurred.

And Henley, ever the perfectionist, did one more run-through and, when it was over, asked for one more.

"Fine by me," said Miller. "If Don Henley wants to do one more, we're certainly not going to stop him."

After they finished, Miller was all praise. "I'm telling ya," he said, "they're gonna blow the house out."

Kragen's only worry was how he should counsel Yearwood about the show. "I have Travis programmed not to win," he explained. "I'm a little more cautious with Trisha. I want her to be prepared if she does win. I don't want to take her down."

By the end of Tuesday evening, he had decided to stay silent. Her victory, he figured, was a virtual certainty.

CHAPTER 26

WEDNESDAY DID NOT BEGIN WELL. NANCY RUSSELL AND
Ken Kragen were both up before seven, waiting for the *Today*
segment Yearwood had filmed in New York three weeks earlier.
There was endless talk about whether Bush and Clinton would
debate, an interview with Ed Harris about *Glengarry Glen Ross*,
six minutes on the troubles of Euro Disney. Nowhere in the
two-hour show, though, was a segment on Trisha Yearwood.

At nine, Russell called Kragen in his hotel room. He was not
happy to hear from her. His phone calls were supposed to have
been held, but the operator put her through, waking his wife.
He was uncharacteristically short with her: Yes, he knew the
show hadn't appeared. Yes, he was unhappy. No, they agreed,
Yearwood shouldn't be told about it unless she asked. Why create
problems?

Russell and McCoy arrived at Yearwood's house at about one.
Gwen and Beth Yearwood had just got in. Yearwood's seamstress
was there, too, for a last fitting of the black jackets. Roseanne
was bounding through the house, barking at strangers, which
meant just about everyone.

"This reminds me of prom night," said Reynolds as he surveyed the scene. "I didn't go to mine."

Backstage at the Opry was a passable imitation of a high school
gym. Lockers lined the hallways. Assorted women in varying
stages of undress filled the half dozen dressing rooms. On the
dressing-room sign for Billy Ray Cyrus, someone had crossed out

the name and written in Travis Tritt. Wynonna Judd wandered through, trailed by a burly man carrying a small dog in a miniature motorcycle jacket. Scores of green-robed choristers snaked through the hallways; they were there for Dolly Parton's finale, "Put a Little Love in Your Heart."

The commissary, three lines of steam table barbecue, was a maelstrom of stars and their handlers. As MCA's publicist, Susan Levy, balanced a plate full of greens, Lyle Lovett walked by, eying her bustline. "My," he said, "you're looking very chesty this evening."

She was dumbstruck. "What am I supposed to say to something like that?"

In the corner by the commissary, a small hand-lettered sign advertised MASSAGE THERAPY UPSTAIRS. "If they don't need me now, they will by the time the show is over," said Jim Ingram, a former physical education teacher who had been hired as the evening's masseur by the CMA.

There was a full dress rehearsal at six. Singing "Walkaway Joe" with a stand-in for Don Henley, Yearwood missed the entrance on the third verse and had to do an extra run-through. It went fine the second time, but still she was terrified. She would not have that margin for error once the show began.

Yearwood's dressing room was straight out of *Steel Magnolias*. Five singers—Yearwood, Pam Tillis, Kathy Mattea, Patty Loveless, and Suzy Bogguss—shared the narrow space, each with her own costumer, cosmetician, and hairdresser, as well as an entourage of well-wishers. Pam Tillis's ten-year-old son sat in the corner playing his Gameboy. Yearwood's mother and sister showed up just before seven.

"Didn't I meet you at Douglas Corner?" Kathy Mattea asked Gwen Yearwood, as her hair was being teased.

"I'm amazed you remember."

"She's come a long way."

The singers were lined up beauty-parlor-style in front of the mirror. As her hairdresser spun her hair into a midsize helmet, Tillis made a sort of kissing sound toward her image in the mirror. "Used to do that when I was in high school," she said. "The boys loved it."

Suzy Bogguss, dressed in a black body suit, short-tiered black velvet skirt, and a broad-brimmed black hat, walked across the room, swinging her hips. "I used to practice walking like this in front of the penitentiary in town," she said. "That way I knew I had an audience. I said that once in an interview, and my mother near died."

At six-thirty Yearwood was dressed, made up, and ready for a whirl of interviews: *USA Today*, *Crook & Chase*, the CBS affiliate from Atlanta, E!, and *Entertainment Tonight*. Just after seven, Russell escorted her back to her dressing room. Backstage was mobbed. Yearwood had a hug for Joe Harris, a tight smile for Bob Doyle. She stopped for a minute to talk with Kragen, duded up for the festivities in a chenille dinner jacket and pewter bow tie, attached with a leather thong.

Just outside the dressing room, Yearwood spotted Johnny Cash. His face was all chiseled cheekbones and crags, Nashville's living, breathing Mount Rushmore. The week before, he had sent Yearwood a note telling her how much he liked her work. Now, she walked up and introduced herself, and Cash pulled her into his dressing room; he wanted her to meet his wife. There wasn't much time. Two minutes later she was back in her dressing room for a last-minute pouffe.

Just after seven, as an Opry assistant swept the halls with a megaphone ("If you want your seats please take them now. If you don't take your seats we are going to give them away."), Yearwood worried.

"If I screw up, there's no going back," she said. "I'll just run off the stage." A minute later: "I'm going to throw up."

"You're going to go out and sing your butt off, and it will be cool," said McCoy.

"The thing is," added Russell, "you really can sing as good as your record."

"Garth Fundis doesn't put stuff in my voice I can't reproduce," said Yearwood.

As if on cue, Reynolds appeared at the door. Yearwood took his arm and stepped out toward the auditorium.

Just behind her, the opening performer, Wynonna Judd, leaned over her headset microphone to kiss her mother. "Mom, I love you," she said as an Opry official grabbed her arm to march her to the stage.

Moments later, Judd was singing "How Did You Get to Me" in a short black leather dress and high black leather boots. Brooks

& Dunn took duo of the year. Garth Brooks won album of the year, and Patty Loveless presented Vince Gill with the male vocalist award.

By the third commercial break, Yearwood was back in the dressing room.

"I'm freaking out," she said. "I need to find a cassette of the edited song."

"You look great," said McCoy.

"That's not what I'm worried about."

Russell ran out to see if she could find a copy of the new version of the song. Miraculously, she reappeared in ninety seconds with a cassette player and a tape.

Yearwood switched on the machine. "This is it," she said. She fast-forwarded to the third verse and listened, sang the line, closed her eyes, and sang it again, committing it to memory. "Has anyone seen my cohort for this?" she asked.

Seconds later, Don Henley was at the door. At 9:30 Trisha Yearwood was singing as she walked out onto the Opry stage.

> *Momma told her baby girl take it real slow*
> *Girl told her momma hey I really got to go*

[She took slow deliberate steps, pausing midstage, just past that patch of scuffed oak from the Ryman.]

> *He's waitin' in the car*
> *Momma said girl you won't get far*

[She finished her slow walk to the front of the stage.]

> *Thus are the dreams of an average Jane*
> *Ninety miles an hour down a lovers' lane*
> *On a tank of dreams*
> *Oh if she could've only seen*
> *But fate's got cards that it don't want to show*
> *And that boy's just*

[Lights illuminated a figure emerging from the wings. Applause rippled through the audience as Henley joined in the harmony.]

> *A walkaway Joe*
> *Born to be a leaver*
> *Tell you from the word go, destined to deceive her*

He's the wrong kinda paradise
She's gonna know it in a matter of time
That boy's just a walkaway Joe.

[The spotlight turned off, leaving Henley in dark silhouette. Yearwood sang the first lines of the next verse alone.]

Now just a little while into Abilene
Pulls into a station and he robs it clean
She's waitin' in the car
Underneath the Texaco star . . .

[She hit the entrance to the third verse perfectly.]

Somewhere in a roadside motel room
Alone in the silence she wakes up too soon
And reaches for his arm
But she'll just keep reachin' on . . .

Henley met Yearwood center stage. By the last chorus, he wasn't just doing harmonies, it was a full-out duet. They sang the lyrics together, nodding into their microphones, looking up and smiling at each other, then out to the audience. They looked as if they had been working together for years. After they sang their last "Walkaway Joe," as the piano played its last sweet lick, Yearwood put her hand behind her partner's waist: "Ladies and Gentlemen, Don Henley."

Henley bowed, then opened his hand toward Yearwood. As the audience applauded, he turned from the stage. Yearwood put her hand through his arm, and the rock star escorted the country singer from the stage.

"It went so fast," she said as they headed into the wings.

"Did you want to add an Eagles medley or something?"

Back in the dressing room, McCoy finally exhaled. "One more song without anything going wrong. Thank you, Lord."

Yearwood was back moments later. As she changed back into her black jacket, Henley poked his head in the door.

"It sounded great," said McCoy.

"Frankly," he said, "I thought we did better at rehearsals. I got to get this stuff off my hands," which were covered with foundation put on to match the color of his face.

"I'm just so proud," said Russell. "I feel like a mother or some-

thing. . . . Trish, I'll see you when you win the Horizon Award."
She headed out into the hallway.

"I haven't thought about what I'm going to say if I win," said
Yearwood, as McCoy patted some powder on her nose. " 'I'd
like to thank Don Henley for agreeing to do this show.' " Strains
of "Achy Breaky Heart" echoed from the stage. "Dang. I'm
missing Billy Ray."

Russell headed to the press room. She watched the monitor as
Lyle Lovett presented Billy Ray Cyrus with the award for single
of the year. The surprise was female vocalist: Mary-Chapin Carpenter, in an upset over the favorites, Wynonna Judd and Reba
McEntire. While Yearwood had been nominated, that wasn't the
award she was expecting. Bogguss, Tillis, and Billy Dean, all
Horizon nominees, did snippets from their latest singles.

Russell passed by Bogguss's publicist just as Reba McEntire
introduced Naomi Judd, who would be announcing the winner
of the Horizon Award.

"Congratulations," the publicist told Russell. "You did a great
job with her."

"It's not over yet," Russell replied.

Out in the audience, Al Teller, the head of MCA Records,
was watching the show next to Sidney Sheinberg, who was in
Nashville for the first time since the premiere of *Coal Miner's
Daughter*.

"I've been in Texas shooting a movie with Kenny Rogers and
Travis Tritt," Judd was saying. "They are still out there on the
set. Travis Tritt was last year's winner. Since he couldn't be
with us, I said, 'Heck, since we put a man on the moon, I think
we can go to Texas.' "

A wide screen rolled down, and, bigger than life, there were
the two singers, live on location in Texas.

"Hi-dee-hi, and a great big howdy, boys," said Judd.

There were a few minutes of patter, and then it was down to
business. "I wish we could be there with you," said Tritt. "Naomi, go ahead and announce those nominees."

In the audience, Teller turned to Sheinberg. "We've got this
one in the bag."

Judd sped through the names: Bogguss, Dean, Brooks & Dunn,
Tillis, and Yearwood. She ripped open the vellum envelope and
pulled out the card.

"The winner," she said, "is . . . Suzy Bogguss."

"I guess I spoke too soon," said Bogguss's publicist, who flew off to find her client.

Russell was too stunned to move.

Kragen was watching in the control room. "It's okay," he said, mostly to himself, "it's okay. It would be one thing if her career were shaky, but she's in good shape. She'll win female vocalist next year."

Russell found Kragen in the hallway. "Are you okay?" he asked. She burst into tears. "You have to be strong for Trisha," he told her, then rushed off to attend to another crisis. He wanted a satellite feed to coordinate Tritt for an interview. Russell headed to the ladies' room, sat in a stall, and cried.

There was half an hour left to the show—awards for disc jockeys of the year (small, medium, and large markets), radio stations of the year, inductees into the Country Music Hall of Fame, and entertainer of the year. Garth Brooks won, and his first thanks went to his bus drivers. ("There are eleven of you, and I know we don't get nothing until you get there.") Yearwood sat through it all as though in a dream. Everyone had told her she would win. It wasn't so much that she was disappointed; she was simply shocked. It was the first time in her fifteen-month career as a recording artist that she had failed.

After the show, Tillis was the first to appear in the dressing room, followed by Bogguss, then Loveless. Finally, Yearwood came to the door. "Has anyone seen my mama?"

There was a chorus of no's. Then she walked over to Bogguss and hugged her.

"Congratulations. Can I just touch it?" said the woman who was supposed to win to the woman who did.

Bogguss handed her the etched crystal.

"Maybe I can borrow it sometime?"

"I'm out of town a lot," said Bogguss. "Anytime."

Russell was folded up in a vinyl chair in the corner, her feet tucked under her long skirt. McCoy put a hand on the publicist's shoulder. "The one thing I've learned," said McCoy, "is that there is life after an awards show."

Yearwood was gone minutes later, off to Henley's dressing room to find her mother and sister.

"You were screwed," said the rock star.

"But at least I should have enjoyed it," Yearwood replied.

"Maybe you should move to L.A.," he said. "We'll get you a Grammy."

By ten o'clock, Yearwood was back in her dressing room, cleaning off her stage makeup, packing up her things. Pam Tillis was the first to head out into the night.

"Girls, y'all have a great evening," she said as she walked out the door. "It's an honor to be in the business with you."

Yearwood's night was not yet over. MCA was throwing a party at Vanderbilt University, and Yearwood had to be there. She drove over with her boyfriend, her mother, and her sister. The first person she saw was Garth Fundis. He pulled her off into a corner, hugged her, and said, "You were great." She stayed there, in the most comfortable spot she'd find all evening, then turned around and headed back out to work the crowd.

Yearwood spent ninety minutes smiling her way through the throng. All the bigwigs showed up: Teller and Sheinberg were there; Michael Hammond, the president of Revlon, had flown in from New York. He was the only person in the room wearing a cowboy hat.

In the center of the room, five television monitors ran a continuous tape of the awards show. She watched her performance with Henley twice over. When the Horizon Award was reannounced, she averted her eyes.

By the time the party was over, she had heard the various theories explaining her loss. According to one, there had been a trade of block votes: Capitol had agreed to throw its female vocalist votes to Mary-Chapin Carpenter if Sony gave its Horizon votes to Suzy Bogguss. According to another, because Yearwood had been nominated for both the vocalist and the Horizon awards, the votes had been split, leaving her a loser in both categories. She had no interest in dwelling on it. "Basically I was okay," she said afterward, "but I felt like I let down the team."

The next morning began early. She had to have Reynolds at the airport by nine, and an hour after that, she was due at the Country Music Hall of Fame. Yearwood was getting her own star in the entry hallway, Nashville's answer to the stars along Hollywood Boulevard. There was a meeting with the Revlon executives, then another run to the airport with her mother and sister. By early evening she was back home with a couple of hours to pack. At midnight, she would be heading out for Warsaw, Indiana.

By eleven-thirty the band started to gather around the bus. Jay Hager was the first on; he brought the evening's entertainment, a video of *Wayne's World*. The talk quickly turned to the awards show. Terry Ford, the driver, offered his review.

"I love Garth, man," he said. "Only guy who's ever thanked his bus drivers."

"I'm really pissed about those awards," said Arnold. "I may have to slap someone around."

Even Lauer was outraged. "She was robbed," he said. "She's better than any of them."

Yearwood appeared just before twelve. She got on the bus and hauled her suitcase down the aisle. "You looked great on the show," Herter said, to nods of agreement. Yearwood shoved her bag into the stateroom, walked back up to the front, and extracted a card from a bouquet sitting on the table, an award from Future Farmers of America. She opened her purse, pulled out the letter from Johnny Cash, and passed it around.

"Meeting him was the second coolest thing that happened all evening," she said. "It's good to be here. This way I might even get a little rest."

As Yearwood headed back to her stateroom, the bus pulled away from the curb, out toward the highway, back on the road. A chiffon ripple of exhaust steamed into the night.

EPILOGUE

*T*O JUDGE BY ITS REVIEWS, *HEARTS IN ARMOR* SHOULD HAVE been one of the biggest success stories of 1992. Along with those glowing notices after the album came out, it ended up on best record lists in a host of publications, including *The Philadelphia Inquirer*, *The Tennessean*, *USA Today*, and *Billboard*. But the critics were but one of the constituencies a Trisha Yearwood had to please. The commercial success of her first album had set expectations high, and on that count *Hearts in Armor* fell short. By mid-January, sales had yet to hit eight hundred thousand. Even though the album would go platinum three months later, Al Teller still considered it a disappointment. "I was hoping to be at one point two or one point three million by *now*," he said.

The trouble was radio play, and it had started back with "Wrong Side of Memphis." "It was never the song that should have been released as the first single," said Walt Wilson, head of marketing at MCA Nashville. "It never gave us out-of-the-box momentum." The next two singles did fairly well—"Walkaway Joe," released the week after the CMA Awards, made it to number three in *Billboard* and two in *Radio & Records* and "You Say You Will" to number twelve in *Billboard* and ten in *Radio & Records*—but neither was a breakaway success. They weren't preteen anthems, like "She's in Love with the Boy," or heart-stopping ballads, the cornerstone of country radio success.

Three singles may have left Al Teller discouraged with *Hearts in Armor*, but his minions in Nashville refused to surrender. In the spring, the marketing department shifted its attention to the release of "Down on My Knees," scheduled for May. It might not have sounded straight country, but it was the sort of high-pitched emotional plea that MCA executives believed could generate the sales momentum that should have been there from the start. Bruce Hinton had Yearwood represent MCA Nashville at its showcase for the National Association of Record Merchandisers in March, and Walt Wilson planned a whole new set of posters and advertisements to create the illusion that the album had just been released.

"Right now we're still in the third inning," said Hinton. "Until we've finished the campaign for 'Down on My Knees,' the game is not over."

Sales, though, were not the only disappointment. Not only did Yearwood fail to win that Horizon Award, she wasn't nominated for a Grammy (much to the surprise of the program's producers, who had called before the nominations were announced to make sure she would be free to perform), and she did not make it to the finals of the Academy of Country Music Awards.

After that third shutout, MCA executives and Ken Kragen tried to diagnose the problem. Hinton felt that her tour schedule had left her too little time on Music Row. "No one here knows her," he said. The other worry was the Revlon deal. Even though Wild Heart's launch had been postponed until April, MCA executives speculated that the much-publicized endorsement so early in her career might have made it appear that she was "getting past her raising." They worried about Nashville xenophobia as well, fretted that the fact that she was managed out of Los Angeles and not Nashville might be alienating local constituencies.

"That doesn't makes sense," Kragen countered. "If that were true, Travis would be suffering as well, and he won a Grammy and was nominated for an ACM." Kragen contended that MCA might be partly (and unintentionally) responsible for Yearwood's slight slump. "They have the two hottest female acts in the business [Wynonna Judd and Reba McEntire]. That leaves Trisha third in line for any money that is spent in a company that can be reluctant to spend a great deal."

Kragen, being Kragen, preferred to accentuate the positive. "We may not be getting exposure from the awards shows," he said, "but we have Revlon, Disney just offered us a one-hour special, and she has a cameo in a Peter Bogdanovich movie that's coming out in July. If the talent weren't there, this is the point when you throw in the towel and go home. But the talent is there, so you don't let if faze you. You look at what's going on, you develop a new game plan, and you move on."

For her part, Yearwood responded with remarkable equanimity. "My experience has been that most critically acclaimed albums never sell well," was how she put it. "I'm not going to worry that 'Memphis' didn't make it to number one, I'm going to worry about making a record I'm proud of." And she was very proud of *Hearts in Armor*. As for Revlon, she was convinced that as long as the image conveyed by the perfume jibed with her aesthetic image, it could do no damage. "They told me that a hundred million people buy Revlon," she said. "That's a potential audience for country music, a potential audience for me—people I can't get to another way. No matter what I do, I'm being marketed. Why shouldn't I try for more exposure?"

In the first months of 1993 Yearwood managed to regain the equilibrium between her professional and personal lives. The relationship with Reynolds had, much to her delight, lasted. In January he moved from Miami to Nashville. Two months later, he drove up to Louisville, Kentucky, to surprise her. After her show, he gave her a slim silver ring and asked her to marry him. She happily accepted.

Her 1993 concert tour was shorter and plusher than her 1992 schedule, making it easier to maintain a home life. She graduated from the dust-bowl circuit, joining Little Texas and Travis Tritt on the Budweiser tour (one reviewer described her as "the highlight of the night"). She had a brand-new customized forty-five-foot Silver Eagle (five feet longer than the one that burned) delivered in January, transportation to her one hundred concert dates. Each one was in an arena, each one at the same time—no more county fairs with uncertain sound systems, no more Rattlesnake Round Ups, and no more worrying about whether she would be paid after the show.

Yearwood was also growing into her role as an executive. "The first year is always rough," said Leonard Arnold. "Some of them learn how to handle it, some don't." By his estimation, Yearwood had been a prize student. At Thanksgiving, she earned her band's gratitude by flying them to the date the next day so they could spend the holiday with their families. Two months later, the band's members received money to pay for their belongings damaged in the fire. (The money came out of Yearwood's own pocket.) "The class of the act came through," said Arnold.

To no one's surprise, Tammy Rogers tendered her resignation in December to try to make it on her own. Tim Lauer had initially decided to stay with the group ("It was time to just shut up and acknowledge it was business"), but in March he got an offer to join Wynonna Judd's band for considerably more money. He gave just four days' notice.

In March, too, Nancy Russell left her employer, Evelyn Shriver, to set up a partnership with Elaine Schock, a New York publicist whose client list included Billy Joel and Sinéad O'Connor. Both Travis Tritt and Yearwood went with her.

Perhaps no one enjoyed the fruits of Yearwood's success more than Garth Fundis. Not only did he buy a BMW, RCA Nashville approached him about taking over as head of its A&R department. His first requirement, he told them, was that he could keep producing Yearwood. If he couldn't, he said, he had no interest in the job.

On February 15, his condition met, he went to work at RCA. The immediate beneficiary of Fundis's new position was Scott Paschall. Not only did Fundis put him in charge of the Sound Emporium, he hired him on as a consultant at RCA.

One of Fundis's first phone calls from his new office at RCA went to Jude Johnstone. He was thinking of starting a label for songwriters, he told her, and he wanted to know if she wanted to make a record. Johnstone told him that she wanted to think about it; she thought she had finally put that dream aside. She had a husband and a child, and she wasn't sure she was up for the road.

Johnstone was still thinking about it on April 8, when Garth Fundis and Trisha Yearwood went back into Studio A at the Sound Emporium to begin recording her third album.

SOURCE NOTES

I spent seven months in the studio and on the road with Trisha Yearwood. I was at meetings with MCA executives when they first heard her album and when they decided on their marketing campaign. I augmented all that reporting with interviews afterward. I witnessed the vast majority of the scenes depicted in this book; the others were drawn from those additional interviews.

This book would not have been possible without the work of scores of writers who came to Nashville before me. The best histories of Music Row are to be found in Bill Malone's *Country Music U.S.A. and Country: The Music and the Musicians*, published by the Country Music Foundation. Those and other books and major newspaper and magazine articles used are cited below.

BOOKS

Adams, Henry. *Thomas Hart Benton: Drawn from Life*. New York: Cross River Press, 1990.

Bart, Teddy. *Inside Music City USA*. Nashville: Aurora Publishers, 1970.

Carnes, Marcia Hayes. *History of Jasper County, Georgia*, ed. John P. Harvey and Irene Roberts Malone. Monticello, Georgia. Jasper County Historical Foundation, 1884.

Cheuse, Alan. *The Tennessee Waltz and Other Stories*. Layton, Utah: Gibbs Smith, 1990.

Corbin, Everett J. *Storm Over Nashville: A Case Against Modern Country Music*. Nashville: Ashlar Press, 1980.

Crabb, Alfred Leland. *Nashville: Personality of a City*. New York: Bobbs Merrill, 1960.

The Country Music Foundation. *Country: The Music and the Musicians*. New York: Abbeville Press, 1988.

The Country Music Foundation. *The Country Music Hall of Fame & Museum*. Nashville: Country Music Foundation Press, 1992.

Crutchfield, James A. *The Tennessee Almanac 1989–1990*. Nashville: Rutledge Hill Press, 1988.

Dannen, Fredric. *Hit Men*. New York: Times Books, 1990.

Doyle, Don. *Nashville Since the 1920s*. Knoxville: University of Tennessee Press, 1985.

Dunkelberger, A. C. *King of Country Music: The Life Story of Roy Acuff*. Nashville: Williams Printing, 1971.

Egerton, John. *Nashville: The Faces of Two Centuries*. Nashville: PlusMedia, 1979.

Ellet, Mrs. *Queens of American Society*. Philadelphia: Henry Coates, 1867.

Escott, Colin, and Martin Hawkins. *Good Rockin' Tonight: Sun Records and the Birth of Rock 'n' Roll*. New York: St. Martins Press, 1991.

Gabhart, Herbert. *Work: Memoirs of a Love Affair with Belmont College*. Nashville: Broadman Press, 1989.

Guralnick, Peter. *Lost Highway: Journeys and Arrivals of American Musicians*. Boston: Godine, 1979.

Halloran, Mark. *The Musician's Business and Legal Guide*. Englewood Cliffs, N.J.: Prentice-Hall, 1991.

Hemphill, Paul. *The Nashville Sound: An Intimate Portrait of the Country & Western Music Scene*. New York: Simon & Schuster, 1970.

Hurst, Jack. *Nashville's Grand Ole Opry*. New York: Abradale Press, 1989.

Lynn, Loretta. *Coal Miner's Daughter*. Chicago: Contemporary Books, 1976.

Malone, Bill C. *Country Music, U.S.A.: A Fifty Year History*. Austin: University of Texas Printing Division, 1965; rev. ed. 1985.

McMurtry, Larry. *Lonesome Dove*. New York: Pocket Books, 1985.

McNutt, Randy. *We Wanna Boogie: An Illustrated History of the American Rockabilly Movement*. Hamilton, Ohio: HHP Books, 1988.

Nash, Alanna. *Behind Closed Doors: Talking with the Legends of Country Music*. New York: Knopf, 1988.

Pohlmann, Ken. *The Compact Disc: A Handbook of Theory and Use*. Madison, Wisc.: A-R Editions, 1989.

Rogers, Jimmie N. *The Country Music Message: Revisited* . Fayetteville: University of Arkansas Press, 1989.

Schwartz, Marily. *A Southern Belle Primer*. New York: Doubleday, 1991.

Shemel, Sidney, and M. William Krasilovsky. *This Business of Music*. New York: Billboard Books, 1990.

Smith, Lee. *The Devil's Dream*. New York: Putnam, 1992.

Stambler, Irwin, and Grelun Landon. *The Encyclopedia of Folk, Country, and Western Music*. New York: St. Martin's Press, 1984.

Stokes, Geoffrey. *Starmaking Machinery: Inside the Business of Rock and Roll*. New York: Vintage Books, 1977.

Tassin, Myron, and Jerry Henderson. *Fifty Years at the Grand Ole Opry*. Gretna, La.: Pelican Publishing, 1975.

Taylor, Peter. *A Summons to Memphis*. New York: Ballantine Books, 1986.

Tosches, Nick. *Country: The Biggest Music in America*. New York: Stein & Day, 1992.

Tosches, Nick. *Dino: Living High in the Dirty Business of Dreams*. New York: Doubleday, 1992.

Vaughn, Andrew. *Who's Who in New Country Music*. New York: St. Martin's Press, 1989.

Wardin, Albert W. Jr. *Belmont Mansion: The Home of Joseph and Adelicia Acklen*. Nashville: Belmont Mansion Association, 1989.

Willis, Ridley II. *The History of Belle Meade*. Nashville: Vanderbilt University Press, 1991.

Williams, Chas. *The Nashville Number System*. Nashville: 1988.

SELECTED MAGAZINE AND NEWSPAPER ARTICLES

Allen, Bob. "Jimmy Bowen is the Most (check one) Respected/ Reviled Man on Music Row." *The Journal of Country Music*. Vol. 13, no. 3.

Coleman, Mark. "No Stranger to the Rain." *The Journal of Country Music*. Vol. 13, no. 2.

Conley, Christopher. "The Second Life of Don Henley." *GQ*, August 1991.

Crovitz, Gordon. "Can Rock Stars Stem Ethiopian Hunger?" *The Wall Street Journal*, April 24, 1985.

Edwards, Joe. "Country Star Keith Whitley Dead at 33 from Alcohol Overdose." Associated Press, May 9, 1989.

Flippo, Chet. "Crossing Over: A Two-Way Street." *Rolling Stone*, November 29, 1979.

Flippo, Chet. "Tanya: The Teenage Teaser." *Rolling Stone*, September 16, 1974.

Fox, William Price. "Grand Ole Opry," *American Heritage*, March 1979.

George, Teresa. "Liner Notes: Garth Fundis." *CMA Close Up*, March 1992.

Goldsmith, Thomas. "Are We Taking Randy Travis for Granted?" *The Journal of Country Music*, Vol. 14, no. 1 (1991).

Gubernick, Lisa, and Peter Newcomb. "Led Zeppelin Meets

Roy Rogers . . . Country Conquers Rock." *Forbes*, March 2, 1992.

"Hands Out Across America." *The Wall Street Journal*, May 23, 1986.

Harris, Melinda. "Is There Life After Garth?" *Atlanta Magazine*, February 1992.

Heron, Kim. "Making Country Music Hot Again." *The New York Times Magazine*, June 25, 1989.

Holley, Deborah. "Trisha Yearwood's Fairy-Tale Rise to Fame." *Billboard*, July 27, 1991.

Hurst, Jack. "The Next Reba." *The Chicago Tribune*, July 14, 1991.

Ingrassia, Lawrence. "At Walden Pond, Two Liberal Causes Seem One Too Many." *The Wall Street Journal*, April 24, 1990.

Keillor, Garrison. "At the Opry." *The New Yorker*, May 6, 1974.

Kragen, Ken. "Letters to the Editor." *Spy*, August 1990.

Kragen, Ken. " 'Naive' Anthem May Make a World of Difference." *The Wall Street Journal*, May 16, 1985.

McKaie, Andy. History of Our Company, Interoffice Memorandum, MCA. December 30, 1985.

Mattingly, Rick. "Eddie Bayers Learns to Adapt." *Musician*, November 1990.

Miller, Jim. "Country Goes Mellow." *Newsweek*, March 30, 1986.

Newcomb, Peter, and Christopher Palmieri. "What's Not to Love?" *Forbes*, September 30, 1991.

Oermann, Robert K. "New Tune: Females Can Sell." *The Tennessean*, August 19, 1992.

Painton, Priscilla. "Country's Big Boom." *Time*, March 30, 1992.

Palmer, Robert. "Nashville Sound: Country Music in Decline." *The New York Times*, September 17, 1985.

"Rolling in Style," *Newsweek*, August 2, 1976.

Ross, David M. "Tying Up: Garth Fundis Interview." *Music Row*, December 23, 1991.

Whitman, Howard. "Jack Kapp: Pulse on the Public." *The New Yorker*, August 24, 1940.

Williams, Bill. "Clement Studios: A Success Story." *Billboard*, June 10, 1972.

Woletz, Robert. "Technology Gives the Charts a Fresh Spin." *The New York Times*, January 26, 1992.

Zibart, Eve. "Country Music's Big Wheels." *The Tennessean Magazine*, October 13, 1974.

INDEX